"Indeed, this matter is well worth dealing with at greater length."

John Calvin on "the greedy person is an idolater"
[Eph 5:5]; *Sermons on the Epistle to the Ephesians*, p. 503

GREED AS IDOLATRY

The Origin and Meaning
of a Pauline Metaphor

Brian S. Rosner

WILLIAM B. EERDMANS PUBLISHING COMPANY
GRAND RAPIDS, MICHIGAN / CAMBRIDGE, U.K.

Published 2007 by

Wm. B. Eerdmans Publishing Co.

2140 Oak Industrial Drive N.E., Grand Rapids, Michigan 49505 /

P.O. Box 163, Cambridge CB3 9PU U.K.

Printed in the United States of America

12 11 10 09 08 07   7 6 5 4 3 2 1

Library of Congress Cataloging-in-Publication Data

Rosner, Brian S.

Greed as idolatry: the origin and meaning of a Pauline metaphor / Brian S. Rosner.

p.   cm.

Includes bibliographical references and indexes.

ISBN 978-0-8028-3374-7 (pbk.: alk. paper)

1. Avarice.   2. Avarice — Biblical teaching.   3. Idolatry — Biblical teaching.

4. Idols and images — Worship — Biblical teaching.   5. Metaphor in the Bible.

6. Bible — Criticism, interpretation, etc.   7. Bible. N.T. Epistles of Paul.   I. Title.

BV4627.A8R67   2007

241'.3 — dc22

2007019549

www.eerdmans.com

For Natalie

Contents

—⟨⟨⟨⟩⟩⟩—

Contents

Preface

—◦◦◦—

The bulk of the research for this book was completed with the generous support of the Alexander von Humboldt Stiftung, Bonn, Germany, which provided a research fellowship to underwrite a year of study at the University of Tübingen. I am most grateful to them and to Prof. Dr. Peter Stuhlmacher, whose recommendation, warm hospitality, and invaluable help made the fellowship both possible and a pleasure to undertake. In addition, I wish to thank the University of Aberdeen, where I was a lecturer at the time, for granting me study leave. Moore Theological College, where I am now happily ensconced, provided the necessary support and encouragement to bring the project to completion. The editors of *Themelios* and *Ex Auditu* kindly gave permission to republish my articles "The Concept of Idolatry" and "Secret Idolatry" in revised and expanded form. Biblical quotations and citations from German secondary sources are my translations unless otherwise indicated.

Greed as Idolatry carries forward my main scholarly interests: the history of scriptural interpretation, Second Temple Judaism, biblical theology, Pauline studies, figurative language and the moral teaching of the New Testament. A whole book on just three words is not unusual in biblical studies. However, it is less common when the words carry a primarily ethical rather than doctrinal import. There is no shortage of monographs on justification, reconciliation, redemption, law, faith, grace, the names of

God, various christological titles, and so on. My hope is that my work will contribute to the current revival of interest in theological ethics and to a recognition that serious treatments of subjects like greed as idolatry have much to contribute to Christian theology, apologetics, and mission and to the building up of the body of Christ.

The most unremarkable century in the history of interpretation of "greed as idolatry" was the twentieth, which gives little evidence of any systematic reflection outside of a few exceptions in liberation theology. Yet, arguably, the modern world gives more evidence of the truth of the judgment than any other period in history. I am convinced that the charge is too serious not to give it a full hearing.

Abbreviations

CRINT	Compendia rerum iudaicarum ad Novum Testamentum
DPL	*Dictionary of Paul and His Letters*, ed. G. F. Hawthorne and R. P. Martin. Downers Grove, IL: InterVarsity Press, 1993
EH	Europäische Hochschulschriften
EKK	Evangelisch-katholischer Kommentar
EncJud	*Encyclopedia Judaica*, ed. G. Wigoder. 16 vols. Jerusalem: Keter, 1971-1972
EvT	*Evangelische Theologie*
ExpTim	*Expository Times*
FAT	Forschungen zum Alten Testament
FRLANT	Forschungen zur Religion und Literatur des Alten und Neuen Testaments
HNT	Handbuch zum Neuen Testament
HTKNT	Herders theologischer Kommentar zum Neuen Testament
HUCA	*Hebrew Union College Annual*
ICC	International Critical Commentary
IDB	*Interpreter's Dictionary of the Bible*, ed. G. A. Buttrick et al. 4 vols. Nashville: Abingdon, 1962
IDBSup	*Interpreter's Dictionary of the Bible, Supplementary Volume*, ed. K. Crim. Nashville: Abingdon, 1976
JAC	*Jahrbuch für Antike und Christentum*
JBL	*Journal of Biblical Literature*
JQR	*Jewish Quarterly Review*
JSJ	*Journal for the Study of Judaism*
JSNTSup	Journal for the Study of the New Testament Supplement
JSOTSup	Journal for the Study of the Old Testament Supplement
JSPSup	Journal for the Study of the Pseudepigrapha Supplement
JTS	*Journal of Theological Studies*
KEK	Kritisch-exegetischer Kommentar
LCL	Loeb Classical Library
LSJ	H. G. Liddell, R. Scott, H. S. Jones, and R. McKenzie, *A Greek-English Lexicon*. 9th ed. Oxford: Clarendon, 1996
LXX	Septuagint
m.	Mishnah
MT	Masoretic text
NCBC	New Century Bible Commentary
NEB	New English Bible
NICNT	New International Commentary on the New Testament
NICOT	New International Commentary on the Old Testament
NIGTC	New International Greek Testament Commentary
NIV	New International Version
NovTSup	Novum Testamentum Supplement

NPNF	Nicene and Post-Nicene Fathers
NTAbh	Neutestamentliche Abhandlungen
NTD	Das Neue Testament Deutsch
NTS	*New Testament Studies*
OBT	Overtures to Biblical Theology
OTG	Old Testament Guides
OTL	Old Testament Library
ÖTNT	Ökumenischer Taschenbuchkommentar zum Neuen Testament
OTP	*Old Testament Pseudepigrapha,* ed. James H. Charlesworth. 2 vols. Garden City, NY: Doubleday, 1983-1985
PG	Patrologia graeca, ed. J.-P. Migne. 162 vols. Paris: Migne, 1857-1891
PL	Patrologia latina, ed. J.-P. Migne. 221 vols. Paris: Migne, 1844-1864
PVTG	Pseudepigrapha Veteris Testamenti Graece
RAC	*Reallexikon für Antike und Christentum,* ed. T. Klauser et al. Stuttgart: Hiersemann, 1950-
RB	*Revue biblique*
REB	Revised English Bible
RSV	Revised Standard Version
SBLDS	Society of Biblical Literature Dissertation Series
SBT	Studies in Biblical Theology
SJT	*Scottish Journal of Theology*
SNTSMS	Society for New Testament Studies Monograph Series
ST	*Studia theologica*
Sup	Supplement
SVTP	Studia in Veteris Testamenti Pseudepigrapha
t.	Tosefta
TDNT	*Theological Dictionary of the New Testament,* ed. G. Kittel and G. Friedrich. Trans. G. W. Bromiley. 10 vols. Grand Rapids: Eerdmans, 1964-1976
TEV	Today's English Version
THKNT	Theologischer Handkommentar zum Neuen Testament
TNTC	Tyndale New Testament Commentaries
TynBul	*Tyndale Bulletin*
WA	Martin Luther, *Kritische Gesamtausgabe* (Weimar edition)
WBC	Word Biblical Commentary
WMANT	Wissenschaftliche Monographien zum Alten und Neuen Testament
WUNT	Wissenschaftliche Untersuchungen zum Neuen Testament
y.	Jerusalem Talmud

PART I

Introduction:
Orientation and Preparation

CHAPTER 1

"Greed as Idolatry":
A Formidable Peak

The judgment that "greed is idolatry" (τὴν πλεονεξίαν, ἥτις ἐστὶν εἰδωλολατρία, Col 3:5) and "the greedy person is an idolater" (ἢ πλεονέκτης, ὅ ἐστιν εἰδωλολάτρης, Eph 5:5) is startling, given that the prohibition of idolatry is so central to biblical religion and that it is the unspeakable sin that alone arouses God's powerful jealousy. The assertion says something not only about greed, potentially condemning a large group who would otherwise plead innocent to the charge of idolatry,[1] but also about God and true worship, since as Moshe Halbertal and Avishai Margalit have observed, different concepts of idolatry create, when reversed, different concepts of God.[2]

Whereas "greed is idolatry" is a suggestive expression susceptible of a variety of interpretations (see chapter 2 below), most commentators offer

---

1. Cf. Chrysostom's 18th Homily on Ephesians, where he anticipates the objections of the reader: Ἀλλ᾽ οὐκ ἐποίησα φησὶν, εἴδωλον, οὐδὲ ἔστησα βωμὸν, οὐδὲ κατέθυσα πρόβατα, οὐδὲ οἶνον ἐπέσπεισα, ἀλλ᾽ εἰς ἐκκλησίαν εἰσῆλθον, καὶ χεῖρας ἀνέτεινα τῷ μονογενεῖ τοῦ Θεοῦ Παιδὶ, καὶ μυστηρίων μετέχω, καὶ εὐχῆς κοινωνῶ, καὶ τῶν ἄλλων ἁπάντων, ὧν προσῆκε τὸν Χριστιανόν (PG, 62:123). ("But I have made no image, erected no altar, slaughtered no sheep, and poured out no libation. Rather I have gone to church and have stretched out my hands to the only begotten Son of God. I have a share in the mysteries and in all other things that belong to Christians.")

2. Halbertal and Margalit, *Idolatry*, 1.

only one and do not acknowledge the possibility of others, and little serious attention has been paid to it in the modern era.[3] Yet a number of historical, exegetical, and, above all, theological issues are raised by the words:

- What does "greed" signify in the expression? Does πλεονεξία here mean sexual greed? If greed in the material realm is its meaning, are the greedy always guilty of oppression and dishonest gain? Who were the greedy in the early church?
- Is only greed equivalent to idolatry? John Chrysostom and Gregory of Nazianzus labeled greed "the second idolatry." Does a third or a fourth form exist? Is sexual immorality or some other vice also idolatry?
- What is the origin of the expression? Can it be traced to biblical and Jewish teaching, to Jesus tradition, or to popular moral philosophy? Or is it original to the New Testament author, his own "creative moral reflection"?[4]
- Do Philippians 3:19/Romans 16:18 and Matthew 6:24/Luke 16:13 mean the same thing as "greed is idolatry"? (Respectively: "their god is their belly" and "No one can serve two masters; for either he will hate the one and love the other, or he will be devoted to one and despise the other. You cannot serve God and mammon.")
- Is "greed is idolatry" a central and profound notion in Christian theology and ethics, distilling much in arresting fashion, or is it just an ill-considered exaggeration?[5]
- What does the judgment that "greed is idolatry" contribute to a Christian response to Western materialism?
- Above all, in what sense are the greedy guilty of idolatry? What is idolatry? What is worship? What constitutes a god?

---

3. Schottroff, "Die Befreiung vom Götzendienst der Habsucht," is an exception. On this article see chapter 2, section 5, "The Meaning of the Expression: Greed Is Slavery Imposed by the Economic System."

4. Barclay, "Ordinary but Different," 37-38.

5. In other words, is the equation of greed with idolatry "rather surprising" (O'Brien, *Colossians*, 183), a "surprising statement" (Delling, 271), "strange" (Clark, *Ephesians*, 167)? Cf. Chrysostom: Τινὲς δὲ ὑπερβολὴν εἶναι φασί τὸ, Ὁ πλεονέκτης εἰδωλολάτρης ἐστιν. Ἀλλ' οὐκ ἔστιν ὑπερβολῆς τὸ ῥῆμα, ἀλλὰ ἀληθείας (PG, 62:122-23; 18th Homily on Ephesians) ("Some say the words, 'the greedy is an idolater,' is a hyperbolic statement. But this expression is no hyperbole; it is pure truth"); and Thomas Manton, *Complete Works*, 19:210: "I confess this staggered me at first."

Before proceeding, I want to comment on two terms from the full title of the book. The first is *idolatry.* In dealing with the subject of idolatry in the Old Testament we immediately confront a problem of definition, for the term can be taken to mean both the worship of foreign gods and the worship of images. The present study takes both senses to be valid. The second commandment extends and applies the first.[6] At least in the Israelite understanding, a pagan deity was present in its image (cf. Exod 20:23, "gods of silver" and "gods of gold"; 32:31, "golden gods"; Lev 19:4, "molten gods"; Josh 24:14, "remove the gods"; 2 Kgs 17:29; 19:18, "remove the foreign gods").

Disagreement over the division of the Ten Words also belies the close relation between the first and second commandments.[7] Whereas the conventional Jewish division takes the opening verse as the first commandment and the prohibitions of worshiping other gods and the worship of images as the second, Augustine, the Roman Catholic, and Lutheran traditions consider all of this material to be the first commandment. In most cases the Old Testament authors do not distinguish between the worship of other gods, the worship of images, and the worship of the Lord using images. While a formal distinction between having gods and having images is possible, and may be useful especially in exploring teaching about the latter, for our purposes idolatry is taken in the broadest sense to include material relating to both.

The second term concerns the *Pauline* authorship of Colossians and Ephesians. Needless to say, the authenticity of both letters is a matter of dispute. This book contributes nothing to this question. While I am not persuaded by the arguments against authenticity, and refer to Paul as the author of both letters, very little in the book's argument depends upon Pauline authorship.

The comparison of greed with idolatry is arguably a high point in New Testament ethics, an alluring but formidable peak. As seen above, its interpretation raises a pile of historical, exegetical, and theological questions. A major thesis of this book is that the notion of greed as idolatry is best understood by analyzing it as a metaphor. Thus, in keeping with the spirit of this approach, one may compare the task of interpreting the words "greed

---

6. Cf. Weinfeld, *Deuteronomy 1–11,* 288.

7. When referring to the Decalogue, I adopt the division supported by Philo, Josephus, and the church fathers and followed in Protestant circles.

is idolatry" to climbing a mountain.[8] As any mountain climber knows, success depends to a large extent on adequate preparation:

- The example of other climbers should be observed and their advice heard (see chapter 2: "The History of Interpretation").
- Maps and supplies need to be assembled and the appropriate climbing techniques learned (see chapter 3: "Method for the Present Study").
- A comparison with similar peaks in the landscape leading up to the summit in question should be undertaken (see part II: "The Origin of the Concept of Idolatrous Greed"), including the distant ranges of the Jewish Scriptures, the tablelands of early Jewish moral teaching, and the foothills of the New Testament.
- Lastly, the surrounding region must be thoroughly explored (see chapter 8: "Understanding Greed"; and chapter 9: "Understanding Idolatry").
- Only then will we be ready to scale the mountain itself (see chapter 10: "Understanding Greed as Idolatry").

I hope the reader will agree with John Calvin: "Indeed this matter is well worth dealing with at greater length."[9]

8. See further analysis of this metaphor as it relates to greed as idolatry in the last section of chapter 3, "'Greed Is Idolatry' as a Metaphor."

9. John Calvin on "the greedy person is an idolater" (Eph 5:5), *Sermons on Ephesians*, 503.

CHAPTER 2

The History of Interpretation:
Lessons from Other Climbers

The task of this chapter is to examine critically the ways in which the words "greed is idolatry" have been understood by interpreters in the past. We shall not concentrate on the meaning of "greed" per se, which has basically been understood as either greed for material things or as sexual greed (see chapter 8),[1] but on the sense in which greed of whatever sort may be said to be idolatry. The standard sources for the history of interpretation of a biblical text will be consulted, including the church fathers (who have more to say than authors in the modern period);[2] important theological figures from across the centuries such as Augustine, Aquinas, and the Reformers Calvin, Luther, and Zwingli; and the biblical commentaries and studies of New Testament ethics from the last two centuries. Furthermore, some sources not normally seen as significant for historical-critical interpretation of the Bible are taken into account, including the

---

1. Until some twentieth-century commentators understood the immediate contexts in Eph 5 and Col 3 to support the meaning of sexual greed, it was taken for granted that "greed" meant greed for material things.

2. Cf. Carpenter, "Popular Christianity," 296, on the preference of the fathers for practical matters: "When Hermas or Second Clement spend a free half-hour in a little theological excursion it is sure to end abruptly in an earnest moral precept." Our stress on the church fathers confirms Hengel's conviction, *Property and Riches*, vii, that studies of such ethical subjects in NT studies should be extended into the early church.

fourteenth-century Viennese Pastor Ulrich von Pottenstein's magnum opus on the first commandment; the Puritans and writers in the tradition of liberation theology, both of which bring unique perspectives to the subject; together with the occasional unwitting interpreter, such as Karl Marx, who supplies a vivid portrait of the alien god of money, and Christian hymns that sometimes succinctly capture the sense of the expression in a striking fashion.[3] Even on a subject as narrow as the relationship between two words in two New Testament texts we cannot hope to present a comprehensive survey. The aim is to cover a broad range of material to ensure that as many views as possible are represented and assessed. The history of interpretation covers first the question of origin, which can be treated relatively briefly, and then of meaning.

The Origin of the Expression

Various authors assume that "greed is idolatry" is a thought original to Ephesians and Colossians and attempt to explain its genesis, or at least the inspiration that led to its formulation. Some assert or at least imply that Paul coined the phrase in order to magnify the sinfulness of greed. For example, John Calvin asks, "why does Paul attribute to covetousness alone what belongs equally to other carnal passions? In what respect is covetousness better entitled to this disgraceful name than ambition, or than a vain confidence in ourselves?" His answer is that the judgment arose from Paul's desire to impress upon his readers the wickedness of greed, which is such a common vice and is commonly held to be a trifle: "I answer, that this disease [greed] is widely spread, and not a few minds have caught the infection. Nay, it is not reckoned a disease, but receives, on the contrary, very general commendation. This accounts for the harshness of Paul's language, which arose from a desire to tear from our hearts the false view."[4]

F. F. Bruce and Richard T. Clifford posit quite specific hypotheses for Paul's desire to condemn greed by labeling it idolatry. Whereas Bruce appeals to Paul's own experience, Clifford stresses his eschatological con-

---

3. The hymns that are cited are mainly from English-speaking Protestant worship. My research indicates that the concept of idolatrous greed is generally neglected in Christian devotion.

4. Calvin, *Ephesians*, 307.

sciousness: "The exceeding sinfulness of covetousness was revealed to Paul, according to Rom. 7:7-13, when he became aware of the commandment 'thou shalt not covet'"; "Pauline theology's radical devaluation of the present age in view of the coming of the new age led it to brand excessive concern with the wealth of this age as idolatry (Col 3:5)."[5] As valid as these considerations may be, the intended effect of the expression may or may not have been the original impulse for its coinage. It is likely that to give a dark assessment of greed is the intended effect (see chapter 10, the section on "Feeling the Metaphor"), but whether this explains the origin of the expression in Colossians and Ephesians is another question. Probably the person who invented the hammer did so in order to drive in nails more effectively. However, to assume that a neighbor hammering nails with a measure of success invented the hammer is to mistake effect or intention for origin.

B. S. Easton, on the other hand, suggests a very specific and almost accidental origin:

> These [vice lists in Ephesians and Colossians] are obviously largely conventional, but Paul has made them serve his immediate purpose excellently. In this way we have the probable explanation for the perplexing phrase "covetousness which is idolatry," . . . it is evident that Paul is citing a formula which concluded with "covetousness and idolatry"; idolatry being the culminating term as in other lists already discussed. But it suddenly occurred to him that the Colossians were in no need of a warning against idolatry, and so he changed the wording, producing a phrase that no doubt lacks clarity but which teaches an excellent moral lesson.[6]

The likelihood of such an ingenious explanation depends upon the strength of evidence for preexisting similar concepts. Such conjecture should only be countenanced in the absence of more historically based explanations.

Two observations suggest that the words "greed is idolatry" are not original to the author of Ephesians and Colossians. The first is that, as Easton observes, Colossians 3:5 is part of the practical section of the letter, much of which is thought to have been derived from traditional sources, as

5. Bruce, *Colossians*, 144, on Col 3:5; Clifford, "Idol," 418.
6. Easton, "New Testament Ethical Lists," 6.

for example does the household code of Colossians 3:18–4:1 (see chapter 3, the section on "Jewish Moral Teaching in Colossians"). Eduard Lohse, for example, asserts: "it is certain that the train of thought explicated in the relative clause ('covetousness' and 'idolatry' are intimately connected) was adopted from the tradition [of the household code]."[7] The second is the expression's compactness, which like proverbs and many titles in the New Testament, it is assumed, suggests a history of usage.

Two traditional sources have been suggested. The first is the words of Jesus in Matthew 6:24/Luke 16:13, which supposedly express a kindred thought. M. Dibelius writes, for example: "The word of the Lord could certainly have given rise to the striking interpretation of greed [as idolatry]."[8]

Some scholars, however, are reluctant to see a dependence on the words of Jesus, which at best expresses a similar thought but in different words. They assert that in ancient Judaism such an assessment of greed was a commonplace. J. B. Lightfoot argues, for instance: "The idea of avarice as a *religion* may have been suggested to St. Paul by our Lord's words, Matt. vi. 24. . . . It appears however elsewhere in Jewish writers of this and later ages."[9] Lohse comes to a similar conclusion.[10] Hans Conzelmann expresses what is perhaps the majority opinion: "In all likelihood, the author has taken over a Jewish precept."[11]

Although not infrequently asserted, the hypothesis that the words have a Jewish background has not been thoroughly investigated. At best a few texts are listed with no attempt at serious comparison. Furthermore, since the charge of idolatry was bound up with the first commandment in Jewish minds, a possible scriptural background cries out for attention that treats the early Jewish texts in connection with and as examples of biblical interpretation. The only way to decide the issue of origin is to examine carefully the tradition out of which the expression could conceivably have arisen, which will be our goal in part II.

7. Lohse, *Colossians*, 139 n. 25.
8. Dibelius, *Kolosser*, 43. Unless stated otherwise, translations of German secondary sources into English are by me.
9. Lightfoot, *Colossians*, 210.
10. Lohse, *Colossians*, 139.
11. Conzelmann, *Epheser*, 116.

The Meaning of the Expression

Nine different responses have been given in answer to the question of the meaning of the words "greed is idolatry":

1. No interpretation, where the commentators' explanations fall short of explaining the meaning of the words.
2. Greed is as bad as idolatry, which holds that the words are intended to assert the equal severity of greed and idolatry, and nothing more.
3. Greed leads to idolatry, which understands the words, along with *Testament of Judah* 19.1, as asserting that greed leads to idolatrous practices.
4. Greed is worship of the god or demon "mammon," which explains the connection between greed and idolatry in terms of demonic influence.
5. Greed is slavery imposed by the economic system, which understands the words not in terms of private and individual morality, but as an indictment of sinful economic and societal structures.
6. Greed is service and obedience to wealth.
7. Greed is inordinate love of and devotion to wealth.
8. Greed is trusting in wealth.
9. Complex interpretations, which adopt two or three of the foregoing interpretations.

Views 6, 7, and 8 are similar in that they treat the words as a metaphor and propose some essential similarity between the way the greedy relate to their possessions and the way believers ought to relate to God.

1. No Interpretation

Many of the modern commentators note (supposedly) parallel sentiments in the ancient world and/or stress the weight given "greed" by the comparison with idolatry, but offer nothing by way of genuine interpretation of the relation between the two. Some give effectively nothing more than a restatement of the words, going no further than the surface meaning of the greedy paying homage to their wealth or replacing God with material things.[12]

---

12. See, e.g., the following commentaries on Colossians: Lohmeyer (1964), Thompson

To say that "greed is idolatry" means that the greedy worship, revere, or concentrate their whole being on money or worldly goods is merely to reiterate the judgment and go no further. Such statements themselves call for interpretation and leave us no better off than with the words they purportedly interpret. Any interpretation worthy of the label must attempt to explain in straightforward terms the sense in which greed and idolatry are being compared.

2. Greed Is as Bad as Idolatry

Although not commonly espoused, this view is perhaps the simplest and most obvious interpretation of the words "greed is idolatry." Rather than looking for some deep or essential similarity between greed and idolatry, this interpretation takes the predication to indicate that the sin of greed is as equally grave as idolatry and no more.

Many commentators note the severe assessment of greed that the words imply as they proceed to explain their meaning. For example, D. Johann Friedrich von Flatt, who thinks the words condemn the love of the greedy for their wealth, nonetheless states: "Greed is just as reprehensible as idolatry."[13] Some, like L. F. O. Baumgarten-Crusius, approach the matter from a different angle, claiming that Paul brands the greedy as bad as the heathen, who are identified by their characteristic vice, idolatry.[14]

Furthermore, in commenting on the words various authors reflect on their intention and the lighter assessment which the sin of greed often receives. Charles Simeon laments: "And as to 'covetousness,' there is no such thing existing in the world, if every person's estimate of himself may be relied on. Men will, indeed, impute it to others; but no one acknowledges it in himself."[15] R. C. H. Lenski recounts a telling experience: "A Catholic

---

(1967), Pokorný (1987), Wolter (1993), Barth (1994); and on Ephesians: Matthies (1834), Ellicott (1855), Foulkes (1963), Vaughan (1978), Mussner (1982), Lindemann (1985), Pokorny (1992).

13. Von Flatt, Epheser, 509.

14. Baumgarten-Crusius, Epheser (on Eph 5:5), 149.

15. Simeon, Works, vol. 17: Galatians–Ephesians, 376. Barnes, Notes, 317, suggests four reasons why greed was in his day often not held to be so grave as, for instance, sexual immorality, by Christians. His observations arguably apply to both Paul's day and ours and help one to appreciate the reason that greed was given such a striking condemnation in Ephesians

priest states that during his long years of service all kinds of sins and crimes were confessed to him in the confessional but never the sin of covetousness."[16]

L. J. Rückert, however, is an early and clear proponent of the view that the equation of greed with idolatry in terms of severity exhausts the meaning of the expression. Rückert mentions a number of rabbinic texts, without supplying details or references, that he claims assert that pride and anger are as bad as idolatry. In this light he surmises that Paul may be doing something similar with greed, expressing disgust for it and consigning the greedy to the company of the heathen.[17]

The equal severity interpretation must be considered a grammatical possibility, since utterances in the form of "*a* is *b*" (or "*a* is like *b*")[18] can in some cases signify "*a* is as bad as *b*," such as in the Sermon on the Mount, where one could summarize some of the teaching as "lust is/is like/is as bad as adultery" and "anger is/is like/is as bad as murder." In these cases the subject is what is normally thought of as a less serious version of the predicate and the intent is to insist that "*a* is no less serious than *b*"; "*a* is tantamount to *b*." Nonetheless, it is conceivable that idolatry, which in Jewish tradition is judged to be such a heinous sin, could be used as the standard against which another sin might be tainted by association. In such circumstances, "greed is (as bad as) idolatry" would be, in terms of the figures of speech, properly labeled hyperbole, and the key to its interpretation would lie in simply clarifying the word "is."

The view is not only grammatically possible, but may also point to the analogous use of idolatry in some contemporary and later Jewish sayings for support. Halbertal and Margarlit note three pertinent examples in their study of idolatry in Jewish tradition, the first two of which are probably the texts Rückert had in mind:

"A proud person is like an idol worshiper."

---

and Colossians: "Because, (1) it is so common; (2) because it is found among those who make pretensions to refinement and even religion; (3) because it is not so easy to define what is covetousness, as it is to define impurity of life; and (4) because the public conscience is seared, and the mind blinded to the low and grovelling character of the sin."

16. Lenski, *Colossians*, 160.

17. Rückert, *Epheser*, 226.

18. Soskice, "Metaphor," 447, rightly insists that similes are semantically equivalent to metaphors.

"If someone tears clothing or breaks utensils in his anger, he should be considered like an idolater."

"One who changes his speech is like an idolater."[19]

We may add two more. First, in 1 Samuel 15:23 Saul's failure to carry out the ban led Samuel, who wished to underscore the seriousness of his sin, to compare it to divination and idolatry. The second instance varies the pattern by comparing the sin to be condemned to the archetypal sin of idolatry rather than to idolatry in general: the minor tractates *Sepher Torah* 1:6 and *Sopherim* 1:7 declare that the day when the seventy elders translated the Torah into Greek for King Ptolemy was as bad a day for Israel as when the golden calf was fashioned.[20]

Roger Brooks argues that it was in fact routine for rabbis to stress the seriousness of sins by equating them with the sin of idolatry and supplies an explanation in terms of the primacy of the first commandment (or in the Jewish reckoning, the first and second commandments):

The rabbis' overwhelming tendency is to equate the transgression at hand with idolatry: "You shall have no other gods besides Me!" Bearing false witness is comparable to worshipping an idol; committing adultery is comparable to worshipping an idol. Why? The rabbis take seriously the first of God's Utterances: "I the LORD am your God who brought you out of the land of Egypt, the house of bondage!" God's zealous desire to be Israel's deity, expressed positively through the special historical relationship between God and Israel, prepares the way for all that follows. Observance of God's Commandments clearly implies the Israelites' recognition of their relationship to God. But, as a corollary, ignoring any one of the commandments would imply an idolatrous disregard: You shall have no other gods besides Me! . . . Any violation of Torah, therefore, constituted an act of idolatry. . . . For the rabbis, any transgression of the Ten Utterances implied a de-

19. Halbertal and Margalit, *Idolatry*, 11, 254 n. 2, citing *t. Baba Qamma* 9 (cf. *b. Shabbat* 105b); *B. Sanhedrin* 92b.

20. This text is cited in Hengel, "Die Septuaginta als 'christliche Schriftensammlung,'" 205, who explains the judgment as underscoring the belief that the Hebrew Torah cannot be translated. Cf. Smolar and Aberbach, "Golden Calf," 106: "it was not unusual to compare any ill-fated day in the annals of the Jewish people to the day on which the golden calf was made."

nial of God's omniscience and omnipotence, and thus constituted an idolatrous act.[21]

In support Brooks cites the detailed comparison of the fourth commandment concerning Sabbath observance with the first commandment in the discussion of appropriate punishment for multiple acts in *y. Nazir* 6:1 54c/24b and *b. Sanhedrin* 62a-b; *b. Shabbat* 70a-b, which in his view establishes "a substantive analogy between one of the Ten Utterances and the absolute prohibition against idol worship,"[22] the equation of perjury or bearing false witness with sexual and idolatrous sin in *y. Ketubot* 3:1; 27b/16b-17a and *b. Yebamot* 90a-b, and the connection between idolatrous belief and sinful action established in *y. Sanhedrin* 10:2; 28d; 51b-52a and *b. Sanhedrin* 106a. Whether or not Brooks's generalizations are too sweeping, his general point stands: "Idolatry clearly was of paramount interest to the rabbis . . . the rabbis widely discussed this transgression and accorded it the most severe gravity"[23] and used it on occasion to condemn a sin that might otherwise be considered less serious.

Whatever interpretation the words are given, they doubtless serve to emphasize the seriousness of the sin of greed. Two examples of them being put to this use by the church fathers suffice to make the point. In a letter to the Chorepiscopi, a class of ministers between the bishops proper and presbyters, Basil the Great responds to a report that some other ministers take money from "candidates for ordination,"[24] which he regarded as nothing less than taking a bribe. Basil concludes his letter of condemnation of the practice by quoting Ephesians 5:5/Colossians 3:5 without interpretation, along with 1 Timothy 1:10, in an effort to impress upon his readers the seriousness of their actions: "One word more, and I have done. These things come of covetousness. And covetousness is the root of all evil and is called idolatry. Do not then prize idols above Christ for the sake of a little money."

Tertullian quotes the words also in tandem with 1 Timothy 1:10 ("love of money, the root of all evil"), in *Idolatry* 1.10, in a discussion of whether trade and commerce are lawful when such activities involve "incense and the other exotic articles, which are a sacrifice to the idols" (11:2). He wishes

---

21. Brooks, *Spirit of the Ten Commandments*, 46-47 (see further 74-90), 74, 80.
22. Ibid., 82.
23. Ibid., 89.
24. Basil the Great, Letter 53 (NPNF, p. 156).

to taint such trade with the motive of greed, and in so doing cites the two Pauline denunciations of greed to make his point more telling. He offers no interpretation of the words. Rather, as J. H. Waszink and J. C. M. van Winden observe, "the intention is to give extra emphasis to the wickedness of covetousness."[25]

However, the issues of function or use (which we will consider in chapter 10, the section on "Feeling the Metaphor") must not be confused with meaning and interpretation. Whether it is right to adopt the minimalist equal severity interpretation of the words "greed is idolatry" depends upon whether it can be demonstrated that something more than the most superficial similarity, their equal gravity, is intended. Either way, the view underscores the impact of the predication in terms of branding greed to be as serious as the most serious sin that characterizes the heathen, namely, idolatry.

3. Greed Leads to Idolatry

The most commonly cited parallel text in discussions of "greed is idolatry" is *Testament of Judah* 19.1: Τέκνα μου, ἡ φιλαργυρία πρὸς εἰδωλολατρείαν[26] ὁδηγεῖ ("My children, love of money leads to idolatry"). While most commentators are simply content to notice it as a kindred thought, some cite it as the key to explaining the Pauline expression.[27]

The immediately preceding verses in *Testament of Judah* 18 help explain the text in question. Judah warns against both sexual immorality and the love of money, as two sins that lead one away from God:

Ὅτι καίγε ἀνέγνων ἐν βίβλοις Ἐνὼχ τοῦ δικαίου ὅσα κακὰ ποιήσετε ἐν ἐσχάταις ἡμέραις. Φυλάξασθε οὖν, τέκνα μου, ἀπὸ τῆς πορνείας καὶ τῆς φιλαργυρίας, ἀκούσατε Ἰουδὰ τοῦ πατρὸς ὑμῶν, ὅτι ταῦτα ἀφιστᾷ νόμου θεοῦ, καὶ τυφλοῖ τὸ διαβούλιον τῆς ψυχῆς, καὶ ὑπερηφανίαν ἐκδιδάσκει, καὶ οὐκ ἀφίει ἄνδρα ἐλεῆσαι τὸν πλησίον αὐτοῦ, στερίσκει τὴν ψυχὴν αὐτοῦ ἀπὸ πάσης ἀγαθοσύνης, καὶ συνέχει αὐτὸν ἐν μόχθοις καὶ πόνοις, καὶ ἀφιστᾷ ὕπνον αὐτοῦ, καὶ

---

25. Waszink and van Winden, in Tertullian, *Idololatria*, 201.
26. Manuscripts β,A,S read εἴδωλα.
27. See, e.g., Conzelmann, *Epheser*, 116; and Gnilka, *Kolosserbrief*, 182.

καταδαπανᾷ σάρκας αὐτοῦ, καὶ θυσίας θεοῦ ἐμποδίζει, καὶ εὐλογίας
οὐ μέμνηται, καὶ προφήτῃ λαλοῦντι οὐχ ὑπακούει, καὶ λόγῳ εὐσεβείας
προσοχθίζει. Δύο γὰρ πάθη ἐναντία τῶν ἐντολῶν τοῦ θεοῦ δουλεύων
θεῷ ὑπακούειν οὐ δύναται, ὅτι ἐτύφλωσαν τὴν ψυχὴν αὐτοῦ, καὶ ἐν
ἡμέρᾳ ὡς ἐν νυκτὶ πορεύεται.[28]

For in the books of Enoch the Righteous I have read the evil things
you will do in the last days. Guard yourselves therefore, my children,
against sexual promiscuity and love of money: listen to Judah, your
father, for these things distance you from the law of God, blind the
direction of the soul, and teach arrogance. They do not permit a man
to show mercy to his neighbor. They deprive his soul of all goodness,
and oppress him with hardships and pain, they take away sleep from
him and utterly waste his flesh. They impede sacrifices to God, he
does not remember the blessings [of God], he does not obey the
prophet when he speaks, and he is offended by a pious word. For two
passions contrary to God's commands enslave him, so that he is un-
able to obey God: They blind his soul, and he goes about in the day as
though it were night.

Since the love of money is a powerful hindrance to obeying and worshiping God, Judah reasons in the next verse, 19.1, that it will lead ultimately to
the worship of false gods. The Old Testament contains related teaching, especially in Jewish interpretation of the Song of Moses, where becoming
rich and powerful leads God's people to forget God and finally to outright
idolatry (see, e.g., Deut 31:20; 32:15ff.).[29] Such teaching may well be of in-

---

28. See de Jonge, *Testaments: Critical Edition,* 71-72.

29. The notion that wealth often leads to apostasy and at the very least can be an obstacle to faith in and fidelity to God is represented in a number of Christian hymns. Note the
following examples, all of which, excluding the last, stem from the nineteenth century:
"Lord, I care not for riches, Neither silver nor gold; I would make sure of heaven, I would enter the fold" ("Is My Name Written There?" by M. A. Kidder and Frank M. David; *Sacred
Songs and Solos,* ed. I. D. Sankey, no. 285); "Vain the world, its pleasures boasting; vain the
charms of life to me; Gold is dross, and riches worthless, If they turn my heart from Thee:
("Welcome, Welcome, O Redeemer," by F. J. Crosby and R. Bottome; *Hymns of Consecration
and Faith,* ed. J. Mountain and Mrs. Evan Hopkins, no. 210); "Come, Saviour, as in days of
old; Pass where the world has strongest hold, And faithless care and selfish greed Are thorns
that choke the holy seed" ("He Sat to Watch o'er Customs Paid," by W. Bright; *Revival
Hymns and Choruses,* ed. S. H. Toy, no. 138); "Search out our hearts and make us true, Wish-
ful to give all their due; From love of pleasure, lust of gold, From sins which make the heart

terest in understanding how a Jew could arrive at the conclusion that "greed is idolatry" and we shall explore it further in part II.

Strictly speaking, however, the notion that greed "leads to" the literal worship of other gods is not the same as judging greed itself "to be" idolatry, as we have in Colossians 3:5 and Ephesians 5:5. J. B. Lightfoot's conclusion is sound: "The passage in *Test. xii Patr.* Jud, 18 [sic] . . . is no real parallel to St Paul's language, though at first sight it seems to resemble it."[30]

4. Greed Is the Worship of the God or Demon "Mammon"

Some scholars have interpreted the words in Colossians 3:5/Ephesians 5:5 in the light of the mammon saying in Matthew 6:24/Luke 16:13 and explain the connection in terms of demonic influence. G. Delling writes: "It [greed] brings him under an ungodly and demonic spell which completely separates him from God through serving an alien power."[31] Ralph Martin concurs. Having cited Delling, he explains: "To that extent it [greed] is no better than a spirit of idolatry, the worship of Mammon (an Aramaic word for wealth which the rabbis personified as a demon, Matt. 6:24)."[32] In support we may note that a few nineteenth-century scholars claimed that mammon was a known Syrian deity, and in some later Christian sources *Mamonas* is depicted as the demon of wealth.[33]

However, solid evidence for either a god or a demon of mammon (or greed) in the first century is lacking.[34] Only a few traces suggest such a link. These include Damascus Document (CD) 4:15-17, where one of the three nets of Belial is wealth, and *Testament of Judah* 19.4, where "the

---

grow cold" ("Before Thy Throne, O God, We Kneel," by William Boyd Carpenter; *The Methodist Hymnbook*, no. 884); "The Voice says, Cry! [cf. Isa 40:6-8] What stops the cry? Our greed of wealth, our love of ease" ("The Voice Says, Cry!" by H. Twells, *The Church Hymnal for the Christian Year*, no. 642); "I want You more than gold or silver, Only You can satisfy; I love you more than any other, So much more than anything" ("As the Deer," by Martin Nystrom, *Spirit of Praise*, no. 13).

30. Lightfoot, *Colossians*, 213.
31. Delling, *TDNT*, 6:271.
32. Martin, *Colossians*, 109-10.
33. See Peterson, "Engel- und Personennamen."
34. Davies and Allison, *Matthew*, 1:643.

prince of error" is blamed for blinding Judah with respect to the harmful effects of the love of money.[35] However, these texts are references to the activity of the evil one in tempting humans to sin in general and do not establish a firm link between greed and a demon or god. In the case of Colossians 3:5 and Ephesians 5:5 one should also not jump to the conclusion that the reference to idolatry necessarily calls to mind the presence of demons. The common Jewish association of idolatry with demons, which Paul shared according to 1 Corinthians 10, need not be read into "greed is idolatry," especially if the expression functions as a metaphor.

As attractive as the demonic explanation is for Matthew 6:24/Luke 16:13 in the light of Jesus' struggle against demonic forces and the inauguration of the kingdom of God, it is more likely that the words in question consist of a personification of wealth as an evil and superhuman power that stands in opposition to God, "possessing" them and distracting them from devotion to God.[36] That wealth can exercise such an enslaving power was a well-known insight among Greeks and Romans,[37] and Jesus was not averse to using such dramatic figures of speech. If demon worship is not the point in Matthew 6:24/Luke 16:13, it is also not an explanation for "greed is idolatry" in Ephesians and Colossians.

The personification of greed brings us to the next interpretation, which also conceives of greed as an alien god.

5. Greed Is Slavery Imposed by the Economic System

In offering his comprehensive critique of capitalism, Karl Marx at one point employs the rhetoric of idolatry. His reflections are not of course concerned with the interpretation of the New Testament. In fact, in his discourse the counterpoint to idolatry is not the true worship of God, but rather human self-fulfillment. Nonetheless, what he says constitutes an unwitting interpretation of the words "greed is idolatry" that tallies with many of the sentiments expressed not only by those espousing the view that greed is slavery imposed by the economic system but also by those

---

35. See 1 Tim 6:9; *T. Jud.* 17.4. Schottroff's generalization, "Befreiung," 143, is slightly exaggerated: "For Jewish and NT texts greed is a work of the devil."

36. Cf. van der Horst, "Mammon."

37. Cf. van der Horst, *Sentences*, 142-43; Frank, "Habsucht."

proposing the related view that greed is service and obedience to wealth (see following section).[38]

Marx reflects on the irony of the capitalist system, where instead of products belonging to their producers, the reverse state of affairs attains, and alienation results. Products are no longer valued for their usefulness, but only for their market value, and money becomes the alien god that confers this value: "Money is the general, self-sufficient value of everything. Hence it has robbed the whole world, the human world as well as nature, of its proper worth. Money is the alienated essence of man's labor and life and this alien essence dominates him as he worships it."[39]

Employing Feuerbach's critique of religion in terms of the projection of human needs and desires, Marx postulates that greed has an analogous dehumanizing effect: "The more the worker exerts himself, the more powerful becomes the alien objective world which he fashions against himself, the poorer he and his inner world become, the less there is that belongs to him. It is the same in religion."[40] In Marx's view, greed is a god because it dominates people's lives and demands an obedience tantamount to slavery.[41] Marx does not view greed as a matter of individual morality but as a structural and societal ill.

Luise Schottroff, who writes in the tradition of liberation theology, builds upon the insights of Marx (and Leonhard Ragaz) in her essay, "Die Befreiung vom Götzendienst der Habgier."[42] She asks: "In the New

38. Marx is treated along with Francis Bacon, Ludwig Wittgenstein, David Hume, Niccolo Machiavelli, Jean-Jacques Rousseau, and Friedrich Nietzsche as case studies of modern discourse on idolatry by Halbertal and Margalit, *Idolatry*, 241-49. Cf. Schottroff, "Befreiung," 139, who cites Marx as saying: "Money is the god of goods and possessions."

39. Marx, *Writings*, 245-46. Halbertal and Margalit, *Idolatry*, 43, explain Marx's view further: "The more man works the more he accumulates money, and the more he externalizes his essence to the alien god of money." See also Lyman, *Seven Deadly Sins*, 253-59, on Marx's characterization of money as "omnipotent . . . like a god" (254).

40. Marx, *Writings*, 289-90.

41. This insight has not escaped the notice of Christian ethicists. For example, Ellul, *Money and Power*, 76, states: "We can, if we must, use money, but it is really money that uses us and makes us servants by bringing us under its law and subordinating us to its aims." Cf. also Francis Bacon: "If money be not thy servant, it will be thy master. The covetous man cannot so properly be said to possess wealth, as that may be said to possess him" (cited in Schimmel, *Seven Deadly Sins*, 165).

42. Ragaz, *Gleichnisse Jesu*. Cf. 42: "Where God does not rule, there rule the idols, the most powerful of which is Mammon."

Testament is greed seen as an offense in terms of individual morality or as a structural sin of the economy in which the individual participates?" Schottroff believes that the latter is true and asks the penetrating question whether Christians in a capitalistic market economy are in any position to avoid such greed. Like Marx, she stresses the slavery that greed imposes.

Other writers in the tradition of liberation theology also take "greed is idolatry" to signify the power greed can exercise over human lives and note its keen relevance to capitalist societies. These include Hugo Assmann and Franz J. Hinkelammert, who write about the god of money and decry "ethical individualism — the privatization of ethics"; Pablo Richard, "Idolatry means the subjugation of people under the power of money"; and Dorothee Sölle, whose comments build upon the concept of sin as a power in Romans: "The real problem does not lie on the level of individual morality. The sin of greed is not a characteristic weakness of individuals, but rather it is a power over the structure of society as a whole."[43]

While it is a helpful corrective to underscore the corporate dimension of the problem of greed, however, I doubt if early Christians and Jews would have stated it in categories that foreshadow Marxist ideology. We shall return to the fact that the condemnation of greed in the early Christian communities had social consequences and was not just a matter of individual behavior when I address the definition of greed in chapter 8. At this point it is noteworthy that Marx, Schottroff, and others are not alone in underscoring the power of greed in making humans its slaves, as the next section demonstrates.

6. Greed Is Service and Obedience to Wealth

The most obvious comment about the utterance "greed is idolatry" is that it is a metaphor: greed is not literally idolatry. The greedy do not bow down before their possessions or set up altars to them. This is the presupposition of the vast majority of interpreters, even if few state it explicitly and no one to my knowledge considers the words in terms of the theory of how metaphors function. Most interpreters assume that the words imply a

---

43. Assmann and Hinkelammert, *Götze Markt;* Richard, "Unser Kampf," 33; Sölle, "Sünde und Entfremdung," 337.

comparison between how the greedy relate to their possessions and how idolaters or believers relate to their gods or God, respectively. The majority of these commentators regard the greedy as guilty of service and obedience, love and devotion (see below), or confidence and trust toward their money and possessions (see below). Thus when the words in question are treated as a metaphor, the question to be answered is: In what sense do the greedy worship their possessions instead of God? In other words, what is the intended point of similarity between the greedy and idolaters? Chrysostom is the most powerful exponent of the service-and-obedience interpretation.

Chrysostom refers to the words "greed is idolatry" no less than forty times in his extant writings, more often than any church father in Greek.[44] He deals with the matter at some length in his 18th homily on Ephesians. Above all, Chrysostom felt the shocking rhetorical impact of the words and sought to impress them upon his hearers with all earnestness. He insists that to call greed idolatry is no exaggeration, but in fact "pure truth." Greed, according to Chrysostom, is "an illness of the soul," "the worst type of decay." He expects his hearers to "shiver" and "shudder" at Paul's words and to "flee from this decay and seize the imperishable." With "preacher's license" he goes as far as to say that greed is "worse than idolatry"; greedy persons are "much worse than an idolater" because whereas idolaters defend their form of worship, greedy persons happily condemn in others the thing they themselves worship.

Chrysostom believes that the greedy are guilty of idolatry because they serve and obey something other than God. Anticipating the objection of the greedy that they do not worship their money, he counters:

Οὐ προσκυνῶ, φησί. Διὰ τί; ὅτι οὐ κάμπτεις σαυτόν; Ἀλλὰ νῦν πολλῷ μᾶλλον προσκυνεῖς διὰ τῶν ἔργων καὶ τῶν πραγμάτων. αὕτη γὰρ μείζων ἡ προσκύνησις. Καὶ ἵνα μάθῃς, θέα ἐπὶ τοῦ Θεοῦ, τίνες μᾶλλον αὐτὸν προσκυνοῦσιν, οἱ ἁπλῶς ἑστῶτες ἐν ταῖς προσευχαῖς, ἢ οἱ τὸ θέλημα αὐτοῦ ποιοῦντες; Εὔδηλον ὅτι οὗτοι. Οὕτω καὶ οἱ ἐπὶ τοῦ μαμμωνᾶ. (PG, 62:123 — 18th Homily on Ephesians)

"I do not worship!" you say. Why? Because you do not kneel in front of it? Yet you now worship all the more by your works and practices,

44. In Homily 8 on Colossians (NPNF, 297), Chrysostom indicates "we have oftentimes explained."

22

and that constitutes greater worship. In order to recognize this, look upon God and tell me: Who worships him more? Those who only stand in prayer or those who do his will? Obviously the latter. So it is also with those who look upon Mammon.

At another point the implicit connection between worship and obedience, which is fundamental to Chrysostom's interpretation of "greed is idolatry," is made clear. The greedy are those who τοὺς θεραπεύοντας αὐτὴν καὶ δουλεύοντας καὶ πειθομένους (PG, 62:125) ("serve it [Mammon] and slavishly obey it").

For Chrysostom, that the greedy serve their own selfish desires comes out in several ways. Chrysostom claims that the "altar of greed . . . strongly smells of human blood," implying that the greedy oppress the poor and needy in their relentless drive for more. With reference to Cain, who "wanted to cheat God due to greed," he explains that greed leads to a lack of love and eventually to pride and even "hatred and contempt of fellow human beings." The unstated premise in Chrysostom's interpretation is that since greed demands behavior that involves disobedience to God, then such service involves "falling away from God" and thus may be justifiably called idolatry. In order to lead the greedy to repentance he stresses the goodness of God in creation in supplying human needs and "inheritance in heaven," a far superior form of riches.

Although he nowhere explicitly says so, Chrysostom appears to interpret "greed is idolatry" in the light of Jesus' saying about serving either God or mammon. He personifies greed in terms of an evil rival master who demands obedience. That this was his consistent interpretation is seen in his Homilies on Colossians where he says that greed is one of the "things which do most of all lord it over the human race."[45]

Cyprian and Jerome confirm Chrysostom's understanding of the enslaving power of riches, although without referring to its idolatrous nature. In what Justo L. Gonzalez describes as "some of the harshest words penned by an early Christian writer against the acquisitiveness of the rich,"[46] Cyprian warns those:

who add forests to forests, and who, excluding the poor from their neighborhood, stretch out their fields far and wide into space

45. Ibid.
46. Gonzalez, *Faith and Wealth*, 127.

without limits. . . . Such a one enjoys no security either in his food or in his sleep. In the midst of the banquet he sighs, although he drinks from a jeweled goblet; and when his luxurious bed has enfolded his body, languid with feasting, he lies wakeful in the midst of the down; nor does he perceive, poor wretch, that these things are merely gilded torments, that he is held in bondage by his gold, and that he is the slave of his luxury and wealth rather than their master.[47]

Likewise Jerome counsels all Christians with means not to become a servant of wealth through greed.[48]

Very few interpreters, however, apart from a few church fathers, express the service-and-obedience interpretation of the words "greed is idolatry." The following six do so, but only in passing:

> Greed has to be compared to idolatry through a certain similitude which greed has with idolatry, because just as idolatry subjects itself to an external creature, so do the greedy, but not in the same way. Through idolatry someone subjects himself to an external creature through an act of divine cult. The greedy however subjects himself to an external creature through desiring it immoderately for one's own use and not for divine cult. (Thomas Aquinas)[49]

> Why is greed idolatry? Because it concerns the veneration of a god, the veneration of the god of money. . . . Money rules the world. Only a king can rule. (Werner Bieder)[50]

> The saying sets up an opposition [between greed and idolatry] in the same way as Jesus sets mammon against God and the slave of mammon against the slave of God. (Adolf Schlatter)[51]

---

47. Cyprian, *Ep.* 1.12.

48. Jerome, Commentary on Matthew 1.6.24, PL; cited by Gonzalez, *Faith and Wealth*, 195.

49. Aquinas, *Summa theologiae* 2-2, q. 118. In context Aquinas is concerned with the question as to whether greed is a mortal sin. His conclusion is that "greed does not have the same weight that idolatry has." Thanks are due to Dr. J. van den Eijnden for help in locating Aquinas's teaching on idolatrous greed.

50. Bieder, *Kolosserbrief*, 186.

51. Schlatter, *Epheserbrief*, 164-65.

The NT also understands idolatry as putting anything in the place that God alone should occupy as the proper focus of obedience and worship (e.g., Col 3:5). (Edward M. Curtis)[52]

Greed is called idolatry, because it turns people into slaves of their addiction always to have more. (Rudolf Hoppe)[53]

Greed is a form of idolatry because it projects acquisitiveness and personal satisfaction as objective go(o)ds to be praised and served. (James D. G. Dunn)[54]

The notion that believers belong to God and must obey him as servants is a biblical theme that has left its mark on many Christian hymns. Only rarely, however, is wealth depicted as a player in the contest of loyalties, as in the first verse of A. B. Simpson and George C. Stebbins's "I Belong to Him": "Tempt me not with sordid gain, Mock me not with earth's illusions, Vex me not with honour vain. I am weaned from sinful idols; I am hence forth not my own; I have given my heart to Jesus, I belong to Him alone."[55]

A nineteenth-century hymn by Joseph Barnby tells the story of the man from Macedonia's cry for help (Acts 16:9-10). Whereas the first two verses expand the call taking Macedonia as a symbol for fallen humanity (e.g., "How mournfully it echoes on! For half the earth is Macedon; These brethren to their brethren call . . . 'O ye that live, behold we die!'"), the third verse takes pains to stress that, paradoxically, the world as a whole neither issues nor hears the call. "By other sounds the world is won than that which wails from Macedon." According to Barnby, the world "cannot heed the alien cry." The cause of people's indifference to their need of God is put down to greed: "The roar of gain is round it [the world] rolled, Or men unto themselves are sold." Not only does the clamor for more drown out the cry from Macedon, but humans are depicted as in bondage to these very lusts. The hymn does not equate greed with idolatry, but rather portrays greed as a pernicious enslaving power. Aptly, as it turns out, the tune to which the hymn is set is called "St. Chrysostom," the major proponent of the view that idolatrous greed amounts to service and obedience to wealth.

52. Curtis, "Idol, Idolatry," *ABD*, 3:381.
53. Hoppe, *Epheserbrief/Kolosserbrief*, 142.
54. Dunn, *Colossians*, 216.
55. *Songs of Challenge*, no. 66.

In English literature the tragic and pitiful figure of Ebenezer Scrooge in *A Christmas Carol* (by Charles Dickens) represents well the slavery that greed imposes. In an encounter concocted by the Ghost of Christmas Past Scrooge is confronted with the awful truth that he worships a golden idol: "I have seen your nobler aspirations fall off one by one, until the master-passion, Gain, engrosses you." As a younger man "there was an eager, greedy, restless motion in the eye, which showed the passion that had taken root, and where the shadow of the growing tree would fall."[56] To his surprise it is made clear to Scrooge that what he needs is nothing short of "release" from his captivity.

The service-and-obedience view is closely related to Marx and Schottroff's understanding of the words (see 5 above). In both cases human beings are conceived of as suffering under the malicious tyranny of money and possessions. The two views may be regarded as complementary, with the first stressing the corporate dimension and the second the individual dimension.

7. Greed Is Inordinate Love of and Devotion to Wealth

The *New Shorter Oxford English Dictionary* defines the verb "to worship" as: "Honour or adore as divine or sacred, esp. with religious rites or ceremonies; offer prayer or prayers to (a god)."[57] By this definition the greedy clearly do not worship their possessions. The "transferred" (or figurative) sense is however more amenable to our purposes: Worship is to "regard with extreme respect, devotion, or love."[58] Similarly, definitions of the German word *verehren,* "worship," frequently involve the notion of love.[59] Thus according to the common usage of the English and German lan-

---

56. Dickens, *Christmas Carol,* 38-39.

57. Edited by Lesley Brown, 4th ed. (Oxford: Clarendon, 1993), vol. 2: *N Z,* 3723.

58. Cf. the definition of "idol" in *Oxford English Dictionary,* ed. J. A. Sampson and E. S. C. Weiner, 2nd ed. (Oxford: Clarendon, 1989), 7:629: "Anything or person that is the object of excessive or supreme devotion or that usurps the place of God in human affection." *Collins English Dictionary and Thesaurus* (Glasgow: HarperCollins, 1993), 1348, defines worship in similar terms as "admiring love or devotion."

59. E.g., *Der Große Duden Synonymwörterbuch,* ed. Paul Grebe and Wolfgang Müller (Mannheim: Duden, 1964), and *Der Sprach Brockhaus: Deutsches Bildwörterbuch von A-Z* (Wiesbaden: F. A. Brockhaus, 1984).

guages, to worship something, figuratively speaking, means then to render it (him or her) an inordinate amount of respect, devotion, or love. It is thus no accident that most interpreters in the modern period attach this meaning to the words "greed is idolatry." It is the most obvious interpretation, understanding worship in the narrowest and popular sense, and it involves little movement up the so-called ladder of abstraction. If to worship something means to have great love for it, then the love of money, for which the greedy are known, constitutes idolatrous worship.

The Viennese pastor Ulrich von Pottenstein (†1416 or 1417) presented late in the fourteenth century an understanding of "greed is idolatry" in precisely these terms.[60] In a massive work written as a catechism handbook, Ulrich undertook an exposition of the Lord's Prayer, the "Hail Mary" (Luke 1:28-33), the Apostolic Creed, and the Decalogue. His exposition of the first commandment alone runs to 360 pages in the edition by Gabriele Baptist-Hlawatsch and considers the subject in relation to faith, hope, love, gluttony, greed, and pride.[61] Chapter 47, "The Second Vice against the First Commandment: Greed," includes section D, entitled "Greed Is Idolatry" (226-29), which is of specific interest for our purposes.

Ulrich explains the relevant words in Ephesians 5:5 as follows:

> "Greed is idolatry." He [Paul] means the greedy person, whose god is the penny, [and who] honors and worships the penny as a god. He loves it more than himself and more than a good Christian loves God. He is willing to give his body, soul, and life for money. Such good Christian devotion toward God one seldom finds. The greedy person will never willingly be parted from his money.[62]

The author says little more by way of explanation, but instead concentrates on describing the excessiveness and callousness of the greedy, who insatiably oppress the poor. He uses graphic similes drawn from the world of nature and human experience, which prove that the greedy person val-

---

60. Schimmel, *Seven Deadly Sins*, 176, claims that an understanding of "greed is idolatry" in terms of love and devotion was quite popular with Christian moralists in the Middle Ages, when "the avaricious person is often equated with the idolater. He is like the Israelites in the wilderness who longed for a god and enthusiastically worshipped the golden calf. So too the greedy suffer from a misdirected and exaggerated love, directed to gods of this world rather than the true God."

61. Ulrich von Pottenstein, *Dekalog-Auslegung.*

62. The translations of von Pottenstein cited in this section are by George S. Rosner.

ues his or her material prosperity above all else. According to Ulrich, the greedy are described by Solomon in Ecclesiastes 2:23: "All his days are full of pain and worry, and his heart never rests at night." The greedy person is a miser whose heart turns to stone when he hears his neighbor's plea for help, for "misers are the hardest people who only have time for themselves. Nothing pleases them more than to cheat the poor and take their goods, thus making the poor sad."

Reflecting on Proverbs 28:15 ("Like an angry lion and a hungry bear, thus is an evil miser toward the poor"), Ulrich asserts that the greedy are even worse than the lion, who eats only when he is hungry and never eats more than he needs. "Therefore they are worse [than lions] when they gulp down whole sheep with skin and hair, although they have at that time no need of them." Continuing the comparison with animals of prey, Ulrich compares the greedy, on the basis of Ezekiel 22.27 ("Her princes in the midst thereof are like wolves ravaging their prey"), to a wolf, which, after entering the sheep pen, kills all the sheep even though he intends to eat only one.

Ulrich condemns the greedy for their selfishness and refusal to engage in charitable deeds: "they do not share their surplus lovingly with the miserable and needy." And he compares the mentality of greed to a serious illness: "It is strange to see that a miser, the more he has, the more he desires, like someone with a fever, who, the more water he drinks, the more he wants."

Augustine presents an understanding of idolatrous greed in terms of the related notions of enjoyment and pleasure (*fruitio*). According to Augustine there is a distinction between those things that are to be enjoyed and those things that are to be used: "To enjoy a thing is to rest with satisfaction in it for its own sake. To use, on the other hand, is to employ whatever means are at one's disposal to obtain what one desires."[63] The failure to observe this distinction results in sin: "Every human evil or vice consists in seeking to enjoy things that are to be used, and to use things that are to be enjoyed."[64] In the strictest sense, only God is to be enjoyed and things are to be used as means to this end. Sin results when we enjoy things, in the sense of finding true and ultimate joy and satisfaction in them, and use God to procure more and more things. Thus the greedy are clearly guilty

63. Augustine, *City of God* 11.25.
64. Augustine, *Eighty-three Different Questions* 30.

of idolatry in that they love money rather than God. Justo L. Gonzalez explains this Augustinian perspective: "The greedy seek to enjoy their possessions and sometimes even to use God in order to increase their wealth. In doing so, they fall into crass idolatry, for only God is to be enjoyed and all things are to be used to attain that enjoyment."[65]

Love and devotion is the most common interpretation of "greed is idolatry," especially in the twentieth century, in which it could be described as the consensus view. It is usually expressed with little explanation or defense. Within the constraints of a commentary, almost without exception, no other views are considered and the meaning of the words is taken to be almost self-evident. Along with the words "love" and "devotion," the interpretation is given most often with reference to the human heart and affections. The following citations offer a representative sample:

Love

God, for each one of us, is what we honour above all else, what we admire and love above all. (Radulphus)[66]

Devotion

The covetous man sets up another object of worship besides God. There is a sort of religious purpose, a devotion of the soul, to greed, which makes the sin of the miser so hateful. (J. B. Lightfoot)[67]

The point is that greedy, covetous persons, those who make their desires their object of devotion, are as much idolaters as are any of those who bow down before an idol in a pagan temple. (P. W. Comfort)[68]

All such greed places at the centre of one's attention and devotion that which is not God. (N. T. Wright)[69]

Obsession with created things instead of devotion to the Creator (e.g., Eph 5:5; Phil. 3:19, where gluttony and covetousness are said to be idolatry). (J. Gray)[70]

---

65. Gonzalez, *Faith and Wealth*, 216.
66. Homily 2.20 (PL, 155:2013).
67. Lightfoot, *Colossians*, 210.
68. Comfort, "Idolatry," 426.
69. Wright, *Colossians*, 134.
70. Gray, "Idolatry," *IDB*, 2:678.

Heart and Affections

[The greedy person] sets all his heart and mind on them [material things], and forgets God. . . . You see then that the covetous abuse their riches by setting their whole heart upon them (which nevertheless is forbidden them by the prophet in the psalm [Ps. 62:10]). (John Calvin)[71]

When it comes to greed, people devote their hearts to that which they desire, as to a god. (Heinrich Schlier)[72]

It [greed] secures the affections which properly belong to God. (Albert Barnes)[73]

Fornication and greed are idolatrous because in such cases a person's heart no longer belongs to God but rather to the objects of desire of their own world. (Dietrich Bonhoeffer)[74]

Covetousness is idolatry because it involves the setting of one's affections on earthly things and not on things above, and therefore the putting of some other object of desire in the place which God should occupy in people's hearts. (F. F. Bruce)[75]

Since a man can serve only one master, God or mammon, but not both (Matt 6:24), then if he sets his heart on wealth, he adores false gods and abandons the one true God. (P. T. O'Brien)[76]

The influential twentieth-century Welsh preacher D. M. Lloyd-Jones, although he does not use the terms "love," "devotion," "heart," or "affections," gives an explanation of "greed is idolatry" that nonetheless qualifies as a description of the inordinate love of the greedy for their possessions. Its value lies in that the description works well in reverse; what the greedy do with money, they should rather do with God; hence the accusation of idolatry: "anything that you and I tend to set up as the big thing, the central thing, in

---

71. Calvin, *Sermons on Ephesians*, 503-4.
72. Schlier, *Epheser*, 235.
73. Barnes, *Notes*, 317 (on Col 3:5).
74. Bonhoeffer, *Nachfolge*, 281-82.
75. Bruce, *Colossians*, 143-44, on Col 3:5.
76. O'Brien, *Colossians*, 183-84.

our lives, the thing about which we think and dream, the thing that engages our imagination, the thing that we *live* for, the thing that gives us the biggest thrill; if it is *anything* other than GOD, it is idolatry."[77]

The love-and-devotion view is also represented in some hymns, perhaps not surprisingly, given the centrality of such affections for Christian worship. Note the following three examples. In the fourth verse of "Be Thou My Vision, O Lord of My Heart," the human affections are presented as necessarily undivided and exclusive in their loyalties:

> Riches I heed not, nor man's empty praise,
> Thou mine inheritance through all my days;
> Thou, and thou only, the first in my heart,
> High King of heaven, my treasure thou art![78]

The second verse of Cecil F. Alexander's nineteenth-century hymn, "Jesus Calls Us," also underscores the competition wealth poses to the Christian's love for God: "Jesus calls us from the worship of the vain world's golden store, From each idol that would keep us, Saying, 'Christian, love Me more.'"[79]

The hymn "St Matthew the Apostle" tells the story of the greedy tax collector's call to discipleship in terms of love for Christ replacing the love of money, but without labeling the latter idolatrous: "Dear Lord, on this Thy servant's day, Who left for Thee the gold and mart, who heard Thee whisper, 'Come away,' And follow'd with a single heart, . . . Let God's great love put out the love of gold, and gain, and low desires . . . the love of Christ is more than gain, and heavenly crowns than yellow dust."[80]

The danger in the love-and-devotion interpretation is its dependence on the (usually modern) interpreter's perception of the concepts of greed and worship, which are perhaps formed more by personal experience and the English and German languages than by the perceptions of Paul and the recipients of Ephesians and Colossians. Furthermore, it is debatable not only whether this sense applies, but also whether only it applies. In other

---

77. Lloyd-Jones, *Darkness and Light*, 340.

78. This hymn derives from an eighth-century Irish poem and was translated from the original Gaelic into English in 1905 by Mary Byrne (1880-1931) and later versified by Eleanor Hull (1860-1935). See Bradley, *Book of Hymns*, 59-61.

79. S. H. Tow, ed., *Revival Hymns and Choruses*, no. 407.

80. W. H. Monk and C. Steggall, eds., *Hymns Ancient and Modern*, no. 420.

words, does the notion of love exhaust the way in which the greedy and idolaters relate to their wealth and idols?

8. Greed Is Trust and Confidence in Wealth

No one in the history of the church placed more importance on the judgment that "greed is idolatry" and made more use of it in their preaching, Bible exposition, and theology than Martin Luther. Luther's understanding of the words may be found at many different points throughout his commentaries and sermons, and even in his catechetical writings and letters. His view is based in part on his interpretation of the Decalogue and the close relationship he perceived to exist between greed and unbelief. Luther believed that the sin of greed consisted in placing confidence and trust in one's possessions rather than in the living God. It is in this sense that money is the greedy person's god and that he or she is guilty of idolatry.[81]

According to Luther the greedy person sins against the second table of the Decalogue, and it is the preacher's task to preach the law and to condemn sins such as greed. It was Christ's condemnation of such sin among the religious leaders of his day that aroused such fierce opposition. Luther also believed that in his day too many of his contemporaries fled from his own preaching of the law because they did not want to have their consciences offended and have to deal with their greed.

The foundation for Luther's understanding of greed as idolatry is laid in his treatment of the first commandment. Luther does not limit the definition of worship and its counterpoint idolatry to adoration and devotion, but takes it broadly to include the idea of trust. In the Shorter Catechism Luther explains how to have no other gods before the Lord: we are to fear, love, and trust God above all things. The extensive exposition of the first commandment in the Larger Catechism, however, expands on the verb "trust." He defines what it means to have a God in a way that fits both true and false worship: "A 'god' means that from which you expect to receive all good things and to which you flee in times of need. 'To have a god' means nothing other than to believe and trust from the heart in something. In

---

81. For a thorough and perceptive treatment of Luther's view of greed see Rieth, *Habsucht bei Martin Luther*. On the relationship between greed and idolatry see esp. 152-58, which the following exposition summarizes and builds upon.

this sense, as I have already said, trust and faith of the heart define both God and an idol."[82] According to Luther, to obey the first commandment is to cling to, rely upon, and look only to God for whatever one needs in any circumstance.

In order to make clear what it means to trust God he adduces some examples that illustrate the contrary. The first concerns the rich person who relies upon his wealth rather than God: "Those who set their whole heart on money and possessions in confidence and trust represent the most common form of idolatry on earth."[83] According to Luther, people set up as their god that from which they expect and hope to obtain help and comfort. Luther observes that even for pagans to have a god means to trust and depend upon something or someone.

In conclusion Luther contends that we learn from the first commandment a stern lesson about God's claim to our exclusive trust and confidence: "Therefore, let us learn well the first commandment: God tolerates no rivals when it comes to our trust and demands, above all, that we put our confidence in him, from whom alone we can expect to receive all good things."[84]

The concluding section of the Larger Catechism on the subject of the Ten Commandments stresses the central role of the first commandment, from which all the others proceed. Using a range of metaphors Luther insists that the first commandment casts its bright light over all the others, is the critical stem running through the varied wreath, and is the source and fountain from which all the others spring. To fulfill the first is to obey all ten.[85] When one obeys the other commandments, it should be done by virtue of the first commandment, out of reverence for God. Although not stated explicitly, this assumption is the basis upon which Luther can understand greed to be a breaking of the first commandment.

Sin for Luther is always an act of contempt for God. It is significant for Luther that when Moses explains the first commandment in Deuteronomy 6:1-13, in terms of what causes someone to break it, he first of all mentions riches and luxurious living, which Luther interprets as mammon and greed. Trusting in riches prevents the human heart from being ruled by

---

82. WA 30,1:133.

83. Ibid.

84. Ibid., 30,1:139.

85. Gestrich, *Return of Splendor*, 181, comments wryly that the logic of Luther's view leads one to conclude that "the reason they are even there [the instructions of the second table] is that God foresaw man's universal failure to keep the first commandment."

faith and love, and consequently the Lord is forgotten. For Luther, Moses himself understood the first commandment in a spiritual sense, as trust in God, and idolatry as a trust in things.[86]

Klaus Bockmuehl's study of Luther's confessional writings confirms that according to Luther's catechisms idolatry occurs when human beings overvalue earthly, created goods and put their trust in them instead of in God from whom we can expect to have all our needs supplied.[87] Bockmuehl asks what conception of God lies behind Luther's interpretation of the first commandment. His answer to this question, which quotes Luther's Larger Catechism, also underscores the notions of confidence and trust: "It is essentially God the creator, upon which Luther's explanation draws, or more accurately, God the sustainer, on whom we depend for our body, life, food, drink, nourishment, health, protection, peace and for all our pressing and eternal needs."[88]

God as sustainer and provider is thus crucial to Luther's understanding of the first commandment. Luther's explanation effectually renders the first commandment a piece of creation ethics. His customary Christocentrism is here conspicuous by its absence. Indeed, the verbs he uses to characterize the human relationship with God here are "trust" and "believe" rather than "love" and "obey."[89]

For Luther, whereas belief is trust in God's help, unbelief is trust in oneself and one's own powers and was often equated with greed. Unbelief and greed grow together. The greater the greed, the more unbelief. The more someone enjoys things of the flesh, without regard for God's will, the more unhappy his or her soul becomes. Sin and material prosperity are matched in that increase by the loss of trust in God and confident hope.[90] The origin of greed is mistrust since the stingy person is prone to worry instead of trusting God for the future.[91] Unbelief consists then in having more faith in one's own deeds and resources than in God's undertaking to preserve humankind and creation.[92]

---

86. WA 14:612, 29–613, 16; in this connection he also mentions 1 Tim 6:10; Bar 3:17.

87. Bockmuehl, *Gesetz und Geist,* 57.

88. Ibid.

89. Cf. ibid., 59.

90. WA 5:415, 28-33; 416, 38–417, 8-9, 24-35.

91. WA 6:272, 13-26.

92. WA 15:370, 5-7; Ps 55:23 and 1 Pet 5:7 are used to support the interpretation; cf. 364, 12–365, 19.

In his commentary on Psalm 127, for instance, Luther understood v. 1 ("unless the Lord builds the house, its builders labor in vain") as a warning against "greed, anxiety, and unbelief" in the family and in society. In his commentary on the Sermon on the Mount he insists in connection with Matthew 6:31 ("So do not worry, saying, 'What shall we eat?' or 'What shall we drink?' or 'What shall we wear?'") that a miser's worry and faith cannot coexist: "Since greed and anxiety are opposed, one must be rid of one or the other."

Christians who engage in business should, according to Luther, carry out their dealings in faith, that is, in the light of the recognition of God's blessing. If pride in human achievement becomes the focus, then greed and worry take over. In a lecture on Genesis Luther commented that Abraham is a model of the relationship between faith and the wrong use of possessions. Abraham does not consistently confess that his goods come from God, and this results in robbery and illicit gain.[93]

Not only does greed cause unbelief but the reverse is also true. This can be seen according to Luther in the last part of Psalm 14:4, which places unbelief next to apostasy, both of which are causes of greed.[94] In an exposition of Psalm 127 Luther stressed his desire that the gospel would produce the fruit of understanding and good works and warned his hearers that the fruit of unbelief, greed, is fighting against this goal.[95] Similarly in his commentary on Matthew 6:28-30 Luther stressed the role of the lily, which by its example refutes human unbelief. Unbelief urges people to "worry and be greedy."[96]

Luther, as already noted, understood worship not in the narrow sense of liturgical process but as the manifestation of faith in all spheres of human life. Often in expositions of the first commandment, the Sermon on the Mount, and Pauline texts that touch on the theme of idolatry, as Ricardo Rieth observes, "Greed and idolatry take the role of counterpart to faith and the worship of God."[97] Luther's comments on Ephesians 5:1-10 explain his understanding of the words "greed is idolatry." Speaking of the greedy miser, Luther explains: "since his confidence and loyalty is based on

---

93. *WA* 15:366, 11-19; 43, 298, 38–299, 5.
94. *WA* 5:422, 34-35, 39; 423, 3.
95. *WA* 115:377, 26–378, 4.
96. *WA* 32:464, 38–465, 7.
97. Rieth, *Habsucht bei Martin Luther*, 156.

money and not on the living God, who has promised him sufficient nourishment, only money is his god and he may well be called an idolater."[98]

Luther was not too shy to apply this teaching to situations in his own day. To cite one clear example from his correspondence, on 26 November 1539 in a letter to Johann Cellarius, he mentions the situation in Dresden, where people, in his opinion because of greed, were not prepared to support church activities financially. He charges them with idolatrous greed and laments that mammon had taken over the land of Meissen.[99]

Indeed, Luther regarded the teaching that greed is idolatry not as a piece of intriguing speculation but with all seriousness, and as a consequence he had much to say about fighting against greed in the human heart by faith.[100] The judgment that "greed is idolatry" accords the vice of greed great weight that calls for both vigilance and urgency in dealing with it. In terms reminiscent of his famous *Streitschrift* written against Erasmus, *The Bondage of the Will,* Luther warned believers against a false sense of confidence in their ability to do good, and instead counseled that they pray for grace in order to be freed from this evil. As Rieth explains: "Luther thought that believers must petition God to learn how to mortify the sin of greed so that their whole being might be rid of it and a new will will exist in its place."[101] In his 1518 exposition of the Ten Commandments he stressed both the depth of human depravity and the effectiveness of contrition and prayer in the fight against greed. Luther took the fourth request of the Lord's Prayer, "give us our daily bread," as a call to shun greed.[102]

Another Reformer who presents a remarkably similar understanding of idolatrous greed is Huldrych Zwingli. In his *Auslegung und Begründung der These oder Artikel 1523* Zwingli concludes his comments on article 20 ("God wants to give all things to Christians in the name of Christ; hence it follows that we need no other mediator than him") with an explanation of the words "greed is idolatry" that is very similar to Luther's view: "Everything in which people put their trust is for them an object of worship."[103]

In view of the profound impact of Luther on Protestant exegesis and

---

98. *WA* 17:11, 211, 4-20. Cited in Rieth, *Habsucht bei Martin Luther,* 156-57.

99. *WA Br* 8:611, 10-17 (3414).

100. See Rieth, *Habsucht bei Martin Luther,* 158-62.

101. Ibid., 162.

102. *WA* 19:96, 7-8. For a contemporary exposition of the first commandment that builds on Luther's interpretation, see Traugott Koch, *Zehn Gebote für die Freiheit,* 157-73.

103. Zwingli, *Schriften,* 2:256.

theology it is surprising that his understanding of "greed is idolatry" in terms of misplaced trust was not picked up more often in later writings.[104] To my knowledge only a handful of authors, mainly Puritans, take trust to be a key feature of the sin of greed, and then usually in combination with love (see 9.b below).[105] Alexander Maclaren is the only other author in my survey to define idolatrous greed chiefly in terms of misplaced trust and confidence: "If we say of anything, no matter what, 'If I have only enough of this, I shall be satisfied; it is my real aim, my sufficient good,' that thing is a god to me, and my real worship is paid to it, whatever may be my nominal religion. The lowest form of idolatry is the giving of supreme trust to a material thing, and making that a god."[106]

Whereas the note of trusting Jesus is struck in countless hymns, it is difficult to find examples in which wealth is a main rival to this trust. The third verse of an anonymous hymn, "All for Jesus!" though not mentioning the charge of idolatry, qualifies: "Worldlings prize their gems of beauty; Cling to gilded toys of dust; Boast of wealth, and fame and pleasure; Only Jesus will I trust."[107] The contrast between boasting in material things and boasting about Christ, which is bound up with the activity of trusting, appears in the second stanza of R. Jude's hymn, "My Heart Is Fixed, Eternal God," reinforced by a reference to the superiority of spiritual over earthly riches: "Let others boast of heaps of gold, Christ for me, Christ for me; His riches never can be told, Christ for me, Christ for me; Your gold will waste and wear away."[108]

Luther's interpretation of "greed is idolatry" has obvious strengths. It is distinguished from the other views surveyed in its impressive explanatory power. Luther supplies a cogent explanation as to the precise sense in which the greedy are guilty of idolatry: they trust in their riches instead of trusting in God. And he develops his view in connection with the Decalogue, Deuteronomy 6, various psalms, and a number of New Testament texts, giving it a biblical-theological foundation that adds to its credibility. Nonetheless, key questions remain largely unanswered. Do the notions of idolatry and its counterpart true worship involve trust as well as

---

104. One exception is Jüngel, "Gewinn," 550, who cites Luther's view with approval.

105. It is intriguing that the words engraved on American bank notes, "In God We Trust," could be read as supplying the implicit message, "and not in money."

106. Maclaren, *Colossians*, 278.

107. J. Mountain and Mrs. Evan Hopkins, eds., *Hymns of Consecration and Faith*, no. 479.

108. Ibid., no. 83.

love and devotion? At what point in the interpretation of the first commandment does such an extension of meaning occur, if at all? Already in the context of Exodus and Deuteronomy? In later Old Testament or Jewish interpretation? At some point in the New Testament? Does Luther's view have genuine biblical roots? Is it credible as an exegesis of the words "greed is idolatry" as they stand in Ephesians 5:5 and Colossians 3:5? Is the misplaced trust of the greedy their defining characteristic? Only a thorough investigation of the relevant texts can hope to answer these questions.

9. Complex Interpretations

A few authors, mainly church fathers and Puritans, present interpretations of "greed is idolatry" that contain elements from more than one category. The most noteworthy is the Puritan David Clarkson, who in comprehensive fashion combines all three metaphorical interpretations (nos. 6-8 above).[109]

a. Love and Service

Gregory of Nyssa's interpretation of "greed is idolatry" in his eighth homily on Ecclesiastes combines the love-and-devotion and service-and-obedience views in striking fashion. His opening remarks on Ecclesiastes 3:8b take the words "there is a time to love, and a time to hate," to mean that one should love the good and hate the evil; and he contends that sin results when we fail to distinguish between the two: "For the confused and erroneous disposition in the soul is the root and source of sin."[110] He then quotes Matthew 6:24, "No one, it says, can serve two masters; for surely he will hate one and love the other," and uses it as a basis for exhortation concerning the consequences of loving and hating good and evil:

> Διαστείλας τοίνυν τῷ λόγῳ τὰ κατ᾽ ἀρετήν τε καὶ κακίαν νοούμενα, ἐπιγνώσει τὴν εὐκαιρίαν, τοῦ τῶς χρὴ πρὸς ἑκάτερον τούτων ἔχειν. Ἐγκράτεια καὶ ἡδονὴ, σωφροσύνη καὶ ἀκολασία, μετριότης καὶ τῦφος, εὔνοια καὶ κακόνοια, καὶ πάντα τὰ ἐξ ἐναντίου νοούμενα,

---

109. Needless to say, some interpreters comment on the equal gravity of greed and idolatry before suggesting a deeper similarity between them.

110. 426, 8–428, 19.

φανερῶς ὑπὸ τοῦ Ἐκκλησιαστοῦ ὑποδείκνυταί σοι ὅπως τῇ ψυχῇ περὶ ταῦτα εὖ διατιθέμενος, λυσιτελῶς βουλεύσῃ. Καιρὸς οὖν τοῦ φιλῆσαι τὴν ἐγκράτειαν, καὶ τοῦ μισῆσαι τὴν ἡδονήν, ἵνα μὴ γένῃ φιλήδονος, μᾶλλον δὲ φιλόθεος, καὶ τὰ ἄλλα πάντα ὡσαύτως, τὸ φιλόνεικον, τὸ φιλοκερδές τε καὶ φιλόδοξον, καὶ πάντα τῇ ἐπὶ τὰ μὴ δέοντα τῆς φιλίας χρήσει, τῆς πρὸς τὸ ἀγαθὸν σχέσεως ἀφορίζοντα.[111]

If you make a distinction in your mind between things thought of as virtue and vice you will recognize the opportunity for the right attitude to each of them. Restraint and pleasure, self-control and indulgence, modesty and excess, goodwill and ill will, and all that are regarded as opposites of one another, are plainly set out for you by the author of Ecclesiastes, so that by adopting attitudes about them in your soul you may make profitable decisions. Thus there is a moment for loving restraint, and for hating pleasure, so that you do not become pleasure-loving rather than God-loving, and likewise in all the other cases, quarrel-loving, gain-loving, glory-loving, and all the rest, which through the use of affection for improper ends separate us from the disposition to good.

In the following remarks Gregory develops the notion that sinful desires can become a rival to God. He observes, alluding to 1 Timothy 4:4, that since God created all things, nothing in creation is wrong if it is accepted with thanksgiving. Problems arise with the improper use of material things: "the ungrateful use of these things turns into a passion, the created means by which fellowship with God comes about; contrary things enter and are set up in God's place, so that for such people their passions become gods."

In applying these thoughts to the specific sins of gluttony and greed, he alludes to Philippians 3:19 and Ephesians 5:5/Colossians 3:5, respectively:

Thus for gluttons the belly becomes God (Phil 3:19). Thus the covetous make their disease into an idol for themselves (Col 3:5). Thus those whose soul's eyes are blinded by error in this present age have made vanity their god. To sum up, whatever a person submits his reason to, making it slave and subject, he has in his sickness made that into a god, and he would not be in this state if he had not attached himself to evil by love.

111. PG, 44:741.

In Gregory of Nyssa's opinion, what one loves, one serves, whether the true God or something put in God's place. His comments on Ecclesiastes 3:8a use Matthew 6:24 as an interpretive key, a verse in which love and service are virtually synonymous.

Origen likewise conceives of the sin of idolatrous greed in terms of false love and service in his Homilies on Jeremiah 5.2. The relevant remarks appear in connection with Jeremiah 3:22 ("come back to me, wayward sons; I will heal your apostasy. O Lord, we come! We come to you; for you are our God"), a text that confronts the nation with its idolatry (see 3:20, 23-24) and reports its repentance. Origen explains what this repentance involves and what, in the case of his hearers, it means to commit idolatry. Like Gregory of Nyssa, his explanation focuses on gluttony, with reference to Philippians 3:19, and greed, in connection with Ephesians 5:5 and Colossians 3:5:

> οὐδενὰ γὰρ θεὸν ἡμεῖς ὁμολογοῦμεν, οὐ τὴν κοιλίαν ὡς οἱ γαστρίμαργοι, ὧν ὁ θεὸς ἡ κοιλία, οὐ τὸ ἀργύριον ὡς οἱ φιλάργυροι, καὶ τὴν πλεονεξίαν, ἥτις ἐστὶν εἰδωλολατρία, οὐδὲ ἄλλο τι ἐκθεοῦμεν καὶ θεοποιοῦμεν, ὧν οἱ πολλοὶ θεοποιοῦσιν, ἀλλὰ ἡμῖν ὁ ἐπὶ πᾶσι θεός, ὁ ἐπὶ πάντων, ὁ διὰ πάντων, ὁ ἐν πᾶσι θεός ἐστιν, καὶ ἐπεὶ ἠρτήμεθα τῆς ἀγάπης τῆς πρὸς τὸν θεόν, ἡ γὰρ ἀγάπη κολλᾷ ἡμᾶς τῷ θεῷ, λέγομεν, ἰδοὺ οἵδε ἡμεῖς ἐσόμεθά σοι, ὅτι σὺ κύριος ὁ θεὸς ἡμῶν.

> For we confess no other god, not to the stomach, like the gluttons, whose god is their stomach [Phil 3:19], not to money, like the lovers of money, nor to greed, which is idolatry [Eph 5:5; Col 3:5]. And we regard nothing else as god. We do not make gods out of things, which many turn into a god. For us there is rather the one who is above all things, God, the one who is above all and through all and in all [Eph 4:6]. If we relate to God through love, for love unites us to God, we say, yes, we will come to you, for you are the Lord our God [Jer 3:22].

According to Origen, those guilty of such idolatry ought to show by their works that they belong to God (δείξωμεν τοῖς ἔργοις, ὅτι ἐπαγγειλάμενοι γενέσθαι αὐτοῦ) and not to other gods, and through their love that they belong only to God. In other words, the obedience and devotion that they had shown either to their belly or their money they must now transfer to God.

b. Love and Trust

Jean Daillé (1594-1670) was a French Protestant who participated in the Calvinistic synods and was minister at Charenton in Paris from 1626 until his death. His sermons on Colossians were delivered in 1639 and published in France in 1648. Cyril J. Barber writes in the foreword to the English edition: "In contrast to some Puritan works of this period, Daillé adhered more closely to the text of Scripture, expounded each verse fully, and generally leaves his readers astonished at his wisdom and insight."[112] His comments on "greed is idolatry" are limited to a short space in one sermon but are nonetheless remarkably full and clear, combining to good effect the notions of love and trust.

At the outset Daillé makes clear the effect of branding greed as idolatry; whereas many regard greed as a light matter, the equation with idolatry impresses upon us its grave seriousness: "he [Paul] qualifies it [greed] with the taint of idolatry, improperly, (I grant) and figuratively, but very fitly for the discovering of its venom in us . . . it is an abominable thing. For in as much as there was nothing in all the horrors of paganism, that was more severely prohibited of GOD, nor more hated or abhorred among the Jews, than idolatry."[113] He aptly compares Paul's denunciation of greed with Samuel's condemnation of Saul in similar terms in 1 Samuel 15:23, which was also intended not literally but to "signify the horridness of disobeying the voice of God."[114]

Daillé is convinced, however, that the equal severity of the two sins is only one of many points of similarity between them. His attempt to draw out such resemblances encompasses two of the three metaphorical interpretations, which we saw earlier, love and trust:

> The idolater looks on his idols with profound veneration; so doth the covetous, on his goods and coin. The one shuts up his idols, so the other does his. The one serves an image; and the other gold and silver and when the idol is of either of these two metals (as they not seldom are) they both serve the self-same thing, with this difference only, that the idolater serves it under one form, and one way figured; the covetous under another; the one offers incense, and sacrifices to this

112. *Exposition of Colossians*.
113. Daillé, *Sermons upon Colossians*, 28.
114. Ibid., 27.

idol; the other immolates his heart and affections to his. Add hereto, that the covetous bears more love to the objects of his passion and renders them more service than he doth to God; he puts his hope in gold, and trust in fine gold, Thou art my confidence.[115]

The prolific Puritan author John Owen, one-time colleague of David Clarkson (whose highly developed views are presented in the next section), presents a similar interpretation when he comments on Hebrews 13:5-6 ("Keep your lives free from the love of money"). With reference to Colossians 3:5, Owen reflects on the severity of the sin of greed ("there is nothing that the Scripture doth more severely condemn, nor denounce more inevitable punishment unto") before explaining idolatrous greed in terms of misplaced love and trust: "[Greed is] such an abominable sin, as there is no name fit to be given unto it but that which intimates a rejection of God himself [i.e., idolatry] . . . covetous persons *adore* their money, and put their *trust* in it in the stead of God."[116]

Five other authors explain "greed is idolatry" in similar fashion:

The greedy person is an idolater in so far as their wealth is their highest love and highest trust. They treat their wealth as their god. (D. Johann Friedrich von Flatt)[117]

Interpretative idolatry is when the creature is set in the place of God; which may be done two ways — by confidence and trust, and by love and delight; for there are two chief respects due to God — love and trust. (Thomas Manton)[118]

Whosoever chiefly and supremely loves any creature, is an idolater; because our chiefest love is due only unto God. . . . Whosoever puts his trust and confidence in any creature more than in God, is guilty of this inward, heart idolatry. (Ezekiel Hopkins)[119]

Idolatry of the heart; it transfers the thoughts, the desires, the affections, the confidence, the expectations and notions of happiness

---

115. Ibid., 28.

116. Owen, *Hebrews*, 6:410. Cf. 411: "It [greed] is always accompanied with a *distrust of God.*"

117. Von Flatt, *Epheser*, 510.

118. Manton, *Complete Works*, 19:211, in a sermon on Eph 5:5.

119. Hopkins, *Works*, 1:356-57, in his exposition of the first commandment.

from God our Creator and Lord, to vile, earthly treasures, to golden dust. Avarice makes a man an idolater, because he does for money, all that he ought to do for God. (Daniel Wilson)[120]

[Greed] is a *desiring* of anything for its own sake, that we may find our happiness in it, rather than in God; and place our *dependence* on it, rather than on God. (Charles Simeon)[121]

c. Love, Service, and Trust

The Puritan David Clarkson (1621 [or 1622]-1686), who was a student and later fellow in Clare Hall, Cambridge, and one-time colleague to John Owen as a minister in a church in London, wrote a sermonic piece on "greed is idolatry" in Ephesians 5:5 entitled "Soul Idolatry Excludes Men out of Heaven." It amounts to some 24,000 words and represents arguably the most comprehensive and theologically penetrating exposition of the words in existence. The editor of Clarkson's works claims that Clarkson's theological writings are characterized by "soundness of reasoning and fervency of appeal and are adorned with the graces of a tasteful eloquence,"[122] a description that fits well the discourse in question.

Clarkson distinguishes between two sorts of idolatry: external, involving actions of the body including bowing and prostrating oneself, which he describes as open and gross idolatry;[123] and internal, consisting of acts of the soul, "when the mind is most taken up with an object, and the heart and affections most set upon it," which he designates "secret and soul idolatry."[124] It is, he claims, the latter variety that Ephesians 5:5 and Colossians 3:5, and for that matter Philippians 3:19 and Matthew 6:24, have in view.

Clarkson analyzes soul worship in terms of thirteen acts, and charges that "to give any one of them to anything besides the God of heaven is plain idolatry."[125] Clarkson contends that it is necessary to define clearly the proper worship of God in order to understand the idolatrous worship

120. Wilson, *Colossians*, 37.
121. Simeon, *Galatians–Ephesians*, 376.
122. Clarkson, *Works*, 1:viii.
123. Ibid., 2:300, 327.
124. Ibid., 300. The Puritan Ezekiel Hopkins, *Works*, 1:354, also distinguishes between external and internal idolatry.
125. Clarkson, *Works*, 2:301.

of the greedy. His taxonomy of worship is indeed broad, but it is supported at various points with proof texts, some of which we will take up in part II. The three characterizations of idolatrous greed, which we found standing alone in other interpretations, namely, love and devotion, service and obedience, and confidence and trust, all appear, with more besides. The following summary draws on Clarkson's own language.[126]

Clarkson contends that God is for every human being, that which (1) we most highly value or esteem; (2) we are most mindful of, be it profits and pleasures or God himself; (3) we most intend (our chief aim or purpose) whether to be rich, great, and powerful or to glorify God; (4) we are most resolved for, whether lusts and outward advantages or God's ways, honor, and service; (5) we most love and adore;[127] (6) we most trust, "for confidence and dependence is an act of worship which the Lord calls for as due only to himself";[128] (7) we most fear; (8) we make our hope; (9) we most desire and enjoy, either worldly enjoyments or "spiritual communion with God";[129] (10) we most delight and rejoice in; (11) we are most zealous for, be it our own things or the things of God; (12) we are most grateful for; and (13) attracts our service and industry, whether mammon or God.

Whereas the final act recalls the service-and-obedience interpretation of idolatrous greed, trust and confidence are explicit in the sixth and implied in the eighth with the notion of hope. Most of the other so-called acts of worship develop what we have called love and devotion. Indeed, Clarkson makes clear that for him the heart of the matter is the question of love: "for wherein does the idolatry of covetousness consist, but in this? That it is an inordinate, an immoderate love of riches."[130] When later in the sermon he lists sixteen ways in which "men make wealth and riches their god," it is this idea of misplaced affections that he amplifies. Note the following verbs and phrases: the greedy value, love, desire, delight in, grieve over, are more affected by, eagerly seek, and prize more highly material things over God.[131]

The breadth of Clarkson's definition of soul idolatry is matched by the

---

126. See ibid., 301-5.
127. Ibid., 302: "Love, whenever it is inordinate, is an idolatrous affection."
128. Ibid.
129. Ibid., 303-4.
130. Ibid., 307.
131. Ibid., 310-11.

size of the net in which he believes the guilty are captured: "Every natural man, let his enjoyments, privileges, accomplishments, be what they will, is an idolater . . . [and] the greatest part of Christians."[132] Comparing this vast throng to Jacob (in Gen 31), who denied the presence of idols in his possession, Clarkson asserts that "though few will own it [soul idolatry], nothing is more common."[133] This grim diagnosis continues in terms of the corruption of human apprehensions, thoughts, goals, supports, expectations, affections, elections, inclinations, and fruitions,[134] through the examination of which Clarkson aims to uncover "the guilt of this secret sin."[135]

Not surprisingly Clarkson takes great pains to stress the gravity of the sin of internal idolatry, which he does not regard as equal to that of external idolatry,[136] but even worse. In seeking to prove this point he exploits further the parallel between true and false worship. Secret idolatry is worse because the Lord is more concerned about inward worship than outward and because "the idols worshipped [with soul idolatry] are more vile, more abominable." Such idols are "the lusts of men . . . there is no goodness at all in the lusts of men."[137] He gives the following advice to those wishing to avoid soul idolatry: (1) "Get new natures. . . . Cry unto God for the spirit of regeneration"; (2) "Mortify your lusts" (cf. Col 3:5); (3) "Get right apprehensions of the things of this world. An overvaluing of outward things is the birth and food of this soul-idolatry"; and (4) "Let your hearts be especially jealous of lawful comforts [pleasures which are permitted]; these are the most dangerous snares."[138]

The danger of Clarkson's scheme is, of course, overinterpretation. Can "greed is idolatry" mean so much? Even if it can be shown that many of the senses in which humans beings secretly worship gods of their own making, which he adduces, are implied in the cluster of texts he labels internal idolatry, can he avoid the charge of illegitimate totality transfer in relation to his interpretation of Ephesians 5:5 and Colossians 3:5?

132. Ibid., 305-6.
133. Ibid., 306.
134. Ibid., 313-25.
135. Ibid., 313.
136. Concerning external idolatry he contends, ibid., 327: "the Lord does most severely, most dreadfully threaten and punish idolatry above other sins."
137. Ibid., 328.
138. Ibid., 331, 332.

Conclusion

As we look back over the history of interpretation, we can make several observations. A virtual consensus exists on only one score, that is, that the expression, however it is understood, serves to condemn greed. However, even here we found that Chrysostom and Clarkson part company with the rest by charging (with poetic license) that greed is not merely as bad as idolatry, but even worse, while Aquinas denies greed's equal gravity with idolatry. When it comes to labeling the sort of idolatry that greed consists of there are several alternatives are on offer, from Chrysostom's *second* idolatry, to the Puritans' *secret, soul, internal,* or *interpretive* idolatry, to Markus Barth's *subtle* idolatry,[139] to *extended* idolatry, a label we will encounter in Sandelin's discussion of analogous notions in Philo, and finally to Luther's description of greed as *the commonest* idolatry of all.

Observing the interpretations of the expression across the centuries reveals few trends, except for a readiness to use it in practical application in exhortations against greed among the church fathers, all-embracing interpretations among the Puritans, and the dominance of the love-and-devotion view in the twentieth century. Luther stands out as the theologian and pastor who made most frequent and effective use of the words, Clarkson as their most comprehensive expositor, and Daillé as the commentator who arguably supplies the fullest exegesis in short space.

We also saw the fundamental theological import of many of the interpretations. How a person conceives of idolatry tells us something indirectly about how they conceive of God and true worship. Indeed, each of the three metaphorical interpretations, when turned around, presupposes a different conception of God. Either God is the Creator and Provider to be *trusted,* or the Savior and Redeemer to be *loved,* or the Ruler and Lawgiver to be *obeyed.*

If the history of the interpretation of "greed is idolatry" teaches anything, it is that in order to understand the expression further work is called for. In what sense are the greedy guilty of idolatry? Six distinctive answers have been given: greed is as bad as idolatry, leads to idolatry, entails the worship of the demon or god of mammon,[140] like idolatry involves forbid-

---

139. Barth, *Colossians,* 205.

140. Here I have combined "greed is worship of the god or demon 'mammon'" and "greed is slavery imposed by the economic system" as essentially equivalent; both emphasize service and obedience.

den service and obedience, like idolatry involves inordinate love and devotion, or like idolatry involves misplaced trust and confidence.

Not only is there a string of different interpretations, but the questions that are fundamental to deciding among them have not been answered. Are the words hyperbole, a metaphor, or literally the case? The nonmetaphorical interpretations were provisionally judged to be inadequate. But how can it be demonstrated that the expression is a metaphor? If it is a metaphor, in what sense is greed like idolatry? How far can the meaning of the metaphor be legitimately extended? What is the origin of the expression? Is it original to Ephesians and Colossians? What is its intended effect in context in the two letters? The following chapter proposes two ways forward in answering such questions.

Chapter 3

Method for the Present Study:
Maps and Supplies

—⟨ɷɷɷ⟩—

In the present study I seek to understand the words "greed is idolatry" by tracing their biblical/Jewish origin and by analyzing them as a metaphor.

A Biblical/Jewish Origin

Whereas several authors note a number of relevant Jewish texts for understanding the words "greed is idolatry," these have not been thoroughly assessed and the judgment has not been set against a biblical and Jewish background in the fullest sense. In the present study I endeavor to examine the relevant texts in Paul's Bible,[1] namely, those that deal with idolatry, greed, or, better still, those where the two are in some way associated, and their early Jewish interpretation in order to grasp as fully as possible the origin of the expression.

Two caveats are needed at this point. First, when seeking the origin of "greed is idolatry," we are not necessarily looking for a specific text to which Paul has alluded or which he is echoing. Teaching in the New Testament, such as the expression "greed is idolatry," may owe its inspiration to the Old Testament in a general sense. Many concepts in biblical theology,

---

1. On Paul's view of the purpose and function of Scripture see Rosner, "Written for Us."

not unlike idolatrous greed, have their roots in the Jewish Scriptures, but not in an explicit and specific sense. The term "the kingdom of God/heaven," for instance, does not occur in the Old Testament. Nonetheless, the idea of the rule of God over creation, all creatures, the kingdoms of the world, and, in a unique and special way, over his chosen and redeemed people, is the very heart of the Old Testament message. Furthermore, the "kingdom of God" in the New Testament can be understood only against the backdrop of this rule and dominion, which is characteristically rejected by the human race, and whose final stage is anticipated in the prophets in terms of radical renewal and completion.[2]

Second, the early Jewish moral teaching to which I will refer is to be understood not as an independent and rival source to Scripture, but as inextricably linked to it. As the lens through which Paul perceived the relevance of Scripture for ethics, Jewish moral teaching refracted the dynamic biblical witness in at least six different ways. As I have argued elsewhere, in Jewish moral teaching certain biblical passages become prominent, certain biblical moral scruples are emphasized, certain biblical ethical concerns are connected, certain biblical forms of parenesis are popularized, certain biblical themes undergo development, and certain biblical exegeses and expositions are promulgated.[3]

Since in the ancient world greed was often taken to be a vice not only in

---

2. Examples could be multiplied. The ascension of Jesus is strictly speaking without precedent, yet it is best understood in the context of the frequent presentation of God in the OT as the great king over all the earth, proud humanity's urge to lift itself up in self-sufficiency and disobedience and the notion of God's enthronement in heaven. Many NT concepts have a relatively slim lexical base and yet can lay no less a claim to be of central importance. The word for "vanity," for instance, occurs only here and there in the Bible. However, the concept captures much of the human predicament of sin under God's wrath. The whole of salvation history, from creation to the ultimate consummation of all things, illustrates the tension that arises between the willful desires of human folly and the benevolent purposes of a loving God. The earliest biblical example of this tension is the divine curse on the ground (Gen 3:17-19), which resulted from the attempt of disobedient humanity to become autonomous, like God. The mutual harmony between God, humanity, and the created order was disrupted, and working the land became a toil and burdensome. The removal of vanity, at the other end of salvation history, is a picture of ultimate redemption. The subject of vanity is noteworthy in the Bible for both its poignancy and its scant explicit mention.

3. See Rosner, *Paul, Scripture, and Ethics*, chap. 2, "Indirect Dependence: Scriptural Influence through Jewish Moral Teaching."

the Jewish tradition but also in pagan moral philosophy,[4] some specific justification for concentrating on the Bible and early Jewish sources in our search for the origin of idolatrous greed is called for. Four observations suggest the biblical/Jewish origin of the words "greed is idolatry" in Colossians 3:5 and Ephesians 5:5: (1) the character of the moral teaching in Colossians and (2) Ephesians is decidedly Jewish; (3) greed is a prominent vice in early Jewish moral teaching; and above all, (4) the fight against idolatry is a distinguishing mark of ancient Judaism. Whereas the third and fourth points will be confirmed in chapter 8 on greed and chapter 9 on idolatry, respectively, the first two points can be treated briefly here, before moving on in chapters 4–6 to a discussion of the biblical and Jewish texts that may have some bearing on the origin of the expression.

Scott Hafemann rightly noted in 1993:

> The fundamental issue still to be resolved in Pauline studies is the determination of the *primary* religious and theological context within which Paul's thought is to be understood . . . whether one interprets his letters primarily against the Greco-Roman philosophical and religious world of Paul's day, as Bultmann argued over fifty years ago, or in the light of the Hellenistic-Jewish world of the first century and its Scripture, as Adolf Schlatter proposed in the early decades of this century.[5]

Whereas scholars such as Adolf Schlatter and W. D. Davies saw Paul and his teaching as essentially Jewish, E. P. Sanders's influential work portrayed Paul as something fundamentally different. Since the publication of Sanders's *Paul and Palestinian Judaism* in 1977, comparisons of aspects of Paul and his thought with early Jewish thought have abounded. Much recent work has stressed the Jewish matrix of Paul's thought and his scriptural inheritance.[6]

---

4. Although not widespread, Horace (*Ep.* 1.6.37) and Juvenal (*Sat.* 1.113) mention *Pecunia*, money being worshiped as goddesses.

5. Hafemann, "Paul and His Interpreters," 678.

6. To be fair, comparisons between Paul and Judaism have not all stressed continuity. For example, Laato, *Paulus und das Judentum*, argues that they differ radically in terms of anthropology, Judaism having a far more optimistic view of the human condition and free will than Paul does. Seifrid, *Justification by Faith*, compares Paul's soteriology with that of 1QS and the *Psalms of Solomon* and concludes that after his conversion it underwent a radical change.

To note a few prominent examples: Paul's identity received fresh treatment in Martin Hengel's *Pre-Christian Paul,* one goal of which is to demonstrate "how deeply his [Paul's] gospel is moulded by the language and spirit of the old people of God"; Karl-Wilhelm Niebuhr's study of "the Jewish apostle to the gentiles" examines the four points in Paul's letters that discuss his Jewish past (Gal 1:13-14; Phil 3:5-6; 2 Cor 11:22-23; Rom 11:1) and concludes that Paul considered himself to be in a central rather than an extreme position within Judaism; and in *Paul — One of the Prophets?* Karl O. Sandnes argues that Paul understood his apostleship in terms of the Old Testament prophetic tradition.[7] Three books stress in particular the continuity between Paul's moral teaching and biblical/Jewish antecedents; the titles give an indication of the contents: Peter J. Tomson, *Paul and the Jewish Law: Halakha in the Letters of the Apostle of the Gentiles;* Eckhard Reinmuth's investigation of "the presuppositions and contents of Paul's parenesis," *Geist und Gesetz;* and my own *Paul, Scripture, and Ethics: A Study of 1 Corinthians 5–7.*[8]

Whether or not we accept every detail of these studies, the general thrust is difficult to miss. It is that Paul is "Jewish to the roots," to use Morna Hooker's words.[9] Likewise N. T. Wright concludes that Paul is "a very Jewish thinker" and not "a thoroughgoing Hellenist."[10] The present study of the expression "greed is idolatry" is set in the context of this rediscovery of the Jewishness of Paul over the last few decades.[11] However, we can be more specific with respect to the background of Paul's depiction of greed as idolatry. The character of the moral teaching of both letters in which the pronouncements appear is decidedly biblical/Jewish.

---

7. See Hengel, *Pre-Christian Paul,* xii; Niebuhr, *Heidenapostel aus Israel;* and Sandnes, *Paul — One of the Prophets?*

8. Several authors have connected Paul with Judaism in more general terms. For instance, without reviewing the above-mentioned studies, two journal articles stress the Jewishness of Paul: Harrington, "Paul the Jew," argues that Paul never disavowed his identity as a Jew; and Stegner, "Jewish Paul," concludes that Paul fits more comfortably today into first-century Judaism than two decades ago.

9. "Paul — Apostle to the Gentiles," 85. In this article Hooker argues that "the popular picture of Paul as anti-Jewish is false," 89.

10. Wright, *What Saint Paul Really Said,* 23.

11. This trend is of course of less interest to those who do not think that Paul wrote Ephesians and Colossians. Nonetheless, if these letters are taken at least to be Pauline in character, this research underscores the "Jewishness" of the Pauline tradition in which they stand.

Jewish Moral Teaching in Colossians

The practical exhortations in Colossians begin in 3:5 and continue up to the final greetings that begin with 4:7ff. In the following section the biblical/Jewish character of the household code in 3:18–4:6 will be observed. The instructions in 3:5-17 bear the same stamp.[12] First we consider the provenance of the form of instruction in which the words "greed is idolatry" appear.

The origin of the catalogues of virtues and vices in the Pauline letters has attracted a good deal of scholarly attention. The main examples are found in 1 Corinthians (5:9-11; 6:9-10), Romans (1:29-31; 13:13), Galatians (5:19-23), and Philippians (4:8). Three chief theories of the "prehistory" of these lists, which are in fact a less specific class of household code (see next section), deserve mention. First, in 1936 Anton Vögtle emphasized the indebtedness of New Testament ethical lists to Stoicism.[13] Whereas the catalogues of Philippians 4:8 and 2 Peter 1:5-7 have more affinities with Stoic parallels than the other New Testament lists, a significant Stoic influence upon the New Testament catalogues in general, especially those in Paul's letters, has not been established to the satisfaction of many scholars. Paul's stress on love and faith is not typical of the Stoic lists, and the four cardinal virtues and corresponding vices of Stoicism are absent from Paul's lists. Furthermore, many of the virtues in Paul's lists were regarded as vices in Stoicism.

Second, in the mid-twentieth century both Siegfried Wibbing and Ehrhard Kamlah found the roots of New Testament catalogues in the dualistic cosmology of Iranian religion.[14] Wibbing considered that the Qumran *Rule of the Community,* which contains virtue and vice catalogues in its section dealing with the governance of humankind by two spirits, found its roots in Iranian religion, and that Paul's ethical lists, also set in a dualistic framework, belong to the same milieu. Kamlah refined Wibbing's theory by distinguishing between "parenetic" catalogues, which describe putting off vices and putting on virtues, and "descriptive" catalogues, which close with a promise of salvation and/or a threat of destruction. He

---

12. Dunn, *Colossians,* is especially helpful in showing the passage's "Jewish frames of reference" (p. 217).

13. Vögtle, *Tugend- und Lasterkataloge.*

14. Wibbing, *Die Tugend- und Lasterkataloge;* Kamlah, *Form der katalogischen Paränese.*

limited the influence of the dualistic cosmology of Iranian religion to the descriptive catalogues (parenetic catalogues were put down largely to Hellenistic syncretism with its dichotomy between the body and the soul).

Third, a number of scholars locate the lists in a broad biblical/Jewish tradition. F. F. Bruce and D. Schroeder offer a critique of the Iranian provenance theory and underscore instead the direct influence of the Old Testament.[15] They rightly question whether dualistic expression in the New Testament (such as found in Eph 5:6ff.) can be taken to reveal dualistic anthropology. Few scholars doubt that the New Testament God is an unrivalled Sovereign. Both the *Community Rule* and Pauline catalogues manifest rather the ethical dualism of the Old Testament prophets' Day of the Lord that promised salvation and judgment for different groups (e.g., Jer 21:8; Ezek 18:5-9, 15-17), and the blessings and curses of Deuteronomy 27–28. Sebastian Brock, who traces the origin of the "two ways" theme (cf. *Did.* 1.1; *Barn.* 18) to the Palestinian Targum of Deuteronomy 30, moves in a similar direction.[16] Finally, E. Schweizer and P. Borgen are examples of those whose stress on the Jewish background to the Pauline vice catalogues has proved to be more convincing.[17] The combined influence of biblical and Jewish sources accounts for much of the background to the Pauline ethical lists such as the ones in which Colossians 3:5 and Ephesians 5:5 appear.

Other features of Colossians 3 also betray a Jewish origin:

1. The emphasis on wrong desire as the root of sin (as evident in 3:5; cf. Rom 7:7-8) is thoroughly Jewish.[18]
2. The belief that sexual immorality and idolatry deserve and will receive God's judgment (Col 3:6) is typically Jewish.[19]
3. The belief in the coming wrath and judgment of God (3:6) is a widespread Jewish tradition,[20] especially in relation to a day of "wrath."[21]

15. Bruce, "Review of Wibbing"; Schroeder, "Lists, Ethical."
16. Brock, "Two Ways."
17. Schweizer, "Traditional Ethical Patterns"; Borgen, "Catalogues of Vices."
18. See Dunn, *Romans*, 1:380.
19. Dunn, *Colossians*, 216, notes esp. Exod 32:10-12; Num 25:1-4; Deut 29:16-28; 2 Chron 24:18; Jer 7:16-20; 25:6; Ezek 22; Mic 5:10-15; 1QS 2:15; 5:12; Matt 3:7. See further the section on "Opposition to Idolatry" in chapter 9.
20. Cf. Isa 34:8; Dan 7:9-11; Joel 2:1-2; Mal 4:1; *Jub.* 5.10-16; *1 En.* 90.20-27.
21. For example, Isa 13:6-16; Zeph 1:15, 18; 2:2-3; 3:8; cf. Dunn, *Colossians*, 217.

4. "Son of disobedience" (3:6) is a Semitism.

5. Walking as a metaphor for conduct is Jewish idiom.[22]

6. The imperative not to lie recalls the ninth commandment.

7. The metaphor of putting on godly virtues (3:10) is common in the Bible and Jewish sources.[23]

8. Renewal both in knowledge and after the image of God (3:10) recalls Genesis 1:26-27.[24]

9. The phrases "Greek and Jew" and "circumcised and uncircumcised" (Col 3:11) clearly indicate a Jewish perspective.[25]

10. The description of the Colossian Christians as "chosen ones, holy and beloved," is highly reminiscent of Jewish self-perception.[26]

11. The five virtues that are to be put on (3:12) are characteristic of Jewish wisdom teaching.[27]

12. The peace of Christ that is to rule in Christian hearts (3:15) was, as Dunn contends, a hope for the future new age tied up with being the people of the Messiah.[28]

13. Being "called" to peace (3:15) is related to the scriptural theme of being a chosen people (3:12).[29]

14. "Psalms" (3:16) may refer to songs from the Scriptures, such as the psalms of David (and "hymns" to praise of a Christian origin).[30]

15. The notion that worship and daily living are bound together is thoroughly Jewish.[31]

---

22. Cf. Lohmeyer, *Kolosser,* 139: "Again it is obvious how deeply determined are those sentences by Jewish dogmatism against heathenism."

23. Cf. "righteousness" in Job 29:14; Ps 132:9; Wis 5:18; "strength and dignity" in Prov 31:25; "the beauty of glory, the robe of righteousness" in Bar 5:1-2; "faith" in Philo, *Conf.* 31; "virtues" in Philo, *Dreams* 1.225; cf. Dunn, *Colossians,* 221; Lohmeyer, *Kolosser,* 140.

24. Cf. Wolter, *Kolosser,* 180: "an unavoidable allusion."

25. Dunn, *Colossians,* 224, perceptively asks, "apart from Jews who else would single out the 'Jews' and lump all the rest together?"

26. See Dunn, *Colossians,* 227-28. Wolter, *Kolosser,* 184, and Dunn, *Colossians,* 228, detect an allusion to Deut 7:6-7.

27. Schweizer, *Kolosser,* 206, notes in particular the parallel in 1QS 4:3.

28. Dunn, *Colossians,* 233-34; cf. Isa 9:6-7; 54:10; Ezek 34:25-31; 37:26; Mic 5:4; Hag 2:9; Zech 8:12; *1 En.* 5.7, 9; 10.17; 11.2; *T. Dan* 5.11.

29. For example, Isa 41:8-9; 42:6; 43:3-4; 48:12; 49:1; 51:2.

30. Cf. Lightfoot, *Colossians,* 223. Cf. the "new song" of Isa 42:10.

31. Cf. Sir 47:8; *m. 'Abot* 2:12; cf. Lohse, *Colossians,* 152 n. 160.

16. "The name of the Lord Jesus" is analogous to the "name of the Lord," which appears throughout Scripture.[32]

A few of these features are not uniquely Jewish but can also be found in Greek thought and in the Jesus tradition. Nonetheless, taken together they point to the biblical and Jewish milieu of the instructions in which the judgment that "greed is idolatry" is found.

Several scholars have suggested a more specific hypothesis for the biblical inspiration for the teaching of Colossians 3:5ff., namely, the Decalogue.[33] Indeed, a number of Jewish and Christian ethical catalogues betray just such an influence, including *Sibylline Oracles* 4.29-39, Pseudo-Phocylides 3-21,[34] Mark 7:21-22/Matthew 15:19, and 1 Timothy 1:8-10.[35] Many elements in the passage can be taken as Decalogue interpretation and application: the vice lists of Colossians 3:5 and 8 recall commandments 1-2, 5, 6, 7, 8, and 10 (taking hatred to be equivalent to murder; cf. Matt 5:21-22; 1 John 3:15);[36] Colossians 3:9a recalls the ninth commandment; the virtues of 3:12-14 may be read as countering commandments 6, 8, 9, and 10 (in a manner reminiscent of Ps.-Phoc. 5, 7), with love as the all-embracing commandment (cf. Rom 13:8-10); the instructions of Colossians 3:16 concerning Christian worship could be seen as relevant to the fourth commandment;[37] and Colossians 3:20–4:1 may represent an application of the fifth commandment, which is quoted at the corresponding point in Ephesians 6:2-3. The only one of the Ten Words missing is the third on taking God's name in vain (which finds what is probably a coincidental parallel in Col 3:17 with the reference to Jesus' name).

32. Cf. Dunn, *Colossians*, 240: "another indication of the extent to which the first Christians understood what they were doing simply as an extension of Israel's ancestral religion."

33. Ernst, *Kolosser*, 223ff.; Gnilka, *Kolosserbrief;* and especially Hartman, "Code and Context," 239-42.

34. On the influence of the Decalogue on Pseudo-Phocylides see Thomas, *Jüdische Phokylides*, 405ff.

35. See Hartman, "Code and Context," 239-40.

36. Ernst, *Kolosser*, 226, takes 3:8 to be a kind of midrash on Deut 5:17-18.

37. Cf. Philo's description of the prayers, singing and instruction of the Therapeutae on the Sabbath in *Cont. Life* 29, 75-80.

Jewish Moral Teaching in Ephesians

The "life worthy of the calling" to which the Ephesian Christians are called (4:1) is expounded in 4:1–6:20. It would not serve our purposes to list and assess the many points of contact between the Scriptures and early Jewish sources in what is the longest section of parenesis in the Pauline corpus. Instead we shall confine ourselves to making some general observations, to examining briefly the exhortations in 5:3-5, and to considering the origin of the household code in 5:21–6:9.[38]

While the teaching of Ephesians has been compared to Gnostic sources, the Dead Sea Scrolls, and Stoicism,[39] Thorsten Moritz is right that "the most predominant and deliberate source of influence on Ephesians [was] the Jewish Bible."[40] In the exhortation to maintain the unity of the church (Eph 4:1-16), a reflection upon Psalm 68:18 in Ephesians 4:8-10 sets up the crucial discussion of gifts in the church. In the exhortation to live as the new humanity as opposed to the old (4:17-24) the lifestyle to be avoided, as in so much Jewish moral teaching, is that of the gentiles. In the practical injunctions about the old and new life (4:25–5:2), the passage immediately preceding the section in which the judgment that "the greedy person is an idolater" appears, the links with biblical and Jewish tradition are manifold and impressive. Scriptural quotations are found in 4:25 (Zech 8:16) and 4:26a (Ps 4:5), an allusion in 4:30 (Isa 63:10) and reminiscences in 4:26b (Deut 24:15) and 4:28 (Lev 19:11, 13, and/or the eighth commandment).[41] In the exhortation to live as the children of light (Eph 5:6-14), the climactic and summary injunction (5:14), possibly part of an early Christian hymn, is a striking christological interpretation of two scriptural texts

---

38. That another household code appears in Colossians singles it out for attention; my conclusions will in effect serve double duty. Furthermore, since scholars think such codes are among the most traditional types of parenesis in Paul's letters, their origin may give some general indication as to the question from where the author customarily draws his moral teaching.

39. Cf. the commentaries by Pokorný and Gnilka.

40. Moritz, *Profound Mystery*, 214.

41. Cf. ibid., 87-96. Sampley, "Scripture and Tradition," 106-7, suggests that the text displays "an antiphonal relationship" between OT material and its "application." In other words, virtually the only material which cannot be paralleled from the OT in the passage can be seen as explanation and expansion. The scheme, though at points rather arbitrary, nonetheless shows the extent of OT influence on the passage. Lindemann's opinion that most of the overlap is coincidental, *Epheserbrief*, is difficult to maintain.

(Isa 26:19 and 60:1ff.).[42] The exhortation to wise and Spirit-filled behavior (Eph 5:15-20) includes a possible echo of Proverbs 23:31 in Ephesians 5:18.[43] Finally, the exhortation to stand firm in spiritual battle (6:10-20) is heavily indebted to passages from Isaiah (most clearly Isa 11:5; 52:7; 59:17 in Eph 6:10, 14-17).

In the list of vices in 5:3-5 sexual sins dominate, a stress that is carried on with the references to "deeds of darkness" and "what is done in se-cret" in 5:11-12. Jews considered sexual immorality, defined broadly, to be a typical pagan vice. It is condemned in the Old Testament and through-out the intertestamental Jewish sources. The appeal to "what is fitting" (5:4) was a feature of Stoic ethics, but it was probably mediated to early Christianity via Hellenistic Judaism.[44] Both avoidance of shameful and foolish talk and the giving of thanks were common Jewish teaching. For example, strict regulations concerning speech are found in the Dead Sea Scrolls, with 1QS 10:21-23 providing a close parallel to Ephesians 5:4.[45] And Philo uncontroversially regarded thanksgiving to be a preeminent virtue that summed up the whole of religious duty (cf. *De Plant.* 126, 131).

Finally, the household codes of Ephesians 5:22–6:9 and Colossians 3:18–4:1, which follow the texts in question (Eph 5:5; Col 3:5), supply good evi-dence for a Jewish inspiration at the level of both form and content. Whereas M. Dibelius and his pupil K. Weidinger argued that the codes in question are lightly christianized forms of earlier lists drawn from Stoic moral philosophers (such as Aristotle, Seneca, Plutarch, and Epictetus),[46] K. H. Rengstorf claimed that the *Haustafeln* (codes of instruction for

42. Moritz, *Profound Mystery,* 115-16.
43. See ibid., 94-95.
44. Lincoln, *Ephesians,* 322.
45. Ibid., 323.
46. Dibelius (*Kolosser,* especially after his comments on 4:1, pp. 48ff.) and Weidinger (*Haustafeln*) appeal to expressions such as ἀνῆκεν (Col 3:18) and εὐάρεστον (3:20), which are common in the Stoic literature. The motivation ἐν κυρίῳ (3:20, etc.) is in their opinion merely a cosmetic Christian pendant. In spite of the popularity of the theory, especially in German scholarship (Crouch, *Origin,* 21, lists many adherents including Bultmann, Thyen, Conzelmann, Lohse, and Merk), several factors weigh against it. There are considerable dif-ferences between the content, motivations, and settings of the Christian and non-Christian material, and their form is markedly different (the Stoic lists use neither direct address nor the imperative mood). The most that can be said is that the *Haustafeln* share certain charac-teristics with some Hellenistic codes.

members of households) are uniquely Christian, inspired by the home life of John and Jesus described in Luke 1–2.[47] James E. Crouch, on the other hand, found the best precedents for the household codes in the literature of Hellenistic Judaism.[48] E. Schweizer, W. Schrage, and W. Lillie to a large extent concur.[49] The main sources to which Crouch points are Philo (*Hypo.* 7.1-9),[50] Josephus (*Ag. Ap.* 2.190-219), and Pseudo-Phocylides (175-227). His opinion is that "each [of these] drew from a store of ethical material which was in current use in Jewish missionary activity."[51] He argues persuasively that the Hellenistic Jewish codes are significantly more similar to the Pauline codes than are the Stoic lists.

The influence of the Scriptures on the Pauline household codes has not escaped the notice of a few scholars. D. Schroeder (who takes an eclectic view of the background to the *Haustafeln*) considers that the content of the Pauline codes is basically Old Testament–Jewish and argues that their form reaches back to Old Testament apodictic law (cf. Deut 5:16), which also uses direct address in the imperative mood supported by statements designed to motivate obedience.[52] Lillie also emphasizes Old Testament–Jewish influences, noting the fifth commandment quotation in Ephesians 6:2-3 (and the example of Sarah cited in the equivalent Petrine code, 1 Pet

---

47. Rengstorf, "Neutestamentliche Mahnungen." In these narratives Joseph and Zechariah are clearly the heads of their respective families (a concept shared with the Ephesian and Colossian codes) and in Luke 2:51 Jesus is submissive, ὑποτάσσω, to his parents (a key term in both codes). Furthermore, an important *Haustafeln* motif, that of ἀγάπη, surely derives, he argues, directly from the example of Jesus. The influence of such Christian factors is difficult to weigh (though one wonders in what sense the family lives of Jesus and John were distinctively "Christian"). As a comprehensive theory of the origin of the *Haustafeln* material, however, this view would become unsatisfying if some ancient sources, with which Paul may have been familiar, could be shown to contain some quite similar elements to the *Haustafeln,* which brings us to the theory of Jewish origin.

48. Crouch, *Origin,* 1972.

49. Schweizer, "Weltlichkeit"; Schrage, "Zur Ethik der neutestamentlichen Haustafeln"; Lillie, "Pauline House-Tables."

50. Schweizer, "Haustafeln," has noted not only the influence of Hellenistic Jewish sources on the *Haustafeln,* but also the impact of the OT on the Jewish sources themselves. For instance, he points out that in Philo's instruction, unlike the (non-Jewish) Hellenistic codes, there are echoes of the biblical concern for the welfare of the weak and disadvantaged in society. Parental authority is limited by the first commandment, Israel is reminded of its slavery in Egypt, and the married life of the neighbor is protected.

51. Texts from 4 Maccabees, Sirach, Tobit, and *Aristeas* are also cited.

52. Schroeder, "Haustafeln"; idem, "Lists, Ethical."

3:6).[53] Finally, Peter Stuhlmacher and Lars Hartman have demonstrated that the Decalogue was a major "point of departure" not only for the relevant texts from Philo, Josephus, and Pseudo-Phocylides but also for the Colossian *Haustafel*.[54]

"Greed Is Idolatry" as a Metaphor

Along with seeking the origin of "greed is idolatry," I contend that only when we recognize that the expression is a metaphor can we properly understand it. To put it another way, a thorough study of "greed is idolatry" involves not only investigating the terms "greed" and "idolatry," but also the word "is."

At this point my major presupposition, that "greed is idolatry" is a metaphor, requires some defense. As we saw in the history of interpretation in chapter 2, to note that "greed is idolatry" is not strictly the case still leaves it open as to whether the expression is a metaphor. It may simply be hyperbole. The line between different types of figurative and literal language is sometimes difficult to draw, especially when the context of the words is meager or itself ambiguous. While certainty may be unattainable, what can be demonstrated with an expression like "greed is idolatry" is the plausibility of regarding it as a metaphor.[55]

Two lines of evidence support this construal. First, it is conceivable that such a comparison between greed and idolatry could have been uttered by a first-century Christian with a Jewish background. Comparable notions exist in ancient Judaism (see chapter 5) and in the Gospels (see chapter 6). Furthermore, the way for such a comparison is paved in literal teaching concerning the danger of wealth leading one away from God. In other words, the expression sharpens and distils sentiments that were common to biblical and Jewish moral teaching. That both greed and idolatry share a

53. Lillie, "Pauline House-Tables."

54. Stuhlmacher, "Christliche Verantwortung," 177-78; Hartman, "Code and Context," 243.

55. Metaphor by its very nature involves a kind of logical incongruity, nonequivalence, or, in Paul Ricoeur's terms, "semantic impertinence," which defines it as nonliteral speech. Aaron, *Biblical Ambiguities*, 28: "Unless we can establish incongruence, we cannot assert the presence of metaphor." Simply put, "greed is idolatry" is not literally the case since normally speaking, impudence aside, greed and idolatry are not equivalent.

fascination for gold and silver (idols often consist of these two metals) renders the comparison all the more likely. The coincidence of such incidental features, though contributing nothing to the meaning of the metaphor, renders it more appealing (see the section on "Preparing the Metaphor" in chapter 10).[56]

Second, "greed is idolatry" makes perfectly good sense when read as a metaphor. As we shall see in the section on "Mapping the Metaphor" in chapter 10, the behavior of the greedy and the idolatrous toward their wealth and idols overlaps in significant ways. As a metaphor, "greed is idolatry" is neither far-fetched, nor strained and obtuse.

The current consensus on the study of metaphor is that metaphors speak directly and "do not need to be translated into 'literal' language to be understood. Indirect metaphorical meaning is accessible in and of itself."[57] As Janet Martin Soskice contends: "It is an indication of a good metaphor if it is unnecessary to spell out its implications for the reader."[58] While this opinion carries a measure of truth, we have seen in the history of interpretation in chapter 2 that in the case of "greed is idolatry," since no consensus exists, interpretation is definitely called for.

Soskice contends that the many theories of how metaphor works fall into three basic groups: (1) those that regard metaphor as a decorative way of saying what could be said literally; (2) those that stress the affective impact a metaphor exerts; and (3) those that consider metaphor to be a unique cognitive vehicle enabling one to say something that can be said in no other way.[59] The first group of theories is clearly mistaken in ignoring the emotive responses that metaphors evoke. The psalmist's description of God as "a rock" cannot be reduced to the literal utterance that God provides the psalmist with protection; feelings of security and safety are also

---

56. Linguists categorize metaphors variously. Black, "More about Metaphor," 33-35, distinguishes between extinct, dormant, and active metaphors. Our point is that "greed is idolatry" falls into the active category, which does not discount its creativity as it appears in Colossians and Ephesians but recognizes its readily comprehensible nature and potential to structure thinking and conduct. Lakoff and Johnson's typology, *Metaphors We Live By*, 53-55, categorizes metaphors as dead, new, and conventional. Depending on how original one takes "greed is idolatry" to be in Colossians and Ephesians (see part II), I would describe it either as new or conventional.

57. Osborne, *Hermeneutical Spiral*, 310.

58. Soskice, *Metaphor and Religious Language*, 23.

59. Ibid., 24ff.

communicated. Simply to "translate" a metaphor into straightforward language is to miss the metaphor's dynamism.[60] Nonetheless, the second group, in denying that a metaphor makes any increment to meaning, go too far in the other direction, for if thoughts and feelings can be expressed in words, then at least part of a metaphor's meaning may be expressed literally, even if by doing so one risks blunting the affective impact. An adequate account of metaphor must consider both cognitive meaning and emotive effect.

Soskice provides us with a workable definition of metaphor: "metaphor is that figure of speech whereby we speak about one thing in terms which are seen to be suggestive of another."[61] It is "a form of language use with a unity of subject-matter and which yet draws upon two (or more) sets of associations."[62] The intelligibility of the metaphor, "man is a wolf," for example, relies on both the speaker and hearer "having a body of shared knowledge or assumptions about the nature of men and the nature of wolves."[63] The meaning of this metaphor, then, will depend on who drew the comparison between man and wolves, to whom he or she was speaking, and the context in which the comparison was made, as to whether the fierceness, persistence, predatory clannishness, cruelty, or cunning of the wolf is meant. It would be wrong to transfer all of these connotations to the metaphor; overinterpretation must be avoided. The two entities, man and wolf, are in all likelihood only meant to overlap in one, or at most a few, respects in any given instance of the metaphor.[64]

With respect to a correct construal of "greed is idolatry" we must decide which of the many connotations are being called on for the purpose of the comparison, or in David H. Aaron's words, resolve its ambiguity:

---

60. In this regard literature in German often speaks of the *Unübersetzbarkeit*, the untranslatability, of metaphors into nonmetaphorical language. Cf., e.g., Röhser, *Metaphorik und Personifikation*, 21-23.

61. Soskice, *Metaphor and Religious Language*, 15. Cf. Lakoff and Johnson, *Metaphors We Live By*, 5: the function of metaphor concerns "understanding and experiencing one kind of thing in terms of another kind of thing."

62. Soskice, *Metaphor and Religious Language*, 49.

63. Ibid., 41, in a discussion of Black's "interactive" theory of metaphor.

64. Cf. Ricoeur, *Interpretation Theory*, 68, who speaks of "the very copula of metaphorical utterance" that calls the reader to distinguish the "is" from the "is not" of poetic assertion.

Most figurative, rhetorical devices thrive on ambiguity. This is especially true of metaphor. Ambiguity in metaphorical expressions results from uncertainty as to how the first part of a nonliteral statement is to be understood in terms of its second, or implied, part. For instance, in the phrase, "all the world's a stage," there is ambiguity with regard to how the world is to be understood as a stage. We might think of this ambiguity as internal to the expression. That is, once you recognize something as figurative, there is ambiguity involved in decoding how its parts evoke meaning. As an aesthetic element, ambiguity contributes to an expression's richness.[65]

To recall some of the interpretations reviewed in chapter 2, does the reference to idolatry connote service and obedience, love and devotion, or confidence and trust? Is it the futility of idolatry or the forgetfulness it normally involves or the jealousy of God that it provokes that Paul had in mind? A clue to answering this question may be present in the other set of associations involved in the metaphor. That is, which connotations of the greedy are in view? Who are the greedy for Paul and his readers? Are they those who trust in their wealth, consume material things hedonistically, make money by ruthlessly oppressing the poor, or meanly cling to their possessions? To understand "greed is idolatry" we must first seek to understand "greed" and "idolatry" in the mind of Paul and his readers.

Furthermore, with some New Testament metaphors assistance with the interpretation is supplied by their established usage in the Old Testament. When Jesus says to the woman at the well in John 4 that if she knew who he was, she would ask him and he would give her "living water," we are not left to our own devices as to whether the refreshing, cleansing, or life-giving qualities of water are in view. As Soskice notes, this is "not a metaphor used at random; in the prophetic literature 'living water' is associated with God as the source of life" (cf., e.g., Isa 55:1; Jer 2:13; Zech 14:8).[66] Thus there is both an historical argument and a literary argument for examining the biblical and Jewish background to the words.[67]

---

65. Aaron, *Biblical Ambiguities*, 1.

66. Soskice, *Metaphor and Religious Language*, 156.

67. Cf. Williams, *Paul's Metaphors*, 2: "If metaphors are an index to their user's world, it is equally true that a knowledge of that world is necessary to understand well and appreciate his or her metaphors."

In the light of these brief theoretical remarks, four main interpretive tasks need to be undertaken in order for us to understand "greed is idolatry" as a metaphor. First, the way in which the stage is set for the metaphor, its *preparation,* needs to be noticed. It is useful with some metaphors to consider the presence of what we might call incidental features, which though adding little or no increment to meaning make the comparison more appealing and compelling and may even have suggested it in the first place. Frank is a wolf, for example, is more likely to be said and will be more readily accepted if Frank's eyes, teeth, or beard imply the comparison or if Frank comes from a region where wolves are present. Such features of "greed is idolatry" will be noted in the section on "Preparing the Metaphor" in chapter 10.

Second, the metaphor needs to be *felt* in terms of its affective impact and rhetorical function (see the section on "Feeling the Metaphor" in chapter 10). As Steven J. Kraftchick observes, "Metaphor is a mode of creating dissonance of thought in order to restructure meaning relationships."[68] The biblical metaphors, especially the extended variety, the parables of Jesus, reorient our perception, sometimes radically. Such metaphors move the hearers to reconsider their attitudes and values. To understand a biblical metaphor like "I am the living bread that came down from heaven" (John 6:51a) is "to allow our life and perception of reality to be changed in light of the 'ontological flash' created by the metaphorical conjunction."[69] The accusation of idolatry carried a far greater impact in first-century than in twenty-first-century Christianity. Some attempt must be made to bridge this gulf and to feel the impact of the comparison of greed with idolatry afresh.

Third, the metaphor needs to be *mapped.* As Kraftchick observes, "metaphor is not an isomorphic mapping of all relationships within one field to another, but a highlighting of some and suppression of others."[70] With respect to "greed is idolatry" several steps are involved in this process of discerning the relevant similarities. An attempt must be made to understand greed and idolatry as separate concepts (see chapters 8 and 9, respectively). A further step will be to attempt to construct an abstract definition of idolatry, which moves away from its strictly literal associations, in order

68. Kraftchick, "Necessary Detour," 302.
69. Hays, *Moral Vision,* 301.
70. Kraftchick, "Necessary Detour," 23.

to see how the concept might function in a metaphorical context. To understand the metaphor "Jesus is a shepherd," it is a useful exercise to formulate a definition of a shepherd that fits both the literal and figurative realms, such as "a shepherd knows, cares for, and leads those under his charge." In similar fashion we must seek to discover the essence of idolatry. Finally, the associations that greed and idolatry throw up, that is, the profiles of the greedy and the idolater, ought to be compared to determine at which level the comparison is most likely to be intended (see the section on "Mapping the Metaphor" in chapter 10).

David Aaron has a similar understanding of the process of understanding a metaphor. He contends that metaphors

> create structure in our understanding of life . . . when we map the schema of one domain onto another. This "mapping" exposes the conceptual activity involved in decoding a metaphor. Metaphor, by mapping otherwise unconnected domains onto one another, can create new meaning. Metaphors do this by highlighting certain features while suppressing others, and by allowing for inferences.[71]

Similarly, Göran Eidevall speaks of the need to "map out . . . the effects of the metaphorical restructuring of the topic domain."[72]

The fourth and final step in analyzing "greed is idolatry" as a metaphor involves *comparing the metaphor* (see the last section in chapter 10). One of the goals of part II on the origin of "greed is idolatry" is to turn up analogous teaching, which compares greed with idolatry in some way. This material may then be placed alongside our interpretation of the Pauline expression and a comparison made. In some cases such denunciations of greed include an explanation or something in the surrounding context that is of assistance in their interpretation, both of which are missing from Colossians 3:5 and Ephesians 5:5. It may be possible to interpret the opaque (Col 3:5; Eph 5:5) in light of the transparent. A best-case scenario would be to tease out the meaning of the figurative in comparison with the literal, a procedure sometimes adopted with the interpretation of the parables of Jesus in the setting of his more prosaic teaching about the kingdom of God. One question we wish to ask is, do the warnings about the dangers of greed in the Jewish and biblical tradition that underscore the damage it

71. Aaron, *Biblical Ambiguities,* 104.
72. Eidevall, *Grapes in the Desert,* 49.

might inflict on faithfulness to God offer some form of explanation about the ways in which this infidelity operates?

By way of review, the four steps for analyzing a metaphor may be illustrated with reference to the comparison of interpreting greed as idolatry with climbing a mountain:

1. *Preparing the Metaphor* — The stage is conceivably set for the comparison of an exercise in scholarly biblical interpretation with mountain climbing in various ways. Both activities are specialized by nature, taking years of elaborate preparation and rigorous training. In both cases, although analogous activities can be undertaken by so-called laypeople, the professionals regard their own endeavors to be of a different order. Neither of these points of comparison is the meaning of the metaphor but they may render it more appealing and facilitate its reception.

2. *Feeling the Metaphor* — The idea of mountain climbing evokes a range of affective responses, some of which are positive, others negative. For some it spells excitement and exhilaration and promises considerable rewards, both on the journey and at its destination. For others, it symbolizes foreboding and danger and may seem self-indulgent and futile. I hope that readers will identify more with the former when feeling the metaphor of mountain climbing as applied to this book.

3. *Mapping the Metaphor* — A number of associations might connect mountain climbing and biblical exegesis. A positive spin on the comparison would note that both take considerable effort but afford handsome returns. The top of a mountain affords a clear perspective over a wide landscape and a glimpse into the heavens. Good theological exegesis has the same aim.

4. *Comparing the Metaphor* — Certain features of this book confirm the intended effect of the comparison. Eleven chapters should convince readers that understanding greed as idolatry requires some effort. It is hoped that new light on various points of exegesis, theology, and ethics will also call to mind the benefits of reaching a major summit.

Richard B. Hays's definition of a metaphor points the way forward for the present study of greed as idolatry: "Metaphors are incongruous conjunctions of two images — or two semantic fields — that turn out, upon reflection, to be like one another in ways not ordinarily recognized. They shock us into thought by positing unexpected analogies."[73] The task before us is to feel the shock and to discern the pertinent similarities that the comparison of greed with idolatry calls upon.

73. Hays, *Moral Vision*, 300. Cf. Kittay, *Metaphor*, 324, who describes the new understanding gained by the unexpected association inherent in a metaphor as a rearranging of the furniture of the mind.

Part II

The Origin of the
Concept of Idolatrous Greed:
A Comparison with Similar Peaks

CHAPTER 4

The Jewish Scriptures:
The Distant Ranges

The search for the origin of the words "greed is idolatry" needs to take
into consideration not only texts that condemn greed as being as bad
as and in some sense comparable to idolatry, but also the notion which un-
derlies this judgment, and may have given rise to it, namely, that greed or
wealth leads people away from God. In this chapter I consider such material in the Old Testament, specifically in the book of Deuteronomy, especially the Shema and the Song of Moses, and in a few texts in Job, Psalms,
and Proverbs.[1] In the following two chapters we consider certain Jewish
and New Testament texts. Philo, the *Testament of Judah,* rabbinic literature,
and the Synoptic Gospels build upon this biblical foundation stressing the
peril that wealth poses as a rival to God. Two texts in Romans and
Philippians that speak of people worshiping their bellies will also be considered. Furthermore, the classic biblical texts on the subject of idolatry
also require attention, in particular the first commandment and the episode of the golden calf, to see whether in some way they pave the way for
the concept of idolatrous greed. As well as suggesting a plausible concep-

1. OT narratives might also be considered. Solomon's extravagance and even self-
absorption, for example, is evident in 1 Kgs 9:10–10:29. Indeed, as Provan, *1 and 2 Kings,* 115,
points out, the only references to Solomon's "splendor" in the NT (Matt 6:25-34 and Luke
12:22-31) occur in passages encouraging believers not to allow concern about material needs
to interfere with seeking the kingdom of God.

tual background for the coinage of the expression "greed is idolatry," chapters 4–7 (along with chapter 10) make a modest contribution to a biblical theology of the dangers of wealth.[2]

The First Commandment

"You shall have no other gods before me"

The first commandment is not a warning against greed, at least not as it appears in the Ten Commandments. Its relevance to our subject lies in the history of its interpretation, or rather application, both in the Old Testament and in ancient Judaism. If the Decalogue contains the epitome of Israelite morality and declares the conditions for membership of the people of God,[3] the first commandment issues the foundational call to absolute loyalty and full devotion that was to be worked out in all areas of life.

One of the clearest findings of research on the Decalogue is that it "early held a central position in Israelite life."[4] Indeed, the first (and second) commandment is echoed in many Old Testament texts (e.g., Exod 34:14; 23:24; 34:17; Lev 19:14; 26:1; Deut 4:16, 23, 25; Ps 97:7; 2 Kgs 17:41; 2 Chron 33:7). According to many versions of the structure of Deuteronomy, chapters 5–11 elaborate the principal command by calling the people to full devotion to the Lord (which means keeping his commandments). It is upon this foundation that all of the other specific commandments in Deuteronomy 12–26 build.[5]

---

2. For a survey of passages that express hostility to wealth, which is a broader theme than that of the present study, in the OT, Jewish noncanonical material, and the Synoptic Gospels, see Schmidt, *Hostility to Wealth.*

3. The narrative framework of Deuteronomy stresses the finality of the Ten Commandments: "These words the Lord spoke . . . and added no more" (Deut 5:22). Weinfeld, "What Makes the Ten Commandments Different?" 38, describes the Decalogue as "a fundamental list of concrete commands applicable to every Israelite, comprising the essence of God's demands from his confederates."

4. Stamm and Andrew, *Ten Commandments,* 22-75.

5. See especially Lohfink, *Hauptgebot;* and Kaufmann, "Structure," 108, who argues that Deuteronomy 12–26 is "a highly structured composition where major topical units are arranged according to the order of the laws of the Decalogue . . . as it appears in chapter 5 [of Deuteronomy]." Cf. Walton, "Deuteronomy." Tomson, *Paul and the Jewish Law,* 152-53, also contends that "Deuteronomy as a whole, both in overall structure and in its details, continually stresses the urgency of the commandment against idolatry."

Not unlike Luther, some Jews came to regard the first commandment as in some sense all-embracing: "Whoever professes idolatry denies the Ten Words . . . Whoever denies idolatry, professes all of the Torah" (*Sifre Num* 111; cf. also *Sifre Deut* 54; *b. Ned.* 28a; *Kid.* 40a; *Hul.* 5a).[6] Indeed, the first commandment was taken by many Jews to be foundational to the rest of the Decalogue. *Mekilta* on Exodus 20:2-3 (*Baḥodesh* 6:1-10) explains the words, "I am the Lord your God, you shall have no other gods before me," in such a fashion: "I am He whose reign you have taken upon yourselves in Egypt . . . you have accepted my reign, now accept my decrees."[7] In Pseudo-Philo 44.6-10 the Ten Commandments are rephrased to make clear that every one is broken by the making of idols.

In this light a metaphorical extension of the prohibition of the worship of other gods, such as we find in Colossians 3:5 and Ephesians 5:5, is not out of keeping with the understanding, apparent at an early stage, that the claim of the first commandment touched all areas of life and that to have "no other gods" involved more than simply refraining from cultic worship of foreign gods.

Deuteronomy

Three texts in Deuteronomy are of particular interest to our subject: the Shema (6:4-5); chapter 8, which elaborates on themes introduced in chapter 6; and the Song of Moses (chap. 32). Since it is in the targumic version of the Shema that the question of wealth in connection with religious loyalty is made clear, we will consider it with rabbinic literature (in chapter 5).

Deuteronomy 8 elaborates on the themes of desert and land that appear in 6:10-19. The chapter is structured in chiastic fashion.[8] The Israelites are exhorted to keep the Law (8:1) and not forget the Lord (8:18-20) in the light of the wilderness journey in the past (8:2-6; 8:15-17) and the promised land in the future (8:7-10; 8:11-14). The central idea, which appears in v. 11,

---

6. In this sense Luther was not, contra Gestrich, "The first person to stress 'the absolute primacy' of the first commandment" (*Return of Splendor*, 180). For the considerable influence of the Decalogue (and the different summaries of the law) upon the literature of early Judaism see Niebuhr, *Gesetz und Paränese*; Berger, *Gesetzauslegung Jesu*, 258-77; and Dexinger, "Der Dekalog im Judentum."

7. Lauterbach, *Mekilta*, 2:237-38.

8. Cf. Lohfink, *Hauptgebot*; and Van Leeuwen, "Structure and Sense."

combines the framing exhortations not to forget the Lord and to obey the law. In vv. 12-14 the nation is warned not to allow their prosperity to lead to forgetting the Lord. The people's own achievements must not result in pride and reliance upon their own power.[9] The danger of forgetting the Lord through reliance on one's own wealth and power is also found in Hosea (see 8:14; 13:6; etc.) and in an Assyrian text regarding Tirhakah, king of Egypt, noted by Weinfeld: "he forgot the might of the god Aššur . . . and trusted in his own strength."[10] Such teaching forges a link between pride and trust in material things (which will also be touched in "Mapping the Metaphor" in chapter 10). The first half of Deuteronomy 8 presents the complementary idea that the people's existence depends not on food and material things but on God's goodness and providence (8:3), a lesson to be learned from the provision of the manna.

Both Deuteronomy 6 and 8 culminate with the threat of annihilation should forgetfulness lead to worshiping foreign gods. Although the juxtaposition of idolatry and the danger of trusting in wealth instead of in God is suggestive, and has led at least one commentator to speak of "the illusory god of wealth,"[11] Deuteronomy 8 does not teach that greed is idolatry. Instead, the lesson is the same one that *Testament of Judah* 19.1 teaches, that wealth can lead to idolatry; trusting wealth instead of God can lead to forgetting God, which in the thought of Deuteronomy leaves a vacuum that only other gods can fill.[12] In the Scriptures the thought that turning away from the way God has commanded is equivalent to turning to other gods is implied by the fact that the reverse state of affairs is true. To turn from evil ways is to turn to God (see 2 Kgs 17:13; 2 Chron 7:14; Isa 30:11; Jer 23:14; 25:5; 33:3; 42:15; Ezek 13:22; 33:8-9, 11; 14:6; 18:28, 30; Jon 3:8, 10).[13]

When we turn to Deuteronomy 32, that "rich and vigorous poem"[14] to which Paul alludes in Romans 10:19; 12:19; and 1 Corinthians 10:14-22,[15]

---

9. Cf. Deut 17:17, 20, where the king is warned not to "multiply to himself silver and gold . . . lest his heart grow haughty."

10. Weinfeld, *Deuteronomy 1–11*, 394.

11. See Olson, *Deuteronomy and the Death of Moses*, 54.

12. Deut 6:16-19 also teach that the people must unswervingly trust the Lord.

13. Cf. Ciampa, "What Does the Scripture Say?" 60.

14. Skehan, "Structure of the Song of Moses," 163.

15. Hanson, *Studies in Paul's Technique*, 115, is right to conclude that Deut 32 is "a passage which we know that Paul studied carefully." On the influence of Deut 32 on 1 Cor 10:22b see my *Paul, Scripture, and Ethics*, 195-203.

we find a depiction of Israel's future in gloomy terms that teaches the same lesson as Deuteronomy 6 and 8: newly acquired wealth will lead the people into apostasy, eliciting severe judgment from the Lord. Following the affirmation that the Lord had graciously led the nation through the wilderness (cf. 32:12, "the Lord alone led him: no foreign god was with him") into the bounty of the promised land in 32:10-14, the song reports Israel's tragic demise: "Jeshurun grew fat and kicked; filled with food, he became heavy and sleek. He abandoned the God who made him and rejected the Rock of his salvation" (32:15). Once again we see that in Deuteronomy to reject God is to worship idols and vice versa: "They made him jealous with their foreign gods and angered him with their detestable idols" (32:16; cf. 32:18, 21a).

The Golden Calf

If in the exodus events the nation of Israel was "created," in the episode of the golden calf Israel experiences its "fall"[16] or "first sin."[17] Indeed, as Scott Hafemann observes, "Israel's sin with the golden calf becomes both determinative and paradigmatic for Israel's future history as God's people."[18] Its unusual importance is seen already in the Old Testament, which retells it in Deuteronomy 9:8-21, Nehemiah 9:16-18, and Psalm 106:19-23 (cf. Acts 7:35-43) and alludes to or echoes it in Deuteronomy 32:24-29, Judges 2:17, and 1 Kings 12:28. For our purposes its significance lies in that, in the words of Brevard Childs, it is "representative of all subsequent idolatry."[19]

Two features of the history of interpretation of the golden calf in ancient Judaism and early Christianity have possible relevance to the notion of greed as idolatry. First, the tragic incident seems to have forged a link in Jewish minds between gold and idolatry, a development that is significant for Philo (see the last section below).[20] Gold came to be asso-

---

16. Hafemann, *Paul, Moses,* 228, who is following Ferdinand Weber.

17. Moberly, *Mountain of God,* 84.

18. Hafemann, *Paul, Moses,* 230.

19. Childs, *Exodus,* 565. As Ciampa, "What Does the Scripture Say?" 62, notes, the language of "turning aside from the way" (Exod 32:8) becomes a standard biblical expression for apostasy. On the history of interpretation see Smolar and Aberbach, "Golden Calf."

20. Indeed, in antiquity in general it was a custom for a wealthy person to have some of his gold cast into an idol (cf. Judg 17:3-5).

ciated with both greed and idolatry. Second, and more importantly, for many Jews, including Paul, the golden calf crystallized an enduring conception of idolatry in terms of evil desire. Already in Numbers 11:4, 34, and Psalm 106:14 (LXX 105:14), the people's sin in the wilderness is described as insatiable greed. The Targumim, furthermore, also stress that the people "reveled licentiously."[21] In 1 Corinthians 10:6-13 Paul also describes the idolatry of the golden calf (along with fornication, provocation, and murmuring) as the desiring of bad things. Philo, as we shall see shortly, builds up an elaborate conception of idolatry as the surrender to sinful passions, in the context of which he treats the sin of greed. It is to the golden calf that we owe the impetus for the idea of idolatry as bad desire.

Psalm 10

That riches can be a substitute for God is suggested at one point in Psalm 10. Paul's use of Psalm 10:7 in Romans 3:14 indicates that he knew the psalm. In Psalm 10:3-11 there is a long and traditional description of the wicked: the wicked deny their accountability to God (10:3-4, 10-11), prosper in arrogant iniquity (10:5-8), and oppress the lowly (10:9).[22] Having complained about God's apparent indifference to the persecution of the poor by the arrogant (10:1-2a), the psalmist offers justification for his petition for God's intervention (10:2b, 12) in terms of the godlessness of the wicked (10:3-11). Verse 3 reads literally: "For the wicked praises the desire of his soul/self, and in his greed gives his blessing."

The material things that the wicked covet in this verse are set up as a substitute for God. As J. W. Rogerson and J. W. McKay note, "He [the wicked] sets his mind on his own desires and makes them his praise instead of God."[23] The practical atheism of v. 4, "he leaves no place for God in all his schemes" (NEB), is not to do so much with his not needing God, as in Deuteronomy and Job 31 (see below), but, as in v. 11, concerns his confidence that God will not interfere with his activities of unjust gain. As in

21. See Bori, *Golden Calf*, 98.
22. Cf. Mays, *Psalms*, 72.
23. Rogerson and McKay, *Psalms 1–50*, 50. Cf. Dahood, *Psalms I*, 60, translation of 10:3b, "the despoiler worships his appetite."

v. 6, he is supremely confident that no misfortune will come upon him in spite of his sin.[24]

The lesson is maintained or even reinforced in the LXX, which reads literally: "Because the sinner praises (ἐπαινεῖται) himself for the desires of his heart; and the unjust blesses himself (ἐνευλογεῖται)." The LXX also interprets the activities of 10:5-8 in terms of oppressing the poor for financial gain by supplying wealthy accomplices in v. 8: "He lies in wait with rich men (πλουσίων) in secret places, in order to slay the innocent; his eyes are set against the poor."

Proverbs 30:7-9

Two things I ask of you, O LORD; do not refuse me before I die: Keep falsehood and lies far from me; give me neither poverty nor riches, but give me only my daily bread. Otherwise, I may have too much and disown you and say, "Who is the LORD?" Or I may become poor and steal, and so dishonor the name of my God.

Proverbs 30:7-9 is unusual in the book of Proverbs both in terms of form and content. The verses constitute a prayer, a unique genre, and qualify the book's dominant teaching on riches as a blessing to the righteous. Only here in Proverbs do we find what R. N. Whybray describes as "a total renunciation of any desire for wealth."[25] Whereas to be free from poverty is in keeping with other teaching in Proverbs, the request not to be given wealth is unprecedented and unexpected. In 10:1–22:16, even if wealth may breed overconfidence and is less desirable than a good reputation (22:1), it is generally regarded as the blessing of God, the righteous person's due reward. In 30:8-9 on the other hand, the dangers of wealth leading to pride and blasphemy mean that it is simply better not to get rich. The pitfalls of both poverty and wealth seem so inevitable that the prayer asks literally for "food of my portion," no more and no less (cf. McKane, "The bread that is my due"; REB, "the food I need"), that is, "a modest sufficiency."[26]

24. Dahood's translation, based on a customary emendation, *Psalms I*, 60, finds the subject of greed and ill-gotten gain also in v. 5: "And his wealth will last for all time."

25. Whybray, *Proverbs*, 412. Cf. Hausmann, *Studien zum Menschenbild*, 334: "This text [30:7-9] makes explicit other sentiments found in the rest of Proverbs."

26. Whybray, *Wealth and Poverty*, 79. Cf. 15:16-17; 16:8; 17:1, where such a condition is preferable to wealth without the fear of the Lord, honesty, or domestic harmony.

The structure of the passage is clear. Verse 7 introduces the prayer in sober terms. Verse 8 supplies two petitions: to be preserved from lying and deceit and from both poverty and wealth. And v. 9 explains why the latter is so important.[27] Verse 9a explains the danger of wealth and why it should be avoided: wealth leads to having no need of God and ultimately to denying him (cf. Deut 8:12-17; Zeph 1:12-13). These verses teach that it is better to be denied wealth than to have wealth and deny God. William McKane explains the conception of God implicit in this motive in terms of dependence and trust: "If I am too well-fed, I shall become self-satisfied and deny God. I shall say: 'Who is God?' i.e., who is this God of whom men speak as if they were dependent on him? God will be declared redundant. A life which is too easy and spacious will create the illusion of self-sufficiency and lead to apostasy."[28]

The LXX, which is noted for its pietistic and moralizing additions in Proverbs, has "Who sees me?" (τίς με ὁρᾶ;) instead of "Who is the Lord?" which strikes a slightly different note. Instead of leading to misplaced trust, these words suggest that wealth inspires a lack of accountability to God.

Job 31:24-28

If I have put my trust in gold or said to pure gold, "You are my security," if I have rejoiced over my great wealth, the fortune my hands had gained, if I have regarded the sun in its radiance or the moon moving in splendor, so that my heart was secretly enticed and my hand offered them a kiss of homage, then these also would be sins to be judged, for I would have been unfaithful to God on high.

Job 31 has been described as "the noblest presentation of individual ethics in the pages of the Bible."[29] In the context of the book of Job the chapter

---

27. Whybray, *Proverbs,* 411-12, relates the first request to the second, and is thereby able to argue that v. 9 supplies a motive for both requests: "The reference may be to deceitfully swearing oaths to other gods, not recognising the true source of wealth." In this case becoming rich would be seen as leading to idolatry. However, it is more natural to read the two requests as unrelated, taking "deceit and lying" more generally as elsewhere in Proverbs. In a later publication Whybray himself adopts this interpretation (see *Wealth and Poverty,* 79).

28. McKane, *Proverbs,* 649.

29. Gordis, *Book of Job,* 542.

represents Job's final and climactic protest of his innocence to his friends in which he asserts his unimpeachable loyalty to God as his sovereign Lord. In 31:24-25 and 26-28 Job denies the sins of greed and idolatry, respectively. The juxtaposition of these two sins raises the possibility that these verses warn against the idolatry of wealth.

Whether 31:24-28 teaches that greed is idolatry depends in part on the structure of the chapter. Are the verses merely unacquainted neighboring items in a list or do they in some sense belong together? Two main options need to be considered: either Job insists he is free from fourteen different sins or he mentions numerous sins listed topically in groups. The former is argued by Robert Gordis on the basis of the numerical literary device of a double heptad that he finds in the passage. Gordis notes that the heptad is an organizing principle in various Old Testament, rabbinic, and New Testament compositions and cites three rabbinic examples from the Mishnah of structures based on the number fourteen (*m. Sanh.* 7:4, fourteen sins punishable by stoning; *'Abot* 5:21, fourteen ages of a man; 6:7, fourteen benefits of studying Torah). In Job 31 the list of two times seven sins would be designed to create the impression of Job's complete innocence. It also militates against finding any significance in the fact that vv. 24-25 are followed by vv. 26-28; these verses are the ninth and tenth sins in Job's code of honor and may be kept separate.[30] Many commentators, even if not subscribing to the double heptad structure, treat the verses as unrelated.[31]

A second way of observing the structure of the material in the chapter supports the view that at the very least 31:24-28 belong together. Some scholars divide it into a number of strophes based on a variety of textual indicators.[32] In particular, the repetition of the particle אִם, which introduces the three offenses in vv. 24, 25, and 26-27, suggests that the penalty stated in v. 28 applies to the four preceding verses. Pieter van der Lugt's summary paraphrase of 31:24-28 spells out the implications, taking greed to be equivalent to idolatry: "If I should have relied on great wealth (vv. 24-

---

30. Cf. Hartley, *Book of Job*, 408, who also lists 14 sins with vv. 24-25 and 26-28 on the ninth and tenth.

31. Cf., e.g., Tur-Sinai, *Book of Job*, 444. The double heptad structure does not however rule out some kind of link between the verses. Gordis himself believes the placing of trust in and love of gold (31:24-25) before the worship of the sun and moon (31:26-28) is intentional. He argues that "Job here repudiates the idolatry of wealth."

32. See especially Ceresko, *Job 29–31*; van der Lugt, *Rhetorical Criticism*, 350ff.; and RSV, TEV, and NIV.

25) or on other 'idols' (v. 26), then, I would be guilty of secret sins and of a *criminal offence* (vv. 27-28)."[33] We may also note that Norman C. Habel ("Although rich, Job has never made his wealth an idol or an obsession. God has been the sole object of his trust and worship") and J. H. Eaton ("He denies making gold his god [31:24-25], congratulating himself on his wealth") draw similar conclusions.[34]

Do the contents of the verses suggest that greed is here regarded as a form of idolatry? The majority of commentators explain Job 31:24-25 in terms of the danger wealth poses to fidelity to God, but without claiming that wealth is a god. Georg Fohrer's comments are typical: "He has not relied on that which is perverse and vain like an ungodly person (cf. Job 8:14) and has not let himself be led away from God by riches."[35] However, it is clear that what the greedy offer gold in vv. 24-25, namely, their trust, confidence, and joy, is considered both in Job and in the Old Testament generally as due God. It is also clear that v. 26 refers to cultic acts of worship: the worship of the sun and the moon was central to pagan religion (cf. 2 Kgs 21:3; 23:4, 5; Ezek 8:16) and the acts of kissing idols (1 Kgs 19:18; Hos 13:2) and throwing kisses to objects of worship were widespread (cf. Deut 11:16, which has the same combination of heart and hand in cautioning against idolatry). Furthermore, the condemnation in Job 31:28 of the sins mentioned in vv. 24-27 shows that greed and idolatry are treated with equal seriousness and describes well the sin of idolatry. The common element in vv. 24-27 is the notion of misplaced trust. The place of the verses in the to-and-fro between Job and his friends also supports the accusation that Job has given to gold what belongs to God. In 22:24-25 Eliphaz had accused Job of raising gold above God as his first love. In 31:24-25 is Job's response.[36]

Surprisingly, no commentary on either Job 31 or on Ephesians 5 or Colossians 3, to my knowledge, notes the parallel between the passages in either direction. Taken together the unit in Job 31 teaches that to trust primarily in riches or idols is to be unfaithful to God. Although this text falls

---

33. Van der Lugt, *Rhetorical Criticism*, 350.

34. See Habel, *Job*, 166-67; Eaton, *Job*, 21.

35. Fohrer, *Studien zum Buche Hiob*, 89.

36. Cf. Rowley, *Book of Job*, 203: "Job is [in vv. 24-25] repudiating the charge which Eliphaz had made against him in 22:24ff." Job 21:7-15 sheds further light on the notion that wealth can lead to apostasy. Job complains that when the wicked prosper they say to God, "Let us alone; we do not want to know your ways! What is Shaddai that we should serve him, or what should we gain by praying to him?" (21:14-15).

short of explicitly branding greed as idolatry, one may safely conclude that the two sins are treated as comparable both in character (both involve trusting a substitute for God) and gravity (both constitute unfaithfulness to God).

Job 22:23-30

That possessions can act as a substitute for God is clear from Deuteronomy 8 and 32 and from Job 31. That the reverse state of affairs can also obtain, with God replacing possessions, is clear from another text in Job and demonstrates from the other side how thoroughgoing is the rivalry between God and money. In Job 22:23-30 Eliphaz warns Job away from excessive attachment to material things ("treat your precious metal as dust and the gold of Ophir as stones from the riverbed," 22:24) and promises that instead God will be gold for Job ("then the Almighty himself will be your precious metal; he will be your silver in double measure," 22:25).

Indeed, it is a commonplace in Scripture to praise the value of knowledge, wisdom and the law of the Lord over against wealth of various kinds (e.g., Prov 3:14; 8:10, 19; 16:16; 20:15; Job 28:15; 1 Kgs 3:10-13; 2 Chron 1:11-12; Pss 19:10; 119:14, 72, 127). Philo eloquently expresses the same thought, which is repeated in other postbiblical Jewish writings,[37] when he asks, "of what riches can we any longer stand in need, when we have you, who alone is true riches?" (*Dreams* 1.179).

---

37. See Schmidt, *Hostility to Wealth,* chap. 5.

CHAPTER 5

Early Jewish Moral Teaching:
The Tablelands

Qumran

I n the Qumran community opposition to both greed and idolatry was taken for granted. The scrolls contain numerous condemnations of the worship of idols (cf. 11QT 54:8–55:21; 59:3-4; 60:16-21; 62:16; 1QM 14:1; 4Q216 2:4-5; 1Q22 1:7; 1QpHab 12:10-15; 13:3), and the sectaries had committed themselves to sharing their possessions. Possible references to the notion of nonliteral idolatry occur in the *Damascus Document* (CD) and the *Rule of the Community* (1QS).

Damascus Document 20 is a critique of apostates from the community. Such people are described as insolent ones, who speak against the community's regulations and despise the covenant of Damascus (20:11-12). A second group appears, along with these despisers (cf. 20:8), in 20:9, namely, those who "have placed idols in their hearts."[1] However, as tantalizing as this phrase at first appears, it is unlikely that it is a reference to the worship of something other than literal idols. *Damascus Document* 20:9 alludes to Ezekiel 14:3 ("Son of man, these men have set up idols in their hearts and put wicked stumbling blocks before their faces. Should I let them inquire of me at all?"), a text that refers to the elders of Israel who came to consult

---

1. On this reading of the passage see Davies, *Damascus Covenant*, 182-86.

the prophet, but were in reality committing idolatry in secret. They are promised swift judgment in order to stop the spread of such infidelity to the Lord in the community.[2] *Damascus Document* 20:9 warns potential apostates that analogous covert rebellion will not go unpunished. As Philip R. Davies observes: "Would-be traitors of the new community are therefore being invited to see themselves in this light, and in particular to contemplate their corresponding fate."[3] Thus, rather than contrasting nonliteral with literal idolatry, idolatry "in the heart" pits those whose rebellion is covert over against those who have physically left the community (20:16-8a, 10b-11a).

The references to the "idols of his heart" in *Rule of the Community* 2:11-18 should be seen in a similar context. The reference again, as Raymond Brown argues,[4] is language of secession in the framework of apostasy. In this case, the "idols of his heart" (2:11) are explained in 2:16-17: "he has turned aside from God on account of his idols and his stumbling block of sin, his lot shall be among those who are cursed forever." Once again an allusion to Ezekiel 14 is evident (and perhaps also to Deut 29:17, 19). In rejecting the community interpretation of the law, the apostate is regarded as an outsider and therefore an idolater.

Although Qumran lacks unambiguous evidence for a metaphorical use of idolatry, such as we find in Colossians 3:5/Ephesians 5:5, texts do appear that underscore the dangers of wealth. In a midrash on Isaiah 24:17 *Damascus Document* 4:17 list the three nets of Belial as fornication, *wealth,* and defilement of the temple. The figure of a net, which suggests that Satan uses these particular sins to "catch Israel" (4:16), removing them from the safety of the covenant and the provision of atonement (4:9-10), is reinforced in 4:17b-18, where the sins are depicted as exercising an inescapable hold. In 4QH 6:20, following an expression of determination not to sin against God (4:17-19), the temptation that greed poses is expressed in the words: "I do not exchange your truth for wealth." A third example occurs in *Pesher Nahum,* 4Q169 frgs. 3 + 4, 1:11, where "I will eradicate the spoils from the earth" (Nah 2:14) is interpreted as "the wealth which [the priests of Jerusalem accu]mulated."[5] In other words, if the text has been correctly

---

2. Cf. ibid., 184.
3. Ibid.
4. Brown, *Epistles of John,* 297.
5. García Martínez, *Dead Sea Scrolls Translated,* 196.

reconstructed,[6] the apostate religious leaders are depicted as being guilty of greedily storing up wealth.

Testament of Judah 19.1

The most commonly cited parallel text to the words "greed is idolatry," namely, "the love of money leads to idolatry" (*T. Jud.* 19.1), was dealt with in context in the section on "Greed Leads to Idolatry" in chapter 2. Seen in the broader context of the biblical and Jewish texts on the danger greed can pose to piety cited in this chapter, this text expresses a thought with which many Jews would have concurred.

Rabbinic Literature

Various passages in the Mishnah, Talmud, and Targumim express a negative attitude toward greed or wealth, regarding it as a threat to proper devotion to God. The most important of these is the targumic tradition relating to the Shema. The possible relevance of the Shema to our subject is suggested not only by the famous affirmation in Deuteronomy 6:4, and by its positive restatement of the first commandment, but because the whole chapter operates as a warning against idolatry; the Israelites are to obey God scrupulously and pass on his teaching diligently lest they forget God and follow the idols of the nations. The Shema in the Targumim bears directly on the relationship between God and wealth.

The Targumim to Deuteronomy offer a fairly literal translation of Deuteronomy 6, with one striking exception. In v. 5, instead of "Love the Lord your God with all your heart and with all your soul and with all your strength," Targum Onqelos has, to quote Bernard Grossfeld's translation, "Now you should love Lord your God with your whole heart, and (with your whole) soul, as well as with all your *possessions*." The Hebrew "strength" is rendered as "possessions/wealth." Targum Pseudo-Jonathan and Targum Neofiti have the related term "money."[7]

Though quite late, the Targumim reliably preserve many ancient tradi-

---

6. The following context, 4Q169 frgs. 3 + 4, 2:1-2, supports the identification of Jerusalem.
7. Cf. the same Targumim to Prov 3:9, which have, "Honor the Lord with your mammon."

tions of scriptural interpretation. Furthermore, since they were transmitted through the synagogues, which were not places of radical innovation but of consensus, these interpretations may well have commanded the support of a wide group. Seeing that the Shema (along with the Decalogue) was read daily in the temple, it is all the more likely that the accompanying Aramaic paraphrase would have been passed on reliably.[8]

Rabbinic support for the interpretation in question, some of which is purportedly from the Second Temple period, also suggests its wide currency. *M. Ber.* 9:5 explains that "'with all your might' (Deut 6:5) means with all your money." Rabbi Eliezer's explanation of the substitution appears in *Sifre Deut* 32 and at four places in the Talmud (*b. Ber.* 61b; *Pes.* 25a; *Yoma* 82a; *Sanh.* 74a):

> If it says "with all your soul" why should it also say "with all your might," and if it says "with all your might" why should it also say "with all your soul"? Should there be a man who values his life more than his money, for him it says: "with all your soul," and should there be a man who values his money more than his life, for him it says: "with all your might."[9]

Furthermore, Moshe Weinfeld has observed that the practice of the Qumran community reflects this understanding of Deuteronomy 6:5: "In the literature of the Qumran sect we find that every member of the sect must bring his mind and his might and *property* into God's community.

---

8. That the Shema exercised a profound influence on early Christianity has been argued at length by Birger Gerhardsson, who contends that it "functioned as an underlying, formative principle at the formulation of a rather impressive series of Early Christian texts" (*Shema in the New Testament*, 303). Most of his examples are drawn from the Gospels and Acts. The main example from Paul's letters, 1 Cor 13 (247-71), may be supplemented by Wright's observations on 1 Cor 8:6 (*Climax of the Covenant*, 120-36) and by Nanos, *Mystery of Romans*, 179-201, who argues more controversially that monotheism and the Shema are the basis of Paul's argument in Romans that gentiles need not become Jews in order to become part of the people of God.

9. This understanding of "might" is defended by Weinfeld, *Deuteronomy 1–11*, 339: "The implication of 'might' is twofold: ability (i.e., power, strength) and means (i.e., wealth)." Cf. especially Sir 7:30-31; Prov 3:9. Calvin, *Sermons on Deuteronomy*, 272, presents a remarkably similar interpretation: "And finally, *thou shalt love God with all thy strength*, importeth among them, that thou must love him with all thy substance and with all thy goods."

This corresponds to the command of Deut 6:5 to love God with all one's mind and force."[10] Two of the clearest texts are as follows:

> All who thus submit freely to his truth will convey all their knowledge, their energies, and *their riches* to the community of God. (1QS 1:11-12)

> And everyone who joins his congregation, he should examine, concerning his action, his intelligence, his strength, his courage and *his wealth.* (CD 13:11)

In other words, at Qumran the demand to love God "with all your wealth" found its practical application in the surrender of private property for the common use of the community.

However one understands the details of Deuteronomy 6:4-5,[11] they express God's claim to the ultimate and full allegiance of his people and a refusal to share this loyalty with another. The Lord alone is Israel's Creator, Redeemer, and Judge and as such calls for total commitment.[12] The rest of the chapter in effect elaborates on this demand for exclusive loyalty to God. In this context it is indeed striking that one of the loyalties singled out in early Jewish interpretation as a threat to faithfulness to God concerns wealth and money. Possessions were apparently considered a potent rival to God.

Another targumic tradition that introduces hostility to wealth in the context of condemnations of idolatry is Targum Jonathan on Jeremiah 19:13, which clarifies that the houses upon whose roofs sacrifices "to other gods" have been offered belong to those who are "rich in possessions." As such it could be seen as an illustration of the dictum that greed leads to idolatry.

Finally, Hillel is attributed with a saying that presents possessions as a

---

10. Weinfeld, *Deuteronomy 1–11*, 339. For details see idem, "Instructions for Temple Visitors."

11. See Achenbach, *Israel zwischen Verheißung und Gebot*, 65-114; or more briefly Weinfeld, *Deuteronomy 1–11*, 337-40, on the interpretive problems.

12. As Weinfeld observes, *Deuteronomy 1–11*, 338, "In Deuteronomy the term *love* has a special meaning of loyalty." Cf. 351: "Indeed, 'love' in the ancient Near East connotes loyalty. Thus, when the suzerain demands loyalty from his vassal, he adjures him that he shall love . . . the king as he loves himself. . . . Similarly, in the treaties and loyalty oaths of the Greek, Hellenistic, and Roman periods, terms for love and affection . . . serve to express loyalty."

hindrance to piety: "the more possessions, the more care; . . . the more Torah, the more life" (*m. 'Abot* 2:7). Similarly, in later rabbinic tradition
wealth is sometimes disparaged or seen as an obstacle to the study of Torah. For example, Rabbah b. Abbahu, in the midst of a discussion of idolatry, advises would-be proselytes to "go and sell your possessions and then
come be converted."[13]

Philo

Given his love of allegory and complex metaphorical interpretation, it is
perhaps no surprise to find in Philo a metaphorical interpretation of idolatry. Idolatry is for Philo a critical subject that he treats repeatedly and
with urgency.[14] He understands idolatry to be the deification of created
things, sees it as intimately bound up with the bodily passions, and believes it calls for the sternest punishment. According to Philo *the inordinate
love of wealth and glory* (or reputation) constitutes idolatry. He expounds
this notion with reference to the first commandment and in his treatment
of the lives of Lot and his wife and Joseph.

In *On the Special Laws* 1, on the first and second commandments, Philo
combats the threat of idolatry in both its literal and figurative senses. In
1:21-22 he condemns those who fashion images of gold and silver which are
used for religious purposes, which he calls "the direct command" and "the
literal prohibition." The other sense, which he describes as "of great value
for the promotion of morality," concerns the idols of πλοῦτος καὶ δόξα,
"wealth and glory."[15] Philo understands the two commandments

> to condemn strongly the money-lovers who procure gold and silver
> coins from every side and treasure their hoard like a divine image in a
> sanctuary, believing it to be a source of blessing and happiness of ev-
> ery kind. And further, all the needy who are possessed by that griev-
> ous malady, the desire for money (φιλαργυρία), though they have no
> wealth of their own on which they may bestow worship as its due,
> pay awe-struck homage to that of their neighbours, and come at

13. For further references see Schmidt, *Hostility to Wealth*, 196.
14. See Sandelin, "Danger of Idolatry," for a useful survey.
15. In subsequent quotations of Philo it may be assumed that "wealth" and "glory" or
"reputation" translate these two Greek words respectively.

early dawn to the houses of those who have abundance of it as though they were the grandest temples, there to make their prayers and beg for blessing from the masters as though they were gods.

According to this passage the greedy and idolaters are comparable in several ways. Both enthusiastically guard their respective treasures and look to them as a source of blessing and happiness. Both focus on something that is ultimately vain and futile (1:25-28). Both assign divine honors to something that aggressively opposes and attempts to replace the worship of the true and living God (1:28).

In *On Drunkenness* 75 Philo commends the fight against the bodily lusts that wage war against the soul, calling such a battle "a great and glorious feat." His tirade picks up the theme of idolatry in the figurative sense. Philo insists: "Neither wealth, nor glory, nor honour, nor office, nor beauty, nor strength, nor all bodily advantages, nor earth nor heaven, nor the whole world, but only the true cause, the Cause supreme among causes, deserves our service and highest honour." That the idea of "service and highest honour" has worship in view is clear from Philo's use of θεραπεία in a cultic context, along with λατρεία, in *On Drunkenness* 144.[16]

In *On Abraham* 208-24 Philo compares Abraham and Lot in the context of the account of the dispute between the herdsmen (Gen 13:5ff.). Whereas Abraham is characterized as a "lover of moral excellence," Lot is seen as "a devotee of external things" (220), who "honours wealth, reputation, office and good birth" (219).[17] Philo associates with Lot the φιλοχρήματοι καὶ φιλόδοξοι, "the lovers of wealth and glory" (221). With reference to the fate of Lot and his wife in *On Dreams* 1.248, Philo warns the reader that "if he pursues the deafness of glory, the blindness of wealth, the stupidity of bodily robustness, and the empty-mindedness of external beauty, and all that is akin to these, he will be set up as a soulless pillar." Even though he does not explicitly say so, in accordance with the description of figurative idolatry in *On the Special Laws* 1.23-27, Lot and his wife, in honoring external things, are for Philo guilty of idolatry.

For Philo another example of the idolatry of worldly things is Joseph, in whom the struggle between divine matters and bodily passions is played

16. Sandelin, "Danger of Idolatry," 119.
17. See ibid., 120-22.

out.[18] Joseph has a mind that is φιλοσώματος καὶ φιλοπαθής, "loves the body and the passions" (*Unchangeable* 111; cf. *Migr.* 16). Although presented more positively in *On Joseph*, Joseph is seen by Philo in *On Dreams* 2.11 as one "who does not indeed take no account of the excellencies of the soul, but is thoughtful for the well-being of the body also, and has a keen desire to be well off in outward things" (cf. *Names* 90). Like Lot, Joseph is a person whose "appetite flows strongly to wealth and reputation and completely masters the interests of body and soul" (*Dreams* 2.12).

In sum, Philo makes good use of the notion of figurative idolatry with reference to the body and its passions. Indeed, for Philo the story of the golden calf, that infamous account of Israel's first idolatrous failure, is a symbol for such sins (see *Posterity* 158-64). As we have seen, his most common terms for the focus of such false worship are "wealth" and "glory," which, because of the second term, is a broader formulation than the one found in Colossians and Ephesians. The power of the temptation which Philo considers wealth and glory exert is seen in *On Drunkenness* 56-58: "For which of us stands up to oppose riches? Who prepares himself to wrestle with glory? When we feel upon our cheeks the breath of hope of such things, though it be but the slightest breath and nothing more, we straightaway submit and surrender and can make no effort of resistance."

Philo's use of figurative idolatry represents an important precedent and point of comparison for the Pauline words in question. In terms of the three metaphorical senses that have been proposed for "greed is idolatry" (see above, chapter 2, sections 6-8), Philo provides clear support for the love and devotion view, with his repeated use of φιλ- vocabulary. The confidence and trust interpretation may also be seen to be implied in *On the Special Laws* 1.23, where the greedy look to their wealth as "source of blessing and happiness of every kind," but could not be said to be an explicit emphasis for Philo. For Philo, the greedy, or more precisely, those whose minds are set on bodily passions, are guilty of idolatry because they love something more than God.

It may be possible to see a distinction between Philo's understanding of the false gods of wealth on the one hand and glory on the other. In terms of the latter, Karl-Gustav Sandelin contends that Philo's warnings against glory are indications that Philo feared that if his fellow Jews sought prominence in Egyptian society, they would inevitably encounter situations of

---

18. Cf. ibid., 134-38.

compromise with literal forms of idolatry.[19] To take a civil office meant possible participation in public sacrifices. Furthermore, sporting contests, theater performances, club meetings, and banquets were also tied up with pagan rituals. Attendance at the gymnasium itself, a prerequisite for those seeking Greek citizenship, also exposed one to idolatrous teachings and activities. While it is tempting to posit for Philo a different rationale for glory-idolatry than for wealth-idolatry, one must say that he himself does not treat them differently.

19. Sandelin, "Danger of Idolatry."

CHAPTER 6

The New Testament:
The Foothills

—⁄σ⁄σ⁄—

The Synoptic Gospels

The Synoptic Gospels supply ample evidence that Jesus and the early church continued the biblical/Jewish tradition of stressing the dangers that wealth poses to a relationship with God. Others have provided full surveys of the material.[1] Here I note those texts in the Synoptics that express a thought somewhat akin to "greed is idolatry," and make some general observations about the theme of riches and poverty in the Gospel of Luke. Since it may shed light on the interpretation of Colossians 3:5/Ephesians 5:5, the treatment of the closest parallel, the mammon saying in Matthew and Luke, will be postponed until "Comparing the Metaphor" in chapter 10.

The only pericope to appear in all three Synoptics that concerns the topic of wealth is the rich young ruler (Mark 10:17-31; Luke 18:18-30; Matt 19:16-30), where dispossession is a prerequisite to inheriting eternal life. Following as it does immediately after the listing of six of the Ten Commandments, several commentators contend that the claim of the first commandment lies behind the call to "sell everything you have," implying

---

1. For an exhaustive survey that traces the origin of the material to biblical and Jewish sources see Schmidt, *Hostility to Wealth,* part 3.

that wealth has become an idol for the ruler.[2] Thomas E. Schmidt suggests that the targumic interpretation of the call to absolute loyalty to God in the Shema in regard to wealth (see the section on "Rabbinic Literature" in chapter 5) informs the teaching reflected in the passage: "the command may reflect a radical application of the consistent targumic tradition that reads חיל in the first commandment as 'wealth' [in Deut 6:4-5]: the man should love God with all his wealth."[3]

While the pericope does not indicate that people worship money instead of God, it does state plainly that it is "hard (δύσκολος) for those who have riches to enter the kingdom," implying that riches may prevent a person from following Jesus and worshiping God in the fullest sense. Similar lessons are taught at several points in the Synoptics, including Mark 8:36 ("for what does it profit a man, to gain the whole world and forfeit his life?"); in the temptation narratives, where becoming the richest of the rich is portrayed as the ultimate satanic temptation that robs God of his rightful worship (Matt 4:8-10; Luke 4:5-8); and Matthew 6:19-21, which as Robert H. Gundry observes, stresses "the importance of treasure as the determinant of the heart":[4] "Do not store up for yourselves treasures on earth, where moth and rust destroy, and where thieves break in and steal. But store up for yourselves treasures in heaven, where moth and rust do not destroy, and where thieves do not break in and steal. For where your treasure is, there your heart will be also." Finally, a warning is issued in the parable of the soils where the danger of wealth is mentioned alongside Satan (Mark 4:15) and apostasy (4:17). A threefold radical renunciation of wealth in Mark 4:19 ("The cares of the world, the deceitfulness of riches, and the craving for other things")[5] reiterates the Old Testament teaching that riches can lead to forgetting God.

When it comes to the teaching of Jesus on the subject of riches and poverty, among the Synoptic Gospels Luke shows the greatest interest.[6]

---

2. See especially Cranfield, "Riches and the Kingdom," 309.

3. Schmidt, *Hostility to Wealth*, 111.

4. Gundry, *Matthew*, 113; cf. Schmidt, *Hostility to Wealth*, 125-26; "there is no more explicit statement in the NT of the integral relation between conduct with regard to possessions and right relation to God."

5. The warning is reduced to two elements in Matthew (13:22; deleting the third member) and sharpened in Luke (8:14; by the omission of "deceitful").

6. Summaries can be found in Seccombe, *Possessions and the Poor;* and Ireland, *Stewardship and the Kingdom,* 161-216.

From the first chapter to the last, economic issues are prominent in Luke. John the Baptist's role in 1:16-17 is announced in terms of Malachi 4:6, where the messenger is sent to restore Israel, whose sins include defrauding laborers of their wages and the oppression of widows and the fatherless (Mal 3:5). The Magnificat in 1:46-55, reminiscent of the Song of Hannah in 1 Samuel 2:1-10, represents God as the one who reverses the fortunes of the oppressed, in particular the humble, who are identified with the poor and hungry: "He has filled the hungry with good things, but has sent the rich away empty" (1:53). When Jesus is born the conditions point to a family that is not well off (2:7; modest clothes and lodgings), an impression confirmed by the sacrifice of the poor they offer in 2:24 (cf. Lev 12:8). John the Baptist's preaching sets the tone for Jesus' own proclamation in insisting that repentance be demonstrated in concrete material ways; he advocates generous sharing of possessions for the well off (Luke 3:11), honesty for tax collectors (3:12-13), and contentment with respect to wages for soldiers (3:14). Jesus models such a disposition when he turns down wealth and the splendor of human power in favor of serving God (4:5-7). While the extent to which the details of his Nazareth manifesto (4:16-21) are to be taken metaphorically is debated, there is no escaping that this programmatic text is couched in economic terms: "The Spirit of the Lord is upon me . . . to preach good news to the poor" (4:18).

At the end of the Gospel, in the passion narrative, there continue to be stark reminders of the prevalence of the theme of riches and poverty to Jesus' mission and purpose. He drives the "robbers" out of the "house of prayer" (19:45-46); insists on not only paying tax to Caesar but also giving God his due (20:20-26), presumably a weightier obligation; warns his followers in view of the nearness of the kingdom not to allow their hearts to be weighed down by "the anxieties of life" (21:34); and reflects back upon the mission of the Twelve and the lesson to trust God to provide for their needs (22:35).

The teaching and example of Jesus in Luke with respect to riches and poverty is too complex a subject to discuss at this point. Suffice it to say, twin emphases stand out: the dangers riches pose to entering the kingdom of God, and the proper use of possessions.[7] The former is underscored

---

7. Of the plethora of historical Jesus reconstructions on offer, the material in question is among the least disputed in terms of authenticity. Few would dispute that the historical Jesus warned against the dangers of riches and advocated the proper use of possessions.

most poignantly in the parable of the rich fool (12:13-21), the encounter with the rich ruler (18:18-30), and the calls to renounce possessions (12:33, "sell your possessions and give to the poor"; cf. 14:33; 18:22). The last is effectively the positive counterpart to these warning passages and receives most explicit treatment in the exhortations not to be anxious but to trust in the Father's providential care (12:22-31; juxtaposed with the rich fool) and in the positive directions concerning possessions in 16:1-31. Both these emphases sharpen what we have seen to be often repeated elements in the moral teaching of the biblical and Jewish tradition in which Jesus stood. That they also could be said to be corollaries of the notion of greed as idolatry is indication that the novelty of the formulation in question lies less in its conceptual underpinnings than in its pointed expression.

Revelation 18:1–19:10

The warning of the fall of Babylon in Revelation is of interest to the present study in four ways. First, it links material acquisitiveness with violence and oppression, a link we will have occasion to explore further with reference to understanding greed in chapter 8. Second, the conception of idolatry that the passage assumes is of interest in understanding the so-called political model of idolatry (see chapter 9). Third, the implicit contrast between the fall of Babylon in 18:1–19:10 and the arrival of the new Jerusalem in all its splendor in 21:9–22:9 brings to mind the promise of true spiritual riches regularly offered in the Bible to those who forgo "treasures on earth," which will be noticed with respect to the section on "The Fight against Greed" in chapter 11. Fourth, of importance at this point is the intriguing association between Babylon's conspicuous wealth and her idolatry.

If Revelation represents Rome's military and political dominance of the empire with the beast from the sea, it portrays Rome's economic exploitation of the empire by the harlot of Babylon.[8] Revelation 18 warns of the fall of imperial Rome and reports the mourning of those who stand most to lose from her demise: the kings (18:9-10),[9] merchants (18:11-17a), and (their employees) the seafarers (18:17b-19). The three classes of

---

8. Bauckham, *Climax of Prophecy*, xvi.

9. The kings may either be leaders of the nations over which Rome rules or the local ruling classes who are manipulated by Rome for financial gain.

mourners are precisely the people who benefit directly from Rome's prosperity. The lamented lost merchandise in 18:12-13 represents the extravagance of the rich of the early empire, much of which was imported into Rome.[10] And 18:14 decries Rome's self-indulgent opulence, ostentatious display, and addiction to consumption.[11] In effect, chapter 18 depicts the destruction of a system of commercial interests that spanned the known world and could only be understood as an expression of unbridled avarice.

What is striking about the passage is the charge that Babylon the city is the great harlot with whom the mighty have committed fornication (18:3, 7, 23).[12] It is not entirely clear whether this sin involves religious or economic activity. Whereas some commentators such as Beasley-Murray understand the image of harlotry in the established Old Testament sense of going after other gods, the kings having adopted Rome's idolatries and emperor worship,[13] others like Christopher Rowland explain fornication in terms of "self-gratification which betrays no concern for God's way and as a result ignores the needs of others."[14]

Richard Bauckham points out that the texts upon which Revelation 17 and 18 draw in their denunciation of Babylon/Rome as the harlot city support both the religious and economic dimensions: "His [the author of Revelation] portrayal of the fall of Babylon is a remarkable patchwork of skilful allusions to Old Testament prophecies of the fall of Babylon and the fall of Tyre."[15] Rome resembled Babylon in its oppression of the people of God and in terms of its idolatry. Tyre, on the other hand, as the greatest trading center of the Old Testament period, influences Revelation's portrayal of Rome in terms of economic exploitation. Significantly, as Bauckham observes, "The Old Testament prophecies do not portray Babylon as a harlot, but Isaiah 23:15-18 uses the image of the harlot for Tyre."[16] Bauckham explains: "The reference there is obviously to the vast trading activity through which the city of Tyre had grown rich. Tyre's commercial

10. Bauckham, *Climax of Prophecy*, 352-66.

11. Ibid., 368.

12. Cf. Sweet, *Revelation*, 264: "the harlot now becomes Babylon."

13. Beasley-Murray, *Book of Revelation*, 266. Rome's idolatry included worship of the divinized emperors and of the goddess Roma.

14. Rowland, *Revelation*, 142.

15. Bauckham, *Climax of Prophecy*, 345. Cf. Jer 50–51 (Babylon), Ezek 26–28 (Tyre), and the shorter oracles against Babylon (Isa 13:1–14:23; 21:1-10; 47; Jer 25:12-38) and Tyre (Isa 23).

16. Bauckham, *Climax of Prophecy*, 346.

enterprise is compared with prostitution because it is association with other nations for the sake of profit."[17]

While one must grant that the primary significance of Babylon as the harlot in Revelation 18 is economic, a number of indications suggest that the economic and religious dimensions are not easily separated. If the worship of the beast is noted in 13:14, the cry of despair over Babylon's demise in 18:18, "what city was like the great city?" also suggests worship. The harlot's clothing in 18:16-17 not only underlines Rome's extravagant luxury but also alludes ironically to the sacred garments of the priests in Exodus 28:5, 15-17.[18] The economic greed of Rome has a peculiarly religious guise. Likewise, the reference to Babylon "deceiving the nations" in Revelation 18:23 evokes the effect of idols on their worshipers. The announcement of judgment in 18:6 in terms of being given back double for what she has given alludes to the same threat in Jeremiah 16:18, where judgment comes because of "detestable idols." Finally, that the counterpoint to Babylon's wealth is the spiritual wealth of the new Jerusalem suggests that there is more to the greed of Rome than meets the eye.

It may be that Revelation 18, with its use of fornication language, condemns the influence of Roman imperial religion, alongside a forthright condemnation of Rome's economic exploitation of the empire. Alternatively, the two emphases may be seen as inextricably bound together, with Rome's economic sins being portrayed in religious terms, in a fashion not unrelated to the judgment that greed is itself idolatry. The interpretation of Revelation is infamously difficult to pin down. Not too much can be hung on these suggestive images. Nonetheless, that Rome came to represent the very embodiment of idolatrous greed for some Christians standing in a biblical and Jewish tradition, as Revelation so clearly does, cannot be ruled out.

Philippians 3:19 and Romans 16:18

Their destiny is destruction, their god is their stomach, and their glory is in their shame. Their mind is on earthly things. (Phil 3:19)

17. Ibid.
18. Choi, "Economic Aspects," 58.

For such people are serving not our Lord Christ, but their own stomach.
By smooth talk and flattery they deceive the minds of naive people.
(Rom 16:18)

In two places in his letters Paul warns his readers about people whose belly
has replaced God: ὧν ὁ θεὸς ἡ κοιλία (Phil 3:19); οἱ γὰρ τοιοῦτοι τῷ κυρίῳ
ἡμῶν Χριστῷ οὐ δουλεύουσιν ἀλλὰ τῇ ἑαυτῶν κοιλίᾳ (Rom 16:18). Both
constitute examples of figurative idolatry, the former case explicitly and
the latter in using a verb that frequently describes the worship of both God
and idols. Unfortunately what Paul means by "belly worship" is not clear.
The two texts are treated here as a possible part of that stream of teaching
that considers wealth or greed to be a hindrance to the worship of God.
Even if Colossians and Ephesians are authentic, as I assume, texts in
Romans and Philippians, since they were written earlier, may be considered to be witnesses to the origin of their teaching in the general sense.

Some take κοιλία quite literally and understand the phrases in question
to be a sarcastic reference to Jewish opponents who are overly preoccupied
with food laws, an interpretation that goes back to Ambrosiaster and was
later put forward by Erasmus and Bengel.[19] However, there is no indication that Paul had Jews in mind. In Philippians he seems to have moved on
from the Jewish-Christian proselytizers of 3:2-11 to those who are morally
lax, "whose mind is set on earthly things" (3:19). Furthermore, as we shall
see below, the idiom possibly had currency in Jewish circles.

Those who take κοιλία as a circuitous way of referring to the "flesh" understand the expressions to refer to egocentrism. Paul's targets are those
whose lives are determined by the flesh (Rom 8:4-5).[20] Such people are
guilty of the sort of sins listed in Galatians 5:19-21, the works of the flesh,
which include all manner of vices. According to this reading not only greed
but also sexual immorality, jealousy, and drunkenness are idolatry.[21] As
M. N. A. Bockmuehl points out, the "shame" (αἰσχύνη, Phil 3:19) in which
those whose god is their belly glory can for Paul "characterise all sorts of
unregenerate excesses, including sexual ones (e.g. Rom 1:27): it generally
denotes the immoral practices of the pagan, pre-Christian life which be-

19. See, e.g., on Rom 16:18, the commentary by Barrett; on Phil 3:19, Hawthorne.
20. See e.g., on Rom 16:18, the commentaries by Cranfield, Käsemann, Wilckens; on Phil
3:19, O'Brien, Caird.
21. Cf. Fee, *Philippians*, 373, who, although he rejects the "flesh" interpretation, suggests
that κοιλία may refer to "bodily desires of all kinds."

lievers have left behind (Rom 6:21; Eph 5:12; cf. 2 Cor 4:2; Jude 13)."[22] Unfortunately, Pauline usage does not supply any support for such a broad, figurative understanding of the κοιλία. Paul uses the word in Galatians 1:15 to refer to a literal belly, namely, his mother's womb, and in 1 Corinthians 6:13 in reference to the stomach ("foods for the belly, and the belly for foods").

A third view takes κοιλία in its most straightforward sense as a reference to gluttony and, as Douglas Moo, explains, "by metonymy, to a greedy and dissipated lifestyle."[23] Cranfield notes that Chrysostom's comment on Romans 16:18 begins by mentioning gluttony before going on to talk of greed in general. Analogous expressions may be found in Euripides (Cyclops 334, 335), where Cyclops says: "I offer sacrifices to no god but myself, and to this belly of mine"; and in Seneca, who refers to people who are "slaves of their bellies" (Ben. 7.26; cf. Xenophon, Mem. 1.6.8; 2.1.2) and praises one who seeks "the good of man, not of his belly" (Seneca, Vit. beat. 9.4).[24] In those cases gluttony seems to be in view (although γαστήρ instead of κοιλία is used).

The closest parallels to Paul's language are, however, to be found in the Cairo Geniza Wisdom Text,[25] a Jewish document, the date of which is highly disputed: "The thoughts of the wise circle the earth; but the thoughts of the foolish are on their belly" (14:6); "Fools are slaves of their bellies and follow after their eyes" (15:7); "The righteous are servants of the Lord, but the godless are servants of their bellies" (17:5). In each case the word for "servant" or "service" is a cognate of עבד, a common word in contexts of worshiping God and idols in the Hebrew Bible. Geniza Wisdom 17:5 stands out from among the three as an explicit instance of figurative idolatry in placing the service of the belly over against the service of the Lord. In Geniza Wisdom belly service is in context linked to various sinful desires and lusts.[26] Whereas the wise shatter their sinful desires, the

22. Bockmuehl, Philippians, 231-32.

23. Moo, Romans, 931; cf. Cranfield, Romans, 2:800: "One might perhaps take it to denote a seeking to live sumptuously or, more generally, greed." Cf. also Godet, Romans, 2:402-3; and Schmithals, Paul and the Gnostics, 231-32.

24. Cited in Fee, Philippians, 372.

25. I am grateful to Markus Bockmuehl for drawing my attention to these references.

26. Indeed, however they are interpreted the Pauline and Geniza Wisdom texts represent clear extensions of the concept of idolatry in terms of evil desire, a notion which as noted above is probably indebted to interpretation of the golden calf episode.

foolish love them (15:4) and think only of them (14:7).[27] As Berger comments, those who serve their bellies are "body-oriented."[28]

Together the three texts, if of an early date, suggest that the references in Philippians 3:19 and Romans 16:18 may well be traditional and represent Jewish idiom.[29] This would be an important result with respect to the question of the origin of the related expression in Colossians and Ephesians, adding considerable weight to the case for a Jewish provenance. Unfortunately the two major recent studies of the Wisdom Text from the Cairo Geniza are at odds on the question of its date. At the turn of the twentieth century it was thought to be a late, medieval composition. However, Klaus Berger's 1989 study argues that it was composed in Egypt around AD 100. In 1991 Hans Peter Rüger's edition of the text, which amounts to an extended correction of Berger's work, attempts to show that the Wisdom Text must be medieval. While Rüger does show the inadequacy of some of Berger's key arguments,[30] he does not provide the detailed exposition of supposed medieval parallels that is needed to establish his own case. As John J. Collins concludes, "What we need is a study of this document by someone who is primarily a medievalist rather than a biblical scholar, to determine how well it fits in the literary genres of medieval Judaism."[31] Wisdom literature is notoriously difficult to date, given its ahistorical and universal character. At this point, although a date in the Tannaitic period has not been ruled out conclusively, it would be unwise to appeal to Geniza Wisdom for help in the interpretation of Pauline "belly worship."

Precisely what sort of sin Paul has in mind with belly worship is difficult to say. A reference to greed is not out of the question, and would give idolatrous greed some prominence in the Pauline corpus, appearing in no

27. Cf. Rüger's translation, *Weisheitsschrift*, 146: "the thoughts of the ungodly revolve around their appetites." In 17:3 the text is incomplete (the verb is missing) but once again the ungodly are characterized in terms of their sinful desires.

28. Berger, *Weisheitsschrift*, 358. Cf. also 3 Macc 7:11, where Jewish apostates have abandoned faithfulness to God's commandments "for the sake of the belly" (cited in Bockmuehl, *Philippians*, 231).

29. Cf. Berger, *Weisheitsschrift*, 356.

30. E.g., Berger believes that the reference to people building houses while the temple lies in ruins (6:11) suggests a date not long after the destruction of Jerusalem. Rüger points out that 6:10b-11a alludes to Hab 1:4 and is no sure reference to the fall of the Second Temple.

31. Collins, "Review of Rüger," 707.

less than four letters. However, a narrower reference to gluttony and a broader one to a range of illicit bodily desires (which is found in the three Geniza Wisdom references) are also possible.[32]

32. Sandnes's study of "belly worship," *Belly and Body*, which appeared after the research for this section had been completed, comes to similar conclusions. He argues that the proper context for the accusation of worshiping the belly is the pagan moral philosophy debate about mastering the desires and the fact that the belly became a catchword for a life controlled by pleasures.

CHAPTER 7

Conclusion:
Debriefing the Trekkers

———⟨⟨⟨⟩⟩⟩———

What is the origin of the words "greed is idolatry"? Whether the expression is original to Colossians and Ephesians we cannot determine with certainty; I have not laid out a case for literary dependence in
the strict sense. Instead I have found ideas in the biblical/Jewish tradition
that are in some way related. The way for the expression seems to have
been paved by *the comprehensive scope of the first commandment*, by *the
characterization of idolatry in terms of evil desire*, and above all by *the association of wealth with apostasy*. Once these three elements are recognized,
the expression comes as no surprise and may be seen to be saying something more innovative in form than in content. The third notion is represented by a small group of passages distinguished by their diversity (various genres including law, poetry, and wisdom) and in some cases
prominence (especially the Shema and the Song of Moses) and is conso-
nant with the warning of *Testament of Judah* 19.1 that "greed leads to idolatry." In chapter 10 biblical and Jewish texts are treated that charge that the
greedy love, trust, and obey their money rather than God. In some cases,
such as the psalms of trust, wealth is explicitly presented as a rival to God.
Such material underscores further the prevalence of regarding wealth or
greed as potentially disruptive of a right relationship with God.

The closest parallels to "greed is idolatry" are in Job 31:24-28, Philo, the
mammon saying in Matthew and Luke, and possibly the belly worship in

Romans and Philippians, which condemn greed in roughly the same way but use more and different words. That Paul learned to equate greed with idolatry from Job or the Jesus tradition cannot be ruled out. However, given the brevity of the expression, the fact that there is no overlap in terminology, and the breadth and strength of the tradition in which it comfortably fits, it is safer to conclude simply that the thought, if not the words themselves, probably have a Jewish origin.

This conclusion is of not only historical but also methodological interest. It points the way forward for our own attempts to understand the words as a metaphor. If the words "greed is idolatry" belong to a Jewish milieu, we are justified in looking at the characterization and common attitudes to greed and idolatry in this setting in order to sense the likely effect of the comparison and to determine the level at which it may be operating. Furthermore, the relevant texts in Job, Philo, and especially Matthew and Luke will serve as a check on our interpretation of "greed is idolatry" (see "Comparing the Metaphor" in chapter 10), since in every case the context in which these texts appear is more informative for their interpretation than is the case in Colossians and Ephesians.

PART III

The Meaning of "Greed Is Idolatry":
Climbing the Mountain

CHAPTER 8

Understanding Greed:
The Surrounding Terrain

━━◦◦◦◦━━

When it comes to understanding πλεονεξία in Colossians 3:5 and πλεονέκτης in Ephesians 5:5, much is at stake. It is not simply a matter of defining a couple of obscure foreign words in two ancient texts. The results will decide the grave issue of who is being accused of the most serious of charges, that of idolatry. In other words, we are seeking not only the sense of πλεονεξία/πλεονέκτης, but also the referent. Who are the greedy? Completely different groups have been proposed. Two questions must be answered if we are to identify the guilty parties safely: (1) Do the terms in context signify greed in the material or the sexual realm? (see "Avarice or Sexual Greed?"); and (2) If they mean greed for money and possessions, does such inordinate desire inevitably bring with it oppression and dishonest gain? (see "Greed, Violence, and Corruption").

Avarice or Sexual Greed?

Commentators on Colossians and Ephesians are divided over whether πλεονεξία and πλεονέκτης refer to greed in the material realm or in sexual matters. The following citations give a representative sample of the two opposing views:

Sexual greed:

Because of the context, πλεονεξία, "covetousness," should also be taken as the sort of unrestrained sexual greed whereby a person assumes that others exist for his or her own gratification. The tenth commandment contains the injunction against coveting one's neighbor's wife; the combination of covetousness and fornication is found in *T. Levi* 14.5, 6; *T. Jud.* 18.2; 1QS 4.9, 10; CD 4.17, 18; and the cognate verb πλεονεκτεῖν has sexual connotations in 1 Thess 4:6. (Andrew T. Lincoln)[1]

It is hard to resist the suggestion that *covetousness* is linked here with sexual immorality; and so speaks of the greed which seeks its satisfaction in what is not lawful. Thus, in Ephesians iv. 19 and v. 5 it is also linked with impurity, while in 1 Thessalonians iv. 6, Paul uses the cognate verb to describe adultery as a defrauding of one's neighbour by possessing that which is especially his. (Herbert M. Carson)[2]

Avarice:

In other contexts the term means grasping greed, possessiveness (Luke 12:15), an insatiable longing to lay hands on another's property — even his wife (Ex. 20:17). The sexual overtone of the word is possibly found in I Thessalonians 4:6 where "wrong his brother" may have this vice in view. But this is not certain since the noun from this verb *(pleonektein)* occurs in I Corinthians 6:10 and means there "greedy." "Covetousness" breaks the sequence in the present list by switching the readers' thought from sexual vices to the sin of avarice. (Ralph Martin)[3]

Accordingly πλεονεξία occurs in close proximity to sins of impurity in several passages. The context in such cases gives a colour to the word; but it does not appear that πλεονεξία can be independently used in the sense of fleshly concupiscence. (J. Armitage Robinson)[4]

These quotations raise the issues that we need to address before we can make any confident decision on the meaning of the terms in question:

1. Lincoln, *Ephesians*, 322.
2. Carson, *Colossians*, 82; cf. Countryman, *Dirt, Greed, and Sex*, 108-9.
3. Martin, *Colossians*, 109.
4. Robinson, *Ephesians*, 199.

1. How frequently does the πλεονε- group of words mean sexual greed and under what conditions?
2. Does 1 Thessalonians 4:6 supply a clear precedent of πλεονεξία/πλεονέκτης having sexual connotations?
3. Are covetousness and fornication combined in early Jewish moral teaching or merely mentioned side by side?
4. Is there evidence in Colossians 3:5 and Ephesians 5:5 that πλεονεξία and πλεονέκτης are to be taken as discrete items in their respective lists?
5. Does the relative clause, "which is idolatry," belong exclusively to πλεονεξία/πλεονέκτης, or are we to understand a broader reference, taking into view the prior sexual sins too?
6. Is the predication of idolatry to avarice or sexual immorality more likely in the milieu of ancient Judaism and early Christianity?

The following paragraphs answer these questions in order. It is my contention that when the evidence is carefully examined it weighs against taking πλεονεξία/πλεονέκτης to signify sexual greed in Colossians 3:5 and Ephesians 5:5.

In their non-Jewish and non-Christian Greek usage the two nouns πλεονεξία and πλεονέκτης and the verb πλεονεκτέω have a broad field of meaning, denoting to want more, whether power, possessions, or sex.[5] Both Aristotle and Plato, for instance, use the nouns to denote not only avarice but also sexual desire. In Jewish and Christian usage, however, the meaning of greed for money and possessions is by far the most common and assured denotation. Of the nineteen New Testament instances only the verb in 2 Corinthians 2:11 cannot mean avarice; and in only three cases, Colossians 3:5, Ephesians 5:5, and 1 Thessalonians 4:6, is sexual greed a possible meaning. Πλεονέκτης occurs in Ephesians 5:5, 1 Corinthians 5:10, 11, and 6:10, where material greed is unambiguously in view (see below). Πλεονεξία occurs ten times. Apart from its appearance in Colossians 3:5, it is universally taken to mean avarice. Luke 12:15 is particularly noteworthy, where Jesus warns, "be on your guard against greed *of every kind* (ἀπὸ πάσης πλεονεξίας)," which is illustrated in the verses following with the parable of the rich fool, who is guilty of wanting to acquire more and more possessions.

Only the verb πλεονεκτέω maintains the broader Classical Greek understanding, carrying the sense of exploit or defraud. Whereas in 2 Corin-

---

5. See LSJ, 1415-16; and Delling, "πλεονέκτης," 266-69.

thians 7:2 and 12:17-18 material things are in view, in 2 Corinthians 2:11 Satan's "taking advantage" of believers is not for financial reasons, but has the sense of a hunger for power. The only reference (apart from Col 3:5 and Eph 5:5) that could mean sexual greed is 1 Thessalonians 4:6.

The interpretation of πλεονεκτέω in 1 Thessalonians 4:6 raises the same issues as the interpretation of πλεονεξία in Colossians 3:5 and πλεονέκτης in Ephesians 5:5. Consider the following comments:

> πλεονεκτέω is the desire to possess more than one should in any area of life, and the nouns πλεονέκτης ("covetous person") and πλεονεξία ("covetousness") repeatedly occur in close association with words denoting fornication or impurity (cf. 1 Cor 5:10, 11; Eph 4:19; 5:3, 5). (F. F. Bruce)[6]

> πλεονεκτέω means "to enlarge, take advantage of," with particular reference to the material realm; so 2 Cor 7:2; 12:17, 18. Noteworthy is 2 Cor 2:11, which also resonates with an unlawful enlargement. Πλεονέκτης (1 Cor 5:10ff.; also Eph 5:5), regularly found in catalogues of vice and in association with sins of injustice, has the sense of material enlargement; likewise πλεονεξία, the most common word in the NT from the word group. (T. Holtz)[7]

The problem concerns whether 1 Thessalonians 4:6 introduces the topic of business dealings between church members (e.g., Holtz) or carries on the discussion of sexual immorality (e.g., Bruce). Is Paul concerned that Christians not "take advantage" of their fellow Christians in matters business or sexual? Both readings of the passage are defensible. As we have seen, avarice was commonly mentioned along with sexual immorality in moral teaching, ὑπερβαίνω and πλεονεκτέω naturally suggest business dealings, and "to wrong his brother in a matter" seems a strange way to refer to a sexual sin.[8] However, the article with πρᾶγμα may indicate a reference to something already mentioned, namely, the πορνεία in the preceding verses. In the summarizing statement of 4:7 ἀκαθαρσία suggests that all of the preceding exhortations concern sexual sin; and, although unusual,

6. Bruce, *1 and 2 Thessalonians,* 84.
7. Holtz, *Erste Brief an die Thessalonicher,* 161.
8. Cf. Merk, *Handeln aus Glauben,* 48: "Verse 6a has neither a linguistic nor conceptual connection to that which precedes."

"wronging one's brother" may well have been an idiom for wronging the husband or father of the woman involved in the sexual liaison.[9] Thus it does appear that 1 Thessalonians 4:6 supplies an example of πλεονεκτέω being used in a sexual context.[10] However, not too much should be made of this. In our investigation it is the lone witness, applying only to the verb and not necessarily to the nouns in question.

At this point it is fair to conclude that avarice is the most frequent and clear meaning of the πλεονε- group of words in the New Testament. Johannes P. Louw and Eugene A. Nida's treatment of the words comes to the same conclusion. They take the two nouns to refer to a strong desire for material acquisition (§§25:22 and 23), and leave open the possibility of a sexual content for the verb, defining it more generally (§88:144: "to take advantage of someone, usually as the result of a motivation of greed — 'to take advantage of, to exploit'").[11]

In no appearance of the two nouns in the Apostolic Fathers is sexual greed a likely translation, and on several occasions the words in question unambiguously denote greed in the material realm. In Polycarp, *Philippians* 2.2, πλεονεξία is followed by φιλαργυρία ("love of money"), and in Hermas, *Mandate* 36.5, "lusts for women and riches and arrogance" (ἐπιθυμίαι γυναικῶν καὶ πλεονεξία καὶ ὑπερηφανία) refers in context to three distinct sins (cf. *Barn.* 10.4; *1 Clem.* 35.5). Finally, in *Didache* 2.6 πλεονέκτης is used in conjunction with ἅρπαξ ("thief"; cf. *Barn.* 19.6).

While it is true that greed turns up in various Jewish vice lists alongside sexual sins, this does not amount to a "combination" (Lincoln) of the two.[12] The four Jewish texts cited by Lincoln, rather than proving

---

9. Cf. Musonius Rufus, Fragment 12, cited in Malherbe, *Moral Exhortation,* 153: "the adulterer who wrongs the husband of the woman he corrupts."

10. So, e.g., Marshall, *1 and 2 Thessalonians.*

11. Louw and Nida, *Greek-English Lexicon,* 1:291-92, 758.

12. Cf. esp. Reinmuth, *Geist und Gesetz,* and the chapter entitled "Die Warnung vor Unzucht und Habgier in der frühjüdischen Literatur," 22-40. Reinmuth's study of the Spirit and the Law in Paul's letters presents the bold thesis that Paul advocated law observance. Two sound observations of Paul's ethics and early Jewish parenesis form the basis for the argument. First, Reinmuth notes that unchastity and greed are prominent vices in both Paul (see Rom 1:29-31; 2:21-22; 1 Cor 5:9-11; 6:9-10; and especially 1 Thess 4:1-8) and early Jewish literature (texts taken from Pseudo-Phocylides, *Testaments of the 12 Patriarchs, Sibylline Oracles, 1 Enoch,* Syriac Menander, Pseudo-Heraclitus, CD, and especially *T. Jud.* 18.2-6). Second, he shows that both Paul (1 Cor 3:16-17; 6:12-20; 2 Cor 6:16; Gal 5:13–6:10; Rom 8:1-11) and various early Jewish texts (*T. Sim.* 4.4; *T. Ben.* 8.2; *Sib. Or.* 3.698-701; 1QS 3:6-8) link the coming

what he supposes, actually make clear that the two sins are distinct. In *Testament of Levi* 14.5-6 "greed" is followed by "married women you profane" and "intercourse with whores and adulteresses." However, the context makes clear that the "greed" is financial since the "gain" that is coveted is procured from "teaching commandments." In *Testament of Judah* 18.2 "sexual immorality" and "love of money" are referred to using the plural pronoun in the following verses ("*they* do not permit"; "*they* provide") and described in 18.6 as "*two* passions contrary to God's commands." In 1QS 4:9-10 "greed" and "appalling acts of lustful passion" are separated by no less than twelve items in the list, including deceit, pride, and impatience. Finally, in *Damascus Document* 4:17-18 the two sins are enumerated as "the first" and "the second" (nets of Belial). Sexual immorality and greed are also cited as distinct sins, using a variety of terms and expressions and in close proximity, in the following Jewish texts: Pseudo-Phocylides 3-6; *Sibylline Oracles* 3.36-40; Syriac Menander B65-66. If the tenth commandment demonstrates that avarice and sexual immorality can be related, in that both involve evil desire, many Jewish texts show that this observation did not lead to a confusion or an amalgamation of the two.

That Paul could include both the πλεονέκτης and the πόρνος in the same list, and mean greed in the material realm with the former, is clear from 1 Corinthians 5–6, where πλεονέκτης occurs three times (the only other NT occurrence is in Col 3:5). The two words appear side by side in 1 Corinthians 5:10 and 11 and appear also in 6:9-10. The fact that in 5:10 an articular πλεονέκτης is linked with ἅρπαξ ("thief/extortioner") by καί

---

of the Spirit with obedience to God. Reinmuth believes that unchastity and greed were a collective code word for general nonobservance of the law among Jews in Paul's day. Since in the latter Jewish texts obedience to God amounts to obedience to the law, Reinmuth concludes that Paul advocates law observance when he opposes unchastity and avarice (remembering the caveat that "the ceremonial law" was abrogated by the Christ event). Unfortunately, the most crucial point in this argument, that by prohibiting the two vices in question one advocated law observance, is the weakest in Reinmuth's scheme. Very few of the Jewish texts offer genuine support for this hypothesis. It does not follow that to cite key moral emphases from the law necessarily means that one is urging wholesale adherence to that code. If this were so one would expect, at least in Paul's case, more explicit indication for the sake of gentile readers. Leaving aside the relevance of Reinmuth's work for the question of Paul's attitude to the law, his major achievement in relation to the present study is the carefully documented assertion that sexual immorality and greed are two key vices in both Jewish moral teaching and Paul's ethics.

shows that the two are regarded as one class of sin.[13] Jean Héring's definition of πλεονέκτης in this text suggests how the two words might be related:
"one who uses brute force to enrich himself at the expense of his neighbor."[14] It is more likely, however, that the first word focuses on the grasping
aspect of avarice, and the latter on the violent and dishonest means employed in carrying it out. What is noteworthy at this point is that the combination of the two words shows that Paul had avarice and not sexual greed in
mind for πλεονέκτης in all three cases in 1 Corinthians 5–6, since in the first
appearance it is clear that greed in the material realm is in view.

There are some clear indications that the introduction of πλεονεξία/
πλεονέκτης represents a new and distinct item in the vice lists in Colossians
and Ephesians. In Colossians 3:5 πλεονεξία is given special emphasis in three
ways: by the addition of καί (which is translated by Lightfoot as "and especially"); by the presence of the definite article (both καί and the article are
absent from the preceding four items in the list); and by the relative clause,
"which is idolatry." Ephesians 5:5 shares only two of the three features, since
of the three items in its list, both the second and third, ἀκάθαρτος and
πλεονέκτης, have a definite article. If in either Colossians or Ephesians the
evidence points toward πλεονεξία/πλεονέκτης introducing something new
to the vice lists, this would favor taking the other in a similar fashion on the
principle that the obscure should be interpreted in the light of the opaque.
Regardless of how one conceives of the relationship between the two letters,
the ethical teachings in Colossians 3:5 and Ephesians 5:5 overlap considerably
in content and belong to the same tradition. In this case Colossians 3:5 is
quite clear. The three features give the list some balance, underscoring avarice, which is mentioned only once, over against sexual immorality, which is
emphasized by the use of four synonyms. Sexual sins are stressed by the
heaping up of synonyms; greed by its comparison with idolatry.

To take πλεονεξία and πλεονέκτης to mean sexual greed is a tempting
conclusion on the basis of the words' apparent etymology. Both the nouns,
as is often pointed out, mean literally to "have more," πλέον ἔχειν. There is
no indication in the words themselves what the πλεονέκτης wants to have
more of. Thus one can reason on the basis of the lists in Colossians 3:5 and

13. Cf. Morris, *1 Corinthians*, 88. Although not cited by Morris, Zerwick (*Biblical Greek*,
59: "the use of but one article before a number of nouns indicates that they are conceived as
forming a certain unity") and Turner (*Syntax*, 181: the phenomenon portrays "a unified
whole") support his point.

14. Héring, *1 Corinthians*, 38.

Ephesians 5:5, which consist of a string of synonyms for sexual immorality, that the words mean the desire to "have more" sex. The problem with this reasoning is that in spite of the admirable appeal to context, it amounts to the etymological fallacy. The usage of the nouns does not support the neutral, flexible sense of "to have more." Nowhere in the New Testament or the Apostolic Fathers is there evidence that the words mean anything else than wanting more in the material realm.

There is another way in which the two texts may be read that links sexual sin with idolatry apart from understanding πλεονεξία and πλεονέκτης to mean sexual greed, namely by taking the relative clause, "which is idolatry," to refer not only to πλεονεξία/πλεονέκτης but also to the preceding four sexual sins in Colossians 3:5 and two sexual sins in Ephesians 5:5. Should the relative pronoun be understood in a particular or a collective sense?[15] Whereas most commentators take the predication to be exclusive to πλεονεξία/πλεονέκτης, some understand a broader reference.[16] The grammars are also divided.[17] The presence of the article can be explained in various ways. Whereas most take the following relative clause to be responsible for its presence,[18] it could also be regarded as anaphoric, pointing to "that πλεονεξία known to all,"[19] or specific instances of greed may be in view.[20] As is often the case in exegesis, gram-

15. Whereas Eph 5:5 has the simple relative pronoun, Col 3:5 has the indefinite relative pronoun, ἥτις. The latter is probably here equivalent to a simple relative pronoun or it may emphasize a characteristic quality, meaning "which, by its very nature" (Harris, *Colossians,* 147), or even have a causal sense, "inasmuch as" (Zerwick and Grosvenor, *Analysis,* 452; cf. Vincent, 913: "seeing it stands in the category of"). In any case, the meaning is clear: greed is in some sense comparable to idolatry.

16. For the former see, e.g., Gnilka, *Kolosserbrief,* 182: "Greed (through the article) is identified and so characterized as a main vice (cf. Blass-Debr 258,1). It alone and not the pentad [of vices] is branded as idolatry." For the latter see, e.g., Gnilka, *Epheserbrief,* 248-49. Those who prefer a collective sense usually understand πλεονεξία/πλεονέκτης to have sexual connotations.

17. See Moule, *Idiom Book,* 130, who contends that the relative pronoun is used "with reference to the 'whole idea' of the preceding clause rather than to the single word which is the immediate antecedent."

18. Cf. Robertson, *Grammar,* 758; BDF 258,1; and Lenski, *Colossians,* 158: "Why is the article used with this fifth noun? Not as has been supposed, because it is the last of the group but because it alone has an attached relative clause."

19. Zerwick and Grosvenor, *Analysis,* 609.

20. Cf. Zerwick, *Biblical Greek,* 176-78: abstract nouns may take the article to indicate "concrete application."

matical considerations throw up the alternatives rather than deciding the case.

Perhaps the best evidence that the words "which is idolatry" refer exclusively to πλεονεξία/πλεονέκτης and that these words denote avarice and not sexual greed is conceptual.[21] Is a person who is greedy any more of an idolater than one who is sexually immoral in the symbolic world of ancient Judaism and early Christianity? While chapter 2 uncovered clear evidence that early Jews and Christians conceived of greed as idolatry (Job, Philo, Matthew, and Luke) and a major result of the present study is that a comparison of greed with idolatry made good sense in the tradition of biblical and Jewish moral teaching, the following section demonstrates that sexual immorality was less readily regarded as such.

Sexual Immorality and Idolatry

Is sexual immorality conceived of as idolatry? It will become clear that the evidence favors assigning sexual immorality a different place than greed in the symbolic world of early Jews and Christians.

In one sense the link between sexual immorality and idolatry could not be more concrete. Pagan temples were often the venue for illicit sexual activities. Religious prostitution was commonly practiced by the cults of the ancient Near Eastern fertility religions, and it was a problem for Israel from the moment they entered the promised land (Num 25:1; cf. Judg 2:17), becoming especially prevalent in Judah and Israel during the divided monarchy (from Rehoboam, 1 Kgs 14:24, to Josiah, 2 Kgs 23:7). According to Exodus 34:11-16 God commanded the extermination of the inhabitants of the land so that the Israelites would avoid the practice. Deuteronomy 23:17 (LXX 18) forbids cult prostitution for Israel (cf. Amos 2:7). Furthermore, the link between apostasy or idolatry and πορνεία that can be found in the Old Testament and is strengthened in early Jewish teaching may also point to the practice of prostitution occurring in the setting of pagan worship. Both idolatry and sexual immorality are associated with demons. Several

---

21. Cf. Braune, "Ephesians," 180, who puts the issue clearly when he comments on the relative clause in Eph 5:5, even if we disagree with his conclusion: "The proof lacks aptness, if that [idolatry] be not attributed to the first two [lust and uncleanness], which is predicated of the third, who is not an idolater more especially than the former. The clause is incorrectly referred to the 'covetous man' alone."

texts in *Testaments of the Twelve Patriarchs, Damascus Document* (CD), and *Rule of the Community* (1QS) associate πορνεία with demons.[22] Sexual immorality in such texts is surrounded by demonic dangers and threats, as in *Damascus Document* 4:15-17, where the three nets of Belial include fornication, wealth, and the defilement of the temple. Paul puts demons and pagan worship together in 1 Corinthians 10 and juxtaposes sexual impurity and idolatry in Romans 1:24-25. In the so-called interconnected triads of cardinal sins of early Judaism, which are attested in many sources, idolatry and sexual immorality are the stable partners sometimes joined by murder, at other times by greed.[23]

Even if sacred prostitution was in all likelihood not practiced in the Greek world,[24] another kind of prostitution that was neither strictly sacred nor strictly secular had associations with idolatry: prostitution at cultic events of a festive nature. It was well attested in places like new Corinth and is even mentioned in the Old Testament. Louis M. Epstein points out that it was common in the ancient Near East for orgies to take place at heathen festivals.[25] Hosea 4:13-14 probably refers to this kind of activity, where mountaintop sacrifices, suggesting a pagan altar, and prostitutes are juxtaposed. E. A. Goodfriend comments that "the presence of prostitutes at reli-

---

22. Cf. Dautzenberg, "Eine Fallstudie," 291. The identification of pagan deities with demons was also a common Jewish and Christian theme. See Deut. 32:17; Isa. 55:11 LXX; *1 En.* 19.1; 99.7; *Jub.* 1.11; 1 Cor. 10; Justin, *Apol.* 1.5. Cf. S. G. Wilson, *Luke and the Law,* 97.

23. Cf. Thomas, *Jüdische Phokylides.*

24. Corinth is the most frequently cited example for sacred prostitution in Pauline studies. However, Strabo's famous account of 1,000 prostitutes in the temple of Aphrodite refers to the Corinth destroyed in 146 BC by the Romans and not to new Corinth, which was refounded in 44 BC by Julius Caesar as a Roman colony. Some even dispute the accuracy of Strabo's remark with reference to old Corinth. For example, Murphy-O'Connor writes that "sacred prostitution was never a Greek custom, and were Corinth an exception, the silence of all other ancient authors becomes impossible to explain" (*St. Paul's Corinth,* 56; cf. Saffrey, "Aphrodite à Corinthe," 359-74). Herter concludes that besides the report of Strabo on Corinth, sacred prostitution was only to be found in Cyprus and eastern Asia Minor, the periphery of the Greek world; it was an "un-Greek practice" ("Soziologie der Antiken Prostitution," 72-73). Fauth's study ("Sakrale Prostitution") likewise concludes that sacred prostitution was rare in the Hellenistic religions. With specific reference to Corinth, Conzelmann, as well as stressing the irrelevance of the Strabo reference to the Corinth of Paul's day, notes that Pausanias's description of Corinth says nothing of sacred prostitution ("Corinth und die Mädchen der Aphrodite").

25. Epstein, *Sex Laws,* 154-55, calls it a "third form of sacred prostitution," the first and second being prostitution as part of idolatrous rites and for the benefit of the temple treasury.

gious festivals could be just one of the excesses such merrymaking would precipitate."[26] As C. D. Ginsburg explains, "inviting prostitutes to the sacrificial banquets was a feature of the festivity rather than of the ritual."[27] The presence of a harlot at such feasts, according to Goodfriend, may be compared to such activity at a modern-day Mardi Gras or All Saints' Day. Further possible references in the Old Testament include Numbers 25:1ff., where Phinehas's slaying of Zimri for sexual immorality occurred in the context of pagan sacrifice, and Isaiah 57:3ff.; Jeremiah 2:20; 3:6. Prostitutes in a temple venue are also spoken of in 2 Maccabees 6:4-5. In Judges 21:19-23 even a feast to the Lord at Shiloh was the occasion for the Benjaminites to take a wife by force.[28]

As Karel van der Toorn sums up, "the OT contains indeed ample evidence of religious feasts that led to sexual excesses. The description of the cult of the golden calf, projected back into the misty times prior to the settlement in Canaan, can be considered as an archetype of the events (Exodus 32). During the celebrations 'the people sat down to eat and drink, and rose up to play' (Exod 32:6). The latter verb . . . is an unmistakable euphemism for sexual activities."[29] According to both pagan and Christian writers feasting and sexual immorality went inevitably together. As A. Booth states, for such authors "eating and drinking and sexual immorality constitute . . . an unholy trinity."[30]

In the Greco-Roman world, prostitution at pagan cultic events was very common. As Catherine Edwards notes, various ancient texts indicate that sexual pleasure was often the expected sequel to a banquet (Cicero, *Phil.* 2.104-5; *De fin.* 2.23; Seneca, *Ep.* 47.7; 95.23), and sometimes prostitutes were explicitly mentioned as part of the after-dinner entertainment (e.g., Juvenal, *Sat.* 11.162-70; Cicero, *Pro Mur.* 13).[31] We may add Dio Chrysostom (*Or.* 77/78.4), who writes that brothel keepers "drag their stock" to the "great festive occasions."[32]

There seems little doubt that the discussion of idol food in 1 Corinthi-

26. Goodfriend, "Prostitution," 509.

27. Ginsburg, *EncJud,* 8:1019.

28. It is not uncommon in Jewish texts for idolatry and sexual license to be linked; cf., e.g., Ep Jer 43; Wis 14:12-27; 2 *En.* 10.4-6; *T. Benj.* 10.10.

29. Van der Toorn, "Prostitution (Cultic)," 510.

30. Booth, "Art of Reclining," 105.

31. Edwards, *Politics of Immorality,* 188.

32. Cited by Winter, *Seek the Welfare,* 174.

ans 8–10 included the problem of πορνεία. Paul's response to the problem of the πόρνη in 1 Corinthians 6:12-20 should probably be read in this light.[33] Apparently some Corinthians were eating in pagan temples and using the prostitutes on offer on such occasions and defending both behaviors with the slogan, "all things are lawful for me" (6:12; 10:23). As already noted, "rise up to play" in 10:7, which alludes to Exodus 32:6, is probably a reference to prostitution on a festive occasion in a pagan temple. Revelation 2:14ff. may supply evidence of such activity in Asia Minor: the church in Pergamum is guilty of eating food sacrificed to idols and of sexual immorality. Acts 15 may also be a witness to the phenomenon. As S. G. Wilson notes, some scholars have argued that "the purpose of the provisions of the [apostolic] decree, including πορνεία, was to discourage Christians from any connection with the idolatrous worship of pagan cults."[34]

All this speaks for a close association of sexual immorality and idolatry. Even though πορνεία often literally took place in pagan temples, however, early Christians conceived of it not as idolatry, worshiping a false god in a pagan temple, but more often as the desecration of the temple of the true God. Dautzenberg points out that sexual prohibitions during the postexilic and early Jewish period were often summarized and systematized by Jews in the frame of thinking about purity.[35] Desecration of the Holy Place and of the priesthood through πορνεία is warned against in many places, including Josephus, *Testament of Levi, Damascus Document* (CD), and *Psalms of Solomon*.[36] For example, *Testament of Levi* 9.9 exhorts its readers: "Beware the spirit of πορνεία. This spirit will desecrate the Holy Place." As Dautzenberg observes, Paul distinguishes himself from early Judaism, which is bound by the law, not by cultic aversion to πορνεία, but rather by a far-reaching spiritualization of cultic thinking.[37] The use of sacral language in 1 Corinthians 6:19 is espe-

33. For a full defense of such temple prostitution as the background to 1 Cor 6:12-20 and a consideration of the main alternatives see Rosner, "Temple Prostitution."

34. S. G. Wilson, *Luke and the Law*, 94 (see further 97-99). Cf. K. Lake, *Additional Notes*, 205ff.; Kümmel, "Die älteste Form des Aposteldekrets"; Siegert, "Gottesfürchtige und Sympathisanten." Kümmel contends that the association of all the terms of the decree with the problem of idolatry and pagan worship is confirmed in later Christian literature, especially the *Pseudo-Clementines*.

35. Dautzenberg, "Eine Fallstudie," 289.

36. Ibid., 288.

37. Ibid., 290.

cially clear, where Paul conceives of πορνεία, which probably occurred in a pagan temple, as desecration of the temple of the Holy Spirit, that is, the believer's body.

It would not be surprising to find Jews and Christians urging that sexual immorality leads to idolatry and vice versa. But in their symbolic world, sexual immorality and greed are conceived of differently. Whereas greed is a sin that involves leaving God's temple altogether and worshiping elsewhere, at least according to texts in Job, Matthew, Luke, Colossians, Ephesians, and Philo (see chapters 4–7 above), sexual immorality constitutes sin in God's temple, perhaps due to sexual immorality often being opposed to categories having to do with purity and holiness.

Greed, Violence, and Corruption

Having established that greed in the material realm is the general meaning of πλεονεξία/πλεονέκτης, we are left with the task of dealing with the finer nuances of the terms. Now that we know where we are fishing, we need to discover how big the net is. One issue that has the potential to narrow drastically the focus of the terms concerns the means used by the greedy person in his or her drive for acquisition. Do πλεονεξία and πλεονέκτης signify merely acquisitiveness, covetousness, the insatiable desire for more and more money and possessions? Or do they inevitably carry with them connotations of dishonest gain and the ruthless oppression of the poor?

As we saw in our discussion of 1 Corinthians 5–6 earlier in this chapter, the greedy person and the thief can have a close association. Furthermore, the cognate πλεονεκτέω can mean to "cheat" or "defraud," as in 2 Corinthians 7:2 and 12:17. In the LXX πλεονεξία occurs in denunciations of violent and dishonest gain (Jer 22:17; Ezek 22:27; Hab 2:9; cf. 2 Macc 4:50). Indeed, a wealth of evidence from the Old Testament and early Jewish moral teaching supports a link between greed and injustice.

Most of the hostility to wealth in the Old Testament is linked to the failure of the rich to act justly toward the stranger, widow, orphan, and the poor.[38] The wealthy man is equated with the wicked (Ps 10:3), the violent (Prov 11:6), and the proud (Prov 15:25; 16:19; Isa 2:7, 11; 13:11, 17; Jer 51:13).

---

38. See Schmidt, *Hostility to Wealth*, 52-60.

The rich are those who "carry out evil plans" (Ps 37:7) and offer bribes (Prov 17:8). Furthermore, wealth is often linked with wickedness (Prov 10:2; 11:28; 22:1; cf. Ps 37:16; Prov 15:16; 16:8; 17:1; 28:6). The first ethical concern mentioned in Proverbs is the band of outlaws whose goal it is to "get all kinds of costly things" and to "fill [their] houses with booty" (1:13); Wisdom warns that such people "run to evil" and are "swift to shed blood" (1:16). In 19:22 it is taken for granted that the greedy are liars. In Micah 2:2 "they that covet fields . . . take them by violence." The false prophet prophesies for personal gain (3:5). Whereas corrupt leaders "judge for a bribe," corrupt priests "teach for a price" (3:11).

Similarly Philo observes that "injustice is bred by anxious thought for the means of life and for money-making" (*Cont. Life* 17). Riches and injustice are associated in 1QS 11:1-2 ("men of injustice . . . who are zealous after wealth"). And *Mekilta Exodus* 20:17 states that "if you desire you will covet; and if you covet you will tyrannize and rob."

In Revelation 18 Babylon's sumptuous wealth and extravagance is tainted in vv. 12-13 when the merchants' list of cargo, which opens with "gold, silver, jewels, and pearls," closes emphatically with "slaves, that is, human souls." As Bauckham notes, this "suggests the inhuman brutality, the contempt for human life, on which the whole of Rome's prosperity and luxury rests."[39] Such a view is confirmed in 18:21, where Babylon is condemned as a blood-shedding city of violence. Wengst contends that the city of Rome was "produced and maintained by military force which is accompanied with streams of blood and tears of unimaginable proportions."[40] In the ancient world Rome represented a powerful object lesson in the ruthlessness of greed.

Is greed then condemned only when it is associated with dishonesty and oppression? If, as was the case, greed was thought to lead almost inevitably to other vices, does that mean that the words for greed carry this taint in their every appearance? These questions touch on the complex issues of how lexical studies relate to analyses of social conditions in the ancient world.

Anthropologists commonly distinguish between societies with a basic perception of unlimited goods and those that understand goods and re-

39. Bauckham, *Climax of Prophecy*, 371. Cf. Rowland, *Revelation*, 134: "In the extravagance and luxury of life and wealth there lies hidden the cost to human lives and societies."
40. Wengst, *Pax Romana*, 13.

sources to be "finite in number and limited in quantity."[41] Put crudely, whereas modern Western economies operate on the assumptions of the former, the collectivist, agrarian Mediterranean societies of the ancient world exemplify the latter. These contrasting views on the availability of resources affect the perception of wealth and poverty, and perhaps also of greed.

In the ancient world the options for getting rich were very limited. For the vast majority of people who worked as peasant farmers or slaves it was not an option at all. Unlike the modern Western world, where at least in theory one can become wealthy through working hard in certain professions, through some business undertaking (or by luck via birth or circumstance, such as winning the lottery), the main ways to become rich in the first century for the vast majority of people were through corruption (note the notorious tax collector), by inheritance, or perhaps by finding a treasure in a field (cf. Matt 13:44).

In a limited goods society, wealth is readily seen as having arisen from an abuse of the poor, for when one person or group has more, then someone else inevitably ends up with less.[42] Bruce Malina explains:

> Since all good exists in limited amounts which cannot be increased or expanded, it follows that an individual, alone or with his family, can improve his social position only at the expense of others. Hence any apparent relative improvement in someone's position with respect to any good in life is viewed as a threat to the entire community. Obviously, someone is being deprived and denied something that is his, whether he knows it or not.[43]

While there is no consensus in studies of the economy of Mediterranean antiquity on the details of the distribution of wealth and the size of the rich and poor classes, all studies emphasize the prevalence of highly stratified class structures that marked off the wealthy elite from agrarian peasants and urban poor. Much of this distinction was rooted in wealth

---

41. Malina, *New Testament World,* 75 (see 71-93). See also Moxnes, *Economy of the Kingdom,* 76-78; and Hellerman, "Wealth and Sacrifice," 149-55.

42. It is not unlike a meal where some guests eat well and others go without because there is only so much food to go around; cf. Paul's dissatisfaction with Corinthian meals in 1 Cor 11:21, "For when the time comes to eat, each of you goes ahead with your own supper, and some go hungry."

43. Malina, *New Testament World,* 76.

consisting principally of family homes and especially land. Particularly in a Jewish way of thinking, land was a finite commodity. In the Pentateuch there were not only strict boundaries for its possession by various tribes (Num 34:1-15; Josh 15–19), based on equitable distribution, but also laws against the abuse of land accumulation (in the laws of the sabbatical year and the year of Jubilee in Lev 25).[44]

Not surprisingly, then, landed wealth is often linked directly to greed: "Woe to you who add house to house and join field to field till no space is left and you live alone in the land" (Isa 5:8). The same viewpoint is spelled out in *Psalms of Solomon* 4. The author targets the Jewish leadership, specifically the priestly aristocracy (see the first line below), for their ruthless accumulation of landed wealth (note the fourfold repetition of οἶκος). He accuses them of blasphemous and hardhearted lawbreaking and envisions a situation of gruesome talionic justice where the Lord "sees and judges" and their covetous eyes will be pecked out by crows; note the threefold repetition of ὀφθαλμοί and the emphasis on greed as wanton desire, ἐπιθυμία, also three times:

Ἵνα τί σύ, βέβηλε, κάθησαι ἐν συνεδρίῳ ὁσίων
καὶ ἡ καρδία σου μακρὰν ἀφέστηκεν ἀπὸ τοῦ κυρίου
ἐν παρανομίαις παροργίζων τὸν θεὸν Ἰσραήλ.

Why are you sitting in the council of the devout, you profaner? And your heart is far from the Lord, provoking the God of Israel by law-breaking. (4:1)

καὶ οἱ ὀφθαλμοὶ αὐτῶν ἐπ' οἶκον ἀνδρὸς ἐν εὐσταθείᾳ
ὡς ὄφις διαλῦσαι σοφίαν ἀλλήλων ἐν λόγοις παρανόμων
οἱ λόγοι αὐτοῦ παραλογισμοὶ εἰς πρᾶξιν ἐπιθυμίας ἀδίκου,
οὐκ ἀπέστη, ἕως ἐνίκησεν σκορπίσαι ὡς ἐν ὀρφανίᾳ
καὶ ἠρήμωσεν οἶκον ἕνεκεν ἐπιθυμίας παρανόμου,
παρελογίσατο ἐν λόγοις, ὅτι οὐκ ἔστιν ὁρῶν καὶ κρίνων.
ἐπλήσθη ἐν παρανομίᾳ ἐν ταύτῃ,
καὶ οἱ ὀφθαλμοὶ αὐτοῦ ἐπ' οἶκον ἕτερον
ὀλεθρεῦσαι ἐν λόγοις ἀναπτερώσεως.

---

44. Cf. Num 33:54, "Distribute the land by lot, according to your clans. To a larger group give a larger inheritance, and to a smaller group a smaller one." Cf. Wright, *Jesus and the Victory of God*, 404: "For most people in the ancient world, the most basic possession was land."

And their eyes are on a man's peaceful house, as a serpent destroys the wisdom of others with criminal words. His words are deceitful that (he) may accomplish (his) evil desires; he did not stop until he succeeded in scattering (them) as orphans. He devastated a house because of his criminal desire; he deceived with words; (as if) there were no one to see and judge. He is satiated with lawless actions at one (place), and then his eyes are on another house, to destroy it with agitating words. (4:9-12)

ὀφθαλμοὺς ἐκκόψαισαν κόρακες ὑποκρινομένων,
ὅτι ἠρήμωσαν οἴκους πολλοὺς ἀνθρώπων ἐν ἀτιμίᾳ
καὶ ἐσκόρπισαν ἐν ἐπιθυμίᾳ.

Let the crows peck out the eyes of the hypocrites, for they disgracefully desolate many people's houses and greedily scatter (them). (4:20)[45]

Interestingly, in Mark 12:38-40 Jesus likewise censures Jewish leaders not only for their ostentatious display but also for devouring widows' houses: οἱ κατεσθίοντες τὰς οἰκίας τῶν χηρῶν (12:40). Jesus' answer to the rich young ruler in 10:17-22 is also revealing; in rehearsing five of the last six commandments of the Decalogue he replaces, or emends, the tenth commandment, "You shall not covet," with "You shall not defraud," μὴ ἀποστερήσῃς, the same verb used in James 5:4 and Sirach 4:1 with reference to failing to pay wages to workmen and depriving the poor, respectively, concepts closely associated with greed and excessive land acquisition.

Given the limited goods nature of ancient society and economics it is not surprising that a connection was regularly made between the landed rich and greed, violence, and corruption. In this light, the question arises: should then πλεονεξία and πλεονέκτης be understood to mean that ruthless drive for more and more material possessions that uses unrighteous means to get them? The following definitions answer this question in the affirmative:

The arrogant and ruthless assumption that all other persons and things exist for one's own benefit (G. B. Caird)[46]

45. Translated by R. B. White, *OTP,* 2:655-56.
46. Caird, *Paul's Letters from Prison,* 205; cited in Vaughan, "Colossians," 212.

Ruthless greed (NEB)

A will to power which expresses itself by oppression and violence to another's detriment (Xavier Léon-Dufour)[47]

A ruthless form of greed, intent to get whatever one desires without regard for the rights, feelings or welfare of others (G. J. Pigott)[48]

The problem in locating the meaning of πλεονεξία and πλεονέκτης is that the words mainly appear in vice lists that supply little context upon which to base a lexical choice. Naturally enough commentators and lexicographers seek to give the words a meaning that justifies their appearance alongside the likes of murder, treachery, wickedness, and workers of evil, as in Romans 1:28-30. "Wanting to get rich, avarice," simply does not seem wicked enough, at least to modern Western sensibilities. Hence definitions such as those listed above are suggested. However, simply wanting more wealth was considered a vice by early Jews and Christians, and other words carried the stronger meanings.

That the two nouns in question can signify just wanting to get rich irrespective of the means employed is suggested by the existence of Christian teaching that condemns just that. Along with Luke 12:15 we may note Matthew 6:9 ("Do not lay up for yourselves treasures on earth"), 1 Timothy 6:19 ("those who want to get rich fall into temptations and snares") and the widespread Jewish and Christian opposition to φιλαργυρία, literally, "loving silver." Furthermore, as we saw in chapter 4, there is a strand of teaching that regards the wealthy per se as having a serious disadvantage with respect to having a relationship with God.

"Ruthless and violent greed" is a better definition of some other words that appear in the New Testament, namely, ἅρπαξ ("pertaining to being violently greedy"), ἁρπαγή ("a state of strong desire to gain things and, if necessary, by violent means — 'grasping, violent greed'"), and αἰσχροκερδής ("pertaining to being shamefully greedy for material gain or profit").[49]

---

47. Léon-Dufour, *Dictionary of the New Testament*, 216.

48. Pigott, "Covetousness," *New Dictionary of Christian Ethics and Pastoral Theology*, ed. David J. Atkinson et al. (Downers Grove, IL: InterVarsity Press, 1995), 268.

49. The definitions of these terms are from Louw and Nida, *Lexicon*, 1:292, respectively, §§25:25; 25:24; 25:26.

Even though the rich were many times regarded as greedy, the two groups were not coextensive. For instance, 1 Timothy 6:17-19 addresses the rich and warns them strongly not to trust their riches instead of God and to be rich in good deeds, motifs associated regularly with parenesis against greed, but it does not condemn them in a blanket fashion for being greedy. Indeed, greed was opposed with appeals, in addition to that it led to violence and corruption, suggesting that the latter, while being a common feature, does not define the concept in practice in every case.

If to define πλεονεξία and πλεονέκτης in terms of sexual greed is in a sense to fall prey to the etymological fallacy, to insist that the words always connote social injustice is to commit a form of illegitimate totality transfer,[50] correctly observing that the concept of greed was often associated with violence and corruption and assuming that every word in the group of synonyms carries this nuance. The evidence for taking πλεονεξία and πλεονέκτης to mean ruthless, violent greed is lacking. The only place in the New Testament where πλεονεξία appears in an illuminating context is Luke 12, where the parable of the rich fool gives no indication that the greed being condemned involves anything other than the accumulation of wealth by legitimate means (his land "yielded heavy crops").[51]

Definitions of Greed

To this point we have established two criteria for understanding πλεονεξία and πλεονέκτης: they concern greed in the material and not in the sexual realm, and they do not per se involve connotations of dishonest and corrupt behavior. Louw and Nida's definitions satisfy both: πλεονεξία: "a

50. Cf. Barr, *Semantics of Biblical Language,* 218: "The error that arises when the 'meaning' of a word (understood on the total series of relations in which it is used in the literature) is read into a particular case as its sense and implication there, may be called 'illegitimate totality transfer.'"

51. "Mammon" supplies an interesting analogy. The word means "possessions" or "wealth" and need not imply wealth gained dishonestly. In the Targumim it often carries the qualifier "of falsehood" in a phrase usually signifying bribes or unjust gain of some description. However, it is also used in the Targumim in the neutral sense (cf. Prov 3:9: "Honor the Lord with your mammon"), and as we saw in chapter 5 with the Shema. In the Dead Sea Scrolls and the Mishnah the equivalent Hebrew word also takes the neutral meaning (France, "God and Mammon," 9-10).

strong desire to acquire more and more material possessions or to possess more things than other people have, all irrespective of need — 'greed, avarice, covetousness'" (§25:22); πλεονέκτης: "one who is greedy or covetous — 'greedy person, covetous person'" (§25:23).[52]

To leave it at that, however, would be to fail fully to understand "greed" in Colossians 3:5 and Ephesians 5:5. Although throughout this book I have chosen "greed is idolatry" as a shorthand way of referring to the words in question in both Colossians 3:5 and Ephesians 5:5, we should not overlook that in the latter it is not greed and idolatry in the abstract that are equated, but the greedy person and the idolater. The sense of a word is prerequisite to discovering its referent, but the characteristics of the referent go beyond that of the sign that points to it. In order to understand not only the sense but also the referent of πλεονεξία and πλεονέκτης, we need to consider opposition to greed in the light of the social setting of early Christianity.

Whereas we may be accustomed to thinking of greed as a private and intangible vice, this was apparently not the case for the early church. The list of offenders in 1 Corinthians 5:10-11 who are to be excluded from the congregation includes five very public and concrete offenses: the sexually immoral, the idolater, the slanderer, the drunkard, and the swindler. It also includes the greedy person, πλεονέκτης, who presumably was just as visible and identifiable as the other five offenders. How was the greedy person to be recognized?

While dispute continues concerning the social structures and constitution of the earliest Christian communities, what is beyond question was their close-knit character, commitment to hospitality and acts of mercy, and, at least to some extent, sharing possessions. We need only consider the marked social dimension of the moral teaching of the New Testament, the description of the communal life of Christians in Acts, and the use of kinship language throughout the New Testament.[53] Michael Wolter is right to stress the threat that greed posed to the very survival of the Christian movement in his comments on the harshness of greed's condemnation in Colossians 3:5: "Here we are dealing with a vice that the whole New

---

52. Louw and Nida, *Lexicon*, 1:291-92. Cf. Delling, "πλεονέκτης," 271: "striving for material possessions"; BAGD, 667: "greediness, insatiableness, avarice."

53. On the social reality of the family metaphor in the early church in terms of the supply of practical help see Sandnes, *New Family*.

Testament sharply rejects above all as a threat to the social harmony of the church."[54]

The expression of love in material terms is a frequent theme in Paul's letters. Along with its explicit injunction in the collection for the saints (2 Cor 8:8: "I want to test the sincerity of your love"), it is implicit in texts such as Philippians 2:1ff. (2:4, "look not only to your own interests, but also to the interests of others") and 1 Thessalonians 1:3 ("your labor of love"), which sound hollow if concrete and costly manifestations are not in view. In recommending self-reliance so strongly, 2 Thessalonians 3:6-13 supplies indirect evidence for the sharing of possessions; the passage addresses a situation where some members of the congregation seem to be living off the largesse of the community. Verse 13 ("do not grow weary of doing good") either exhorts the readers not to behave like those in the community who are abusing the generosity of their fellows; or, just as likely, it seeks to ensure that charitable behavior continues in the community to those who are the truly needy.[55]

The very language of kinship that the early church adopted suggests that the practical help and support that individuals normally expected from their family might now be expected from brothers and sisters in Christ. This is certainly the implication that can be drawn from Justin Martyr's use of such language in *Dialogue with Trypho* 47:2-3. Speaking in a context about hospitality and table fellowship, Justin refers to those who believe in Christ but take differing positions with respect to the law of Moses: "I declare that we must fully receive such, and have fellowship with them in all respects, as being of one family and as brothers."

The New Testament emphasis on hospitality (concrete, personal expressions of Christian love to fellow believers, especially strangers) served as a positive practice to counter and expose greed.[56] As well as meeting the pressing physical needs of strangers, traveling Christians,[57] and the local poor, and providing somewhere for believers to meet (Rom 16:3-5, 23; Col 4:15), hospitality was a concrete way of expressing the respect and recogni-

54. Wolter, *Kolosser*, 175.

55. Cf. Wanamaker, *Thessalonians*, 288.

56. The Greek word φιλοξενία (Rom 12:13; Heb 13:2; 1 Pet 4:9; 1 Tim 3:2; Titus 1:8) literally means love for the stranger. Cf. Koenig, *New Testament Hospitality*; and Malherbe, *Social Aspects of Early Christianity*.

57. The first missionaries traveled widely and were welcomed in a variety of homes (Acts 16:15, 32-34; 18:1-11).

tion called for in groups that were often socioeconomically and religiously diverse.[58] Hospitality was not a mere practical expedient, however, since it was clearly based on theological grounds. The notion of the incarnation with Jesus as a stranger on earth (cf. Luke 2:7; 4:16-30; 9:58; John 1:10-11), dependent on the generous support of others (cf. Luke 8:1-3; 9:1-6; 10:3-12, 38-42), made a permanent impression on early Christians. Not surprisingly Matthew 25:31-46, Luke 14:12-14, and Hebrews 13:2 stress hospitality to strangers. In the Gospels the presence of the kingdom is revealed in shared meals, such as in Luke 24:13-35, where Jesus turns the tables and appears not as guest but as host, and the disciples recognize him as their risen Lord. Paul urged believers to "welcome one another," as Christ had welcomed them (Rom 15:7).

The related responsibility to show mercy in almsgiving (ἐλεημοσύνη, a term developed from ἔλεος) likewise had a profound theological basis. Such acts of compassion were to distinguish Christians as living emblems of God's mercy in Christ. As a proper response to God's mercy, charitable giving was considered a mark of true spirituality (see Tob 4:7; 12:8-9; Sir 3:30; 7:10; 17:22; 29:8, 12; 35:2; 40:17, 24). In Luke 11:41 almsgiving is valued more highly than matters of ritual purity, and in Luke 12:33 it is a mark of true discipleship. Such acts of mercy were highly regarded in the early church (Acts 9:36; 10:2) and taken to be the regular obligation of Christians (cf. 24:17).

Characterizations of Christian life in the second century maintain this stress on sharing possessions with brothers and sisters in the community. Aristides puts the emphasis on the practical ways in which Christians expressed their love for one another: "if they hear that any of their number is imprisoned or oppressed for the name of their Messiah, all of them provide for his needs. . . . And if there is among them a man that is poor and needy, and they have not an abundance of necessaries, they fast two or three days that they may supply the needy with their necessary food" (*Apology* 15.7-10). Lucian of Samosata, a pagan traveling lecturer and rhetorician with no direct interest in Christianity, supplies remarkable confirmation of this picture. In *On the Death of Peregrinus* 1, he comments incredulously on the eager willingness of Christians to support their traveling delegates "at their own expense . . . for in no time they lavish their all." His explanation stresses Christian belief in resurrection:

---

58. Shared meals sometimes also served to expose tensions and inequalities (Acts 10–11; 1 Cor 11:17-34; Gal 2:11-14; Jas 2:1-13).

The poor wretches have convinced themselves, first and foremost, that they are going to be immortal and live for all time. . . . Therefore they despise all things indiscriminately and consider them common property, receiving such doctrines traditionally without any definite evidence. So if any charlatan and trickster, able to profit by occasions, comes among them, he quickly acquires sudden wealth by imposing upon simple folk.

Addressing an audience of some means, Clement of Alexandria wrote a treatise on the rich young ruler of Mark 10, "Who Is the Rich Man That Is Being Saved?", that insists that the church as a family must share its possessions with those in need. The whole tractate can be cited in support, since in his attempt to interpret for his wealthy students Jesus' command to the rich young ruler to sell all his possessions and give the proceeds to the poor, he eschews the literal sense because it would not benefit the family of God.[59] Instead, he recommends the sharing of possessions in the household of faith. For Clement, the rich person who is saved is marked by generous giving and contentment, and is not enslaved to the passions of always wanting more for selfish ends:

ὁ μὲν γὰρ ἔχων κτήματα καὶ χρυσὸν καὶ ἄργυρον καὶ οἰκίας ὡς θεοῦ δωρεάς, καὶ τῷ τε διδόντι θεῷ λειτουργῶν ἀπ' αὐτῶν εἰς ἀνθρώπων σωτηρίαν, καὶ εἰδὼς ὅτι ταῦτα κέκτηται διὰ τοὺς ἀδελφοὺς μᾶλλον ἢ ἑαυτόν, καὶ κρείττων ὑπάρχων τῆς κτήσεως αὐτῶν, μὴ δοῦλος ὢν ὧν κέκτηται, μηδὲ ἐν τῇ ψυχῇ ταῦτα περιφέρων, μηδὲ ἐν τούτοις ὁρίζων καὶ περιγράφων τὴν ἑαυτοῦ ζωήν, ἀλλά τι καὶ καλὸν ἔργον καὶ θεῖον ἀεὶ διαπονῶν, κἂν ἀποστερηθῆναι δέῃ ποτὲ τούτων, δυνάμενος ἵλεῳ τῇ γνώμῃ καὶ τὴν ἀπαλλαγὴν αὐτῶν ἐνεγκεῖν ἐξ ἴσου καθάπερ καὶ τὴν περιουσίαν, οὗτός ἐστιν ὁ μακαριζόμενος ὑπὸ τοῦ κυρίου καὶ πτωχὸς τῷ πνεύματι καλούμενος, κληρονόμος ἕτοιμος οὐρανοῦ βασιλείας, οὐ πλούσιος ζῆσαι μὴ δυνάμενος.[60]

For he who holds possessions and gold and silver and houses as gifts of God, and from them ministers to the salvation of men for

---

59. Cf. Clement of Alexandria, *Salvation of the Rich* 13: "How could we feed the hungry and give drink to the thirsty, cover the naked and entertain the homeless, with regard to which deed he threatens fire and the outer darkness to those who have not done them, if each of us were himself already in want of all these."

60. Ibid., 16.

God the giver, and knows that he possesses them for his brothers' sakes rather than his own, and lives superior to the possession of them; who is not the slave of his possessions, and does not carry them about in his soul, nor limit and circumscribe his own life in them, but is ever striving to do some noble and divine deed; and who, if he is fated ever to be deprived of them, is able to bear their loss with a cheerful mind exactly as he bore their abundance — this is the man who is blessed by the Lord and called poor in spirit, a ready inheritor of the kingdom of heaven, not a rich man who cannot obtain life.

In his exposition and subsequent exhortation, Clement highlights both the grasping and the keeping dimensions of greed that are to be avoided by rich Christians. With reference to the former he speaks of the need "to banish from the soul its opinion about riches, its attachment to them, its excessive desire, its morbid excitement over them."[61] Clement calls on his students to "strip the soul itself and the will of their lurking passions (παθῶν)" and warns them of the danger of greed inflaming "inbred desires (παθῶν)."[62]

Clement's emphasis in the sermon, however, given his focus on the command to give all your possessions to the poor, is on opposing the keeping aspect of greed:

Φύσει μὲν ἅπασαν κτῆσιν, ἣν αὐτός τις ἐφ᾽ ἑαυτοῦ κέκτηται ὡς ἰδίαν οὖσαν καὶ οὐκ εἰς κοινὸν τοῖς δεομένοις κατατίθησιν, ἄδικον οὖσαν ἀποφαίνων, ἐκ δὲ ταύτης τῆς ἀδικίας ἐνὸν καὶ πρᾶγμα δίκαιον ἐργάσασθαι καὶ σωτήριον, ἀναπαῦσαί τινα τῶν ἐχόντων αἰώνιον σκηνὴν παρὰ τῷ πατρί.[63]

Thus he [Jesus] declares all possessions are by nature unrighteous, when a man possesses them for personal advantage as being entirely his own, and does not bring them into the common stock for those in need; but that from this unrighteousness it is possible to perform a deed that is righteous and saving, namely, to give relief to one of those who have an eternal habitation with the father.

61. Ibid., 11.
62. Ibid., 12, 15.
63. Ibid., 31.

Striking evidence that the early church made the connection between the refusal to give and the sin of greed is given in Paul's speech to the Ephesian elders at Miletus in Acts 20. The end of the speech (20:32-35) concentrates on the subject of working in order to share material possessions with those in need. Paul appeals to his own example in this regard and to the teaching of Jesus: "It is more blessed to give than to receive" (Μακάριόν ἐστιν μᾶλλον διδόναι ἢ λαμβάνειν 20:35).

The "words of the Lord Jesus" in question consist of two contrasting elements, involving the verbs δίδωμι and λαμβάνω. The saying, which is not found anywhere else in the New Testament, but which does echo elements of Jesus' teaching (e.g., Luke 6:38), is commonly translated as comparing the states of the giver and the beneficiary: "It is more blessed to give than to receive" (NIV). However, λαμβάνω can also mean "to take hold of," and in this context this makes better sense. The "receiving/taking" that is being unfavorably compared to "giving" is not that of the needy who are being supported, "the weak," but rather of the ones who have worked and have the opportunity of sharing their possessions and pass up the opportunity (cf. Eph 4:28). The verb λαμβάνω here is roughly synonymous with πλεονεκτέω. Acts 20:35b might be translated: "It is more blessed to give than to amass [wealth]."

A small number of commentators support this exegesis. Richard Roberts paraphrases the saying as asserting that "generosity brings more happiness than acquisitiveness" and reasons: "Giving and receiving are the obverse and reverse sides of one and the same transaction; and there is no reason why both should not be equally blessed."[64] I. Howard Marshall comments on the traditional interpretation: "But clearly this is not what is meant, and the point is rather that it is better for a person who can do so to give help to others rather than to amass further wealth for himself."[65] John B. Polhill concurs: "the saying should not be seen as a judgment against gracious receiving but rather against acquisitiveness, against actively 'taking' for oneself."[66] Understood in this way the saying captures succinctly the point that the early church contrasted with greed (not only acquisitiveness but also) the failure to share one's possessions.

Greed is often defined by German commentators with reference to the

---

64. Roberts, "Beatitude of Giving and Receiving," 439, 438, respectively.
65. Marshall, *Acts*, 336.
66. Polhill, *Acts*, 430.

etymology of the words, as *Mehr-haben-wollen,* literally "wanting to have more." Perhaps the point in the first century was not just wanting to have more (in the sense of getting more), but wanting to keep more for yourself, both acquiring and retaining.[67] We may surmise that the greedy in the churches in Colossae and Ephesus were those who refused to do "good to the household of faith" (Gal 6:10; cf. 1 John 3:17), or those who did not share their food with those who had less to eat at the community meals (1 Cor 11:20-22).[68]

In conclusion we may say that the charge of idolatry potentially falls upon a large group: not the sexually immoral, nor those who violently, corruptly and ruthlessly seek material gain, but simply *those who have a strong desire to acquire and keep for themselves more and more money and material things.* While the latter dimension of greed is commonly neglected in modern definitions, in 1909 D. MaCrae Tod defined "avarice" similarly as "an absorbing passion for earthly possessions *and* a selfish gratification in their retention."[69] In the early church such people were probably identified in the first instance as those who refused to share their possessions.

In our attempt to understand greed, however, the questions to ask include not only what does greed mean and who are the greedy, but also what does greed involve? I have argued that greed is best understood in the context of sharing possessions in the family setting of the early church. Greed, however, may be even more broadly defined in terms of its driving motivations. As we saw in "'Greed Is Idolatry' as a Metaphor" in chapter 3, the metaphor of greed as idolatry compares not just two words but two sets of associations.[70] In chapter 10 I attempt to construct a profile of the

67. Hays, *Moral Vision,* 313, considers "the sharing of possessions" to be one of the "four ethical matters at the heart of Christian discipleship as spotlighted by the New Testament." (The other three are the renunciation of violence, the overcoming of ethnic divisions and the unity of men and women in Christ.)

68. Dante took this point a step further taking greed to be the main obstacle to the realization of peace and justice in society (Gino Casagrande, "Avarice," *Dante Encyclopedia,* ed. Richard Lansing, 76-77).

69. Tod, "Avarice," 261; italics added.

70. Only a few commentators recognize this fact and define greed accordingly. The Puritan John Owen, *Hebrews* (on 13:5-6), 6:410, is one example. When defining greed with reference to Col 3:5 he emphasizes the inordinate love of the greedy for their riches: "Covetousness is an inordinate desire, with a suitable endeavour after the enjoyment of more riches than we have, or than God is pleased to give unto us; proceeding from an undue valuation of them, or love unto them."

greedy over against that of the idolater. In other words, I shall try to ascertain what attitudes went along with being greedy in the first century according to Jewish and Christian moral teaching. To anticipate the results of that inquiry, it emerges that *the greedy are those with a strong desire to acquire and keep for themselves more and more money and possessions, because they love, trust, and obey wealth rather than God.*

CHAPTER 9

Understanding Idolatry:
The Surrounding Terrain

In order to understand the words "greed is idolatry," we must first have some idea of the status of idolatry in the Jewish Scriptures, ancient Judaism and early Christianity. An examination of the ways in which idolatry was opposed and the strength of this opposition must be undertaken, since, as all interpreters assume, it is with the sinfulness of idolatry that greed is being compared. Further, in order to discern the similarities between greed and idolatry to which the expression points, we must also attempt to get beyond defining idolatry simply in terms of literally worshiping other gods, a sense that does not fit the expression in question, and see in what ways the concept of idolatry is understood in the biblical and Jewish tradition. Thus in this chapter I attempt to answer two questions: How serious a charge was idolatry? And, what is idolatry?

Opposition to Idolatry

Put simply, in the biblical and Jewish tradition there is no more serious charge than that of idolatry. Idolatry called for the strictest punishment, elicited the most disdainful polemic, prompted the most extreme measures of avoidance, and was regarded as the chief identifying characteristic of those who were regarded as the very antithesis of the people of God, namely, the gentiles.

Idolatry is the ultimate expression of unfaithfulness to God and for that reason the occasion for severe divine punishment (cf. Lev 26:27-33; Num 33:51-56; Deut 29:16-28). In Judith 8:18-19 idolatry explains "why our ancestors were handed over to our enemies to be slaughtered and pillaged, and great was their downfall." Indeed, the prohibition on idolatry was for Jews axiomatic and absolute. It is mentioned in the Mishnah only to clarify the question of culpability and punishment (e.g., *m. Sanh.* 7:4, 6-7, 10; 11:1, 6). The majority opinion accorded idolatry the punishment of stoning, the severest punishment of all, and it was ranked first of the three commandments never to be transgressed by a Jew (the other two were illicit sexuality and bloodshed).[1]

The portrayal of the kings in 1 and 2 Kings is especially revealing. Kings are assessed as either good or bad purely on religious grounds, that is, on the question of whether they destroyed or introduced idols. Omri is a case in point. By all accounts he was a "vigorous and capable ruler . . . [and] must be regarded as one of the greatest kings of Israel."[2] In spite of his political achievements and the "might that he showed" (1 Kgs 16:27), he is only mentioned briefly, for "he led Israel to . . . provoke the anger of the LORD their God with their worthless idols" (1 Kgs 16:26). The theme of judgment on idolatry is also widespread in the New Testament (Acts 7:41-43; 17:31; Rom 1:18-23; 1 Cor 5:10-13; 6:9; 10:5-8, 22; Gal 5:19-21; Eph 5:5-6; Col 3:5-6; 1 Pet 4:3-5; Rev 2:20-23; 14:9-11; 16:1-2; 19:20; 21:8; 22:15).

The theological grounds for the judgment of idolatry is the jealousy of God. The belief that idolatry arouses God's jealousy is a sturdy Old Testament theme with a long history. It is introduced in the second commandment (Exod 20:5; Deut 5:8-10), and in Exodus 34:14 ("Do not worship any other god, for the LORD whose name is Jealous, is a jealous God") it is the explanation of the divine name "Jealous." In fact, all the pentateuchal references to God's jealousy have to do with idol worship (cf. also 1 Kgs 14:22 and the references below). An idol worshiped in Jerusalem in Ezekiel 8:3 is called "the image of jealousy, which provokes to jealousy" (cf. Ezek. 16:38, 42; 23:25).

Furthermore, the conviction that God's jealousy inevitably leads him

---

1. See Tomson, *Paul and Jewish Law*, 50, 154.
2. Maclean, "Omri, King," 601.

to stern action is also deeply rooted in the Old Testament.[3] God's jealousy, based upon his love for those he has redeemed at great cost, motivates him to judge his people; see Nahum 1:2, "The Lord is a jealous God and avenges." The Old Testament is replete with texts in which God's jealousy leads him to destroy the faithless among his people:

> Do not follow other gods . . . for the Lord your God, who is among you, is a jealous God and his anger will burn against you, and he will destroy you from the face of the land. (Deut 6:14-15)

> He is a jealous God. . . . If you forsake the Lord and serve foreign gods, he will turn and bring disaster on you and make an end of you. (Josh 24:19-20)

> They aroused his jealousy with their idols. When God heard them he was very angry; he rejected Israel completely. (Ps 78:58-59)

> In the fire of his jealousy the whole world will be consumed. (Zeph 1:18)

The sin of idolatry was treated with great seriousness not only in the Jewish Scriptures, but intertestamental evidence also suggests that it remained for Jews in the first century a matter of grave concern. As Louis Jacobs observes, "Opposition [among Jews] to anything which savoured of idolatry was fierce during the Roman period."[4] We have already noted the prominence of the first commandment in early Judaism and in the New Testament. Further evidence can be readily gathered from Josephus, who recounts the strong Jewish opposition to certain developments in the first centuries BC and AD that they regarded as idolatrous. These include: Herod's introduction of pagan athletic contests that utilized three-dimensional images (*Ant.* 15.267-91); Herod's placing of an image of an eagle at the gate of the temple (*Ant.* 17.149-54; *War* 1.641-50);[5] the marching of Pilate's troops into Jerusalem carrying portraits of the em-

---

3. In Prov 27:4 ("Wrath is cruel, anger is overwhelming, but who can stand before jealousy") the power of jealousy is almost proverbial.

4. Jacobs, *Jewish Religion*, 263. Cf. Feldman, *Jew and Gentile*, 41: "Opposition to idolatry turned bitter during the first century C.E."

5. Cf. *Ant.* 15.267, where Josephus accuses Herod of corrupting the ancient way of life of the Jews through such practices.

peror (*Ant.* 18.55-59; *War* 1.648-50);[6] the readiness to die rather than allow the statue of the Emperor Caligula to be brought into the temple (*Ant.* 18.257-309; *War* 2.184-203); and the destruction of the palace of Herod Antipas in Tiberias upon the outbreak of the war with the Romans in AD 66, on the grounds that it contained representations of animals (*Life* 66-67).[7]

That Philo considered idolatry to be a serious sin can be seen from his treatment of the subject of its punishment in *On the Special Laws* 1.54-57 and 316, with reference to Numbers 25:1-13 and Deuteronomy 13:2-12. He states bluntly that anyone who betrays the honor of God in idol worship "should suffer the utmost penalties . . . all who have a zeal for virtue" should exact such a penalty without delay (*Spec.* 1.54-55), adducing the example of Phinehas (*Spec.* 1.56). According to Philo it is "a religious duty to seek his [the idolater's] death" (*Spec.* 1.316). If such apostates escape punishment on earth, Philo is convinced they will receive their due beyond the grave: Such a one "will be dragged right down and carried into Tartarus itself and profound darkness" (*Rewards* 152).[8]

A common strategy in the Old Testament for opposing idolatry was that of ridiculing polemic, in which the idols are portrayed as powerless and deceptive. The main examples include Psalms 115:4-8; 135:15-18; the words of Elijah (1 Kgs 18:27); the prayer of Hezekiah (Isa 37:17-20; 2 Kgs 19:16-19); and especially the prophets (Hab 2:18-19; Jer 14:22; 10:3-4; Isa 44:9-20; Hos 8:4-6). The ploy continues to appear in later Jewish moral teaching, in the Apocrypha (Epistle of Jeremiah; Wis 15:7-9; Tob 14:6), the Old Testament Pseudepigrapha (*Sibylline Oracles; Jos. Asen.* 8.5; 11.8; 12.5; 13.11), Philo (*Moses* 2.205; *Decalogue* 7.66; *Posterity* 165), and Josephus (*Ag. Ap.* 2.236-54). Such material stresses the perishable nature of the idols, their human origin (in the mind and skills of the maker) and lifelessness, and insists that idol worship leads only to the disappointment and embarrassment of those who trust in them.[9] Habakkuk 2:18-19 contains all these elements:

---

6. In *Ant.* 18.212-22 Josephus notes the opposition of Vitellius, the Roman Governor of Syria, to allowing such images into the land of Israel.

7. Cf. Feldman, *Jew and Gentile*, 41.

8. Cf. Sandelin, "Danger of Idolatry," 122-23.

9. Jer 16:19-20, for example, warns that our ancestors have inherited nothing but lies, worthless things in which there is no profit.

Of what value is an idol, since a man has carved it?
Or an image that teaches lies?
For he who makes it trusts in his own creation;
he makes idols that cannot speak.
Woe to him who says to wood, "Come to life!"
Or to lifeless stone, "Wake up!"
Can it give guidance?
It is covered with gold and silver;
there is no breath in it.

Griffith observes that the term εἴδωλον, which occurs almost a hundred times in the Greek Old Testament, lends itself to such polemic: "The established association of the word with insubstantiality and falsehood provided the pejorative element in the description of an image as an εἴδωλον. Finally, the shared semantic domain of 'representation' and 'statue' provided the linguistic bridge, by which the word could carry all that the Jews wanted to say about cultic images."[10] It is effectively a term of derision. By contrast, the usual Greek term for cultic image, ἄγαλμα, had positive associations of joy and beauty. Paul reflects such teaching in Romans 1:18-32 and in 1 Corinthians 12:2 ("dumb" idols; cf. Rev 9:20). To worship idols is both an error and a foolish vanity (cf. 1 Thess 1:9-10; Acts 14:15; and especially 1 John 5:21, which contrasts idols with the living and true God).

Disgust and contempt for idolatry is also communicated in several derogatory terms used to describe the idols. Idols are: גלולים, "unclean things," a common designation in Ezekiel; אלילים, "weak/worthless things"; הבל, "that which is insubstantial"; and שוא, a "vanity" or "emptiness." The Israelites were not simply to avoid idolatry; the language of prohibition could hardly be more emotive and urgent; they are to "utterly detest and abhor" the heathen gods (Deut 7:25-26).

The call to resist pagan pressure for Jews to compromise their religion by contact with idolatry is nowhere more clear than in Daniel, where the king's rich and presumably idolatrous food is shunned (chap. 1), Daniel's three companions refuse to worship the king's golden image (chap. 3), and Daniel refuses to pray to the king (chap. 6). According to the book such

---

10. Griffith, "Little children," 70. The next most common term is γλυπτός, "carved image" (55 times).

earthly kingdoms will ultimately give way to the everlasting kingdom of the one true God (cf. 2:44; 4:3, 34; 6:26; chap. 7).[11]

Jubilees 22.16-17 calls for the absolute avoidance of idolatry: "Separate yourself from the nations, and eat not with them, and do not perform deeds like theirs; and do not become associates of theirs; because their deeds are defiled, and all of their ways are contaminated, and despicable, and abominable." This impurity, it goes on to say, is caused by idolatry. Mishnah *Abodah Zarah,* a tractate devoted to halakot concerning social and economic relations with such idolatrous gentiles, recommends extreme caution in connection with anything to do with idolatry.[12] Business with pagans three days before pagan festivals was forbidden (1:1). Selling articles to pagans before such festivals which might be used by them for idolatrous worship (e.g., fir cones, white figs, frankincense, or a white cock) was also forbidden (1:5). Forbidden too was the practice of casting a stone at a *Merkolis* (apparently a pillar to Mercury, the Roman equivalent of Greek Hermes, the patron deity of travelers; 4:1). Rabbinic abhorrence of idolatry in later talmudic materials did not diminish.[13]

Such aversion to idolatry is even evident in the Septuagint translation (LXX), which avoids the use of Greek terms commonly used in the context of pagan worship in passages that describe the religion of Israel, apparently out of a revulsion for other religions, or at least out of a desire to maintain some distance from them. The pagan terms βωμός (altar), σηκός (sacred enclosure), and ἄδυτον (innermost sanctuary) are used in the LXX only with reference to heathen worship. On the other hand, θυσιαστήριον, which is used to describe the altar in Israelite worship, has no precedent in pagan literature. The LXX uses εἷς in contexts of God's incomparability, whereas the words μόνος and πρῶτος were commonly used in Greek prayers that stress the superiority of one god over others. Furthermore, the meaning of certain terms seems to change. For example, ἀνάθεμα, which for pagans referred to a votive offering, is used in the LXX to mean a vow; δῶρον is used for votive offering. Whereas εὐλογία in Greek religion meant "praise," in the LXX it denotes "blessing." While a heathen soothsayer in the LXX is a μάντις, a true prophet is

---

11. Wright, *New Testament and People of God,* 293-97.

12. Schürer, *History of the Jewish People,* 2:82: "Everything with even a possible connection with idolatry was forbidden."

13. Cf. Jacobs, *Jewish Religion,* 263-64.

a προφήτης.[14] The LXX translators did not translate the figure of a "rock" referring to God presumably since in the Hellenistic religions a stone or a rock was a symbol or embodiment of a god. In the approximately 28 instances, a variety of alternatives are used, including θεός, κύριος, and βοηθός ("helper"; Pss 19:14 [LXX 18:15]; 78:35 [LXX 77:35]; 94:22 [LXX 93:22]).[15]

Evidence from a non-Jewish source, Tacitus's *Histories*, confirms the impression of Jewish disdain for gentile worship and lifestyle, the details of which could have been written by a Jew and cross-referenced to various laws from Torah:

> Whatever their origin, these rites are maintained by their antiquity. . . . The Jews are extremely loyal toward one another, and always ready to show compassion, but toward every other people they feel only hate and enmity. They sit apart at meals . . . they abstain from intercourse with foreign women. . . . Those who are converted to their ways follow the same practice, and the earliest lesson they receive is to despise the gods *(contemnere deos)*, to disown their country. . . . The Egyptians worship many animals and monstrous images; the Jews conceive of one god only, and that with the mind alone: they regard as impious *(profanos)* those who make from perishable materials representations of gods in man's image.[16]

According to Tacitus, "the earliest lesson" a Jewish proselyte receives concerns opposition to idolatry.

One piece of counterevidence, the LXX ban on cursing the gods, may turn out to be the exception that proves the rule.[17] Exodus 22:27 (LXX 28) gives the prohibition: "Do not curse אלהים." Usually understood as a ban on either blasphemy or insulting judges, the LXX takes it quite literally: "Do not speak ill of gods." Philo and Josephus offer a number of rather unconvincing explanations for the law. Even while defending it Philo cannot restrain himself from attacking pagan religion, referring to it as an error and delusion.[18] Rabbinic literature contains some rather

---

14. Cf. Feldman, *Jew and Gentile,* 53; and Bickermann, *Jews,* 114.
15. Cf. Tauberschmidt, "MT and LXX Compared," 98-99.
16. Tacitus, *Hist.* 5.5 (LCL translation).
17. See Goldenberg, "Septuagint Ban."
18. See ibid., 383.

flamboyant mockery of gentile gods.[19] The patristic allusions to the law also reflect embarrassment rather than affirmation.[20] Both van der Horst and Goldenberg suggest plausibly that the LXX here represents an early Alexandrian attempt to improve Jewish relations with gentiles. That it failed reveals again the fundamental Jewish hostility to idolatry. Apparently the ban on mocking idols exercised little influence and was quickly forgotten.

The prohibition of idolatry was, as Dunn contends, "no doubt burnt into the heart and mind of the typical first-century Jew . . . [and] could be taken for granted."[21] Even though "little of this actually appears on the surface,"[22] a closer look, as we have seen, confirms that the evils and dangers of idolatry were never far from view. More subtle traces can occasionally be found in the LXX, Targumim, and midrashim where idolatry is sometimes added to clarify or underscore its prevalence or gravity. For example, LXX Hosea 13:4-6 adds to the phrase "the heavens that God created," that the heavens are not meant to be worshiped. *Sifra* on Leviticus 20:6-9 (*Parashat Qedoshim, Pereq* 10) comments that "consecrate yourselves, therefore, and be holy" (Lev 20:7) "refers to the sanctification achieved through separation from idolatry." And Targum Jonathan on Jeremiah 2:4-8 changes "you made my heritage an abomination" into "you made my inheritance into the worship of idols."

The *Biblical Antiquities* of Pseudo-Philo, which dates from the first century AD and probably represents "general synagogal piety,"[23] provides clear evidence of strong Jewish antipathy to idolatry. Pseudo-Philo retells the biblical stories from Adam to the death of Saul. A major and consistent theme of the work is the danger and evil of idolatry. Israel's history is interpreted in terms of the struggle with idolatry. Where idolatry appears in the biblical material it is highlighted (e.g., the golden calf episode of Exod 32 is developed extensively in *Bib. Ant.* 12) and it is added at several points where it does not (e.g., cf. 1 Sam 6:9 and *Bib. Ant.* 55.7, where Philistine idolatry is made an issue in the return of the ark). In 44.6-10 the Ten Commandments are rephrased to make clear that every one is broken by the making of idols. The dangers inherent in contact with gentiles are under-

19. See ibid., 387.
20. See van der Horst, "Thou Shalt Not Revile the Gods."
21. Dunn, "Judaism in Israel," 253.
22. Ibid.
23. Murphy, "Retelling the Bible," 275.

scored and resistance to idolatry is seen as the essence of Israel's identity. As Frederick J. Murphy observes, in this way "Pseudo-Philo reminds Israel that its identity as a nation is founded upon its exclusive and uncompromising loyalty to God."[24]

The unique status of idolatry as the most serious of sins is evident in a number of rabbinic traditions. In the Talmud idolatry is one of the three cardinal sins, along with incest and murder, which it is worth suffering martyrdom to avoid (cf. *b. Sanh.* 74a). To abstain from idolatry is to fulfill all the commandments of the Torah (*b. Hor.* 8a). On the other hand, the person who recognizes an idol breaks the whole Torah (*Sifre Deut.* 54). There is also a tradition that in the age to come the earth will be free from idolatry.[25] Where there is idolatry, so will all other evils be present. It is both a root and a consequence of various forms of evil. In *b. Shabbat* 105b in a saying attributed to Johanan ben Nuri (ca. AD 120-140) idolatry is presented as the height of sin: "This is the device of the evil impulse: Today it says 'Do this', tomorrow 'Do that', till at last it says 'Worship an idol.'" R. Yishmael expressed a typical Jewish sentiment: "Which is the commandment that was said first? None but the one on idolatry" (*b. Hor.* 8a-b).

It is not just that idolatry was one vice among many of which the heathen were guilty, but rather that idolatry is a defining feature of the heathen, whose way of life is characterized inevitably by this sin. Read in conjunction with 1 Thessalonians 1:9, 4:3-5 is an early Pauline witness to this conviction.[26]

The characterization of the heathen by the two sins of sexual immorality and idolatry comes through consistently in the Pauline vice catalogues. Furthermore, sexual immorality and idolatry are the only vices in the undisputed Pauline letters that are considered to be such a threat that one

---

24. Ibid., 284. Pseudo-Philo's preoccupation with the dangers of idolatry can of course be interpreted in two ways with respect to the situation it addresses in the first century, as either evidence for or against Jewish problems with what some perceived to be the idolatry of the Romans. It probably indicates that some Jews regarded the integration of other Jews to be a step too far. For our purposes, the *Biblical Antiquities* provide further support for the point that the charge of idolatry was as serious a charge as a first-century Jew could muster, powerfully symbolizing infidelity to God (cf. Murphy, "Retelling the Bible," 286).

25. See Tomson, *Paul and Jewish Law,* 155. On the demonic view of idolatry in Judaism, see ibid., 156-57.

26. Heckel, "Das Bild der Heiden," 269-70.

must flee from them (1 Cor 6:18 and 10:14, respectively). In Romans 2:22 Paul takes for granted that a Jew is a person who abhors and detests (βδελυσσόμενος) idols.

Opposition to idolatry was in effect an exercise in redrawing group boundaries for both Jews and Christians. As Terry Griffith observes: "Jewish polemic against idols is set within the wider framework of issues to do with identity and self-definition."[27] In texts such as *Joseph and Asenath* idolatry is indeed the essence of gentile existence. Elias J. Bickerman's opinion, even if a little overstated, makes the point, stressing the function of self-definition in Jewish attacks on idolatry: "The endless, monotonous, and unjustified attacks on idolatry in virtually every Jewish book of the Hellenistic age could hardly have offended or persuaded a Greek. . . . These attacks were needed, rather, to bolster the faith of those Jews who through too much contact with Greeks might be persuaded to transgress the divine commandments."[28]

In *Joseph and Asenath*, Asenath's life prior to her conversion is depicted as utterly bound up in idolatry. As Randall D. Chesnutt contends, the text presents a "repudiation of idolatry as the quintessence of conversion . . . the very self-definition of Judaism that emerges from the story is formulated vis-à-vis idolatry and the things associated with idolatry."[29] Even the *Letter of Aristeas,* which represents non-Jews as honoring the God whose providence benefits all humankind, rejects their idolatrous worship without mincing its words (such "fabrications and myths" [137] are "profitless and useless" [136]) and points to this as distinguishing Jews from gentiles (134-38).[30]

In the second century Christians continued to regard idolatry as the hallmark of pagans (cf., e.g., Justin Martyr, *Dialogue with Trypho* 11.4; 69.4; 130.4) and to define Christian identity in terms of the absence of idolatry (cf. 34.8; 35.7-8; 46.6-7; 130.4, where he accuses the Jews of idolatry and portrays Christians as those who steadfastly stand against it, even to the point of death).[31]

For both Jews and Christians in the ancient world the charge of idolatry evoked horror and alarm. The strength of feeling we have traced in this

27. Griffith, "Form and Function," 60-61.
28. Bickerman, *Jews in the Greek Age,* 256.
29. Chesnutt, *From Death to Life,* 171.
30. Cf. Barclay, *Jews in the Mediterranean Diaspora,* 430.
31. See Lieu, *Image and Reality,* 115-17.

section must not escape our notice when we read the words "greed is idol-atry." In chapter 10 it will be of vital assistance in "Feeling the Metaphor."

The Concept of Idolatry

The concept of idolatry in the Jewish Scriptures is powerful and com-plex, diverse and problematic. Moshe Halbertal and Avishai Margalit rightly assert that even though "the central theological principle in the Bible [i.e., the Jewish Scriptures] is idolatry," it is ironic that that "cate-gory that is supposed to be the firmest and strictest of all . . . [exhibits] an astonishing fluidity."[32] It is indeed only by recognizing and distin-guishing the different conceptions of idolatry that one can progress in interpreting the comparison of greed with idolatry in Colossians and Ephesians.[33]

Idolatry is defined by a number of twentieth-century theologians, in-cluding Reinhold Niebuhr, Karl Barth, the Roman Catholic New Testa-ment scholar Luke T. Johnson, and the Sri Lankan evangelical Vinoth Ramanchandra, in terms of making that which is contingent absolute.

For Reinhold Niebuhr idolatry occurs when we "make some contin-gent and relative vitality into the unconditioned principle of meaning."[34] He gives a number of examples, the most cogent of which is the deifica-tion of reason.[35] Niebuhr observes that the human mind is incapable of perfectly comprehending the total meaning of the world. Under these circumstances when someone refuses to acknowledge the need for self-transcendence, to look beyond themselves, they are in danger of replac-ing God with that which is finite and contingent: "Man is constantly tempted to the sin of idolatry and constantly succumbs to it because in contemplating the power and dignity of his freedom he forgets the de-gree of his limitations."[36] Such idolatry manifests itself in various ways. With reference to Nazi Germany, for example, he notes "the spiritual character of national pride" and the "temptation to idolatry implicit in

32. Halbertal and Margalit, *Idolatry*, 10, 250.
33. The following analysis builds on their ground-breaking work, especially chapters 1 and 8.
34. Niebuhr, *Nature and Destiny of Man*, vol. 1: *Human Nature*, 178.
35. See ibid., 176ff.
36. Ibid., 178.

the state's majesty."[37] The essence of idolatry for Niebuhr is the attribution of "final and ultimate value, the cause which gives human existence meaning"[38] to anything or anyone other than God. Indeed, Niebuhr defines not just idolatry but sin itself in such terms: "sin is the vain imagination by which man hides the conditioned, contingent and dependent character of his existence and seeks to give it the appearance of unconditioned reality."[39]

Karl Barth's comments on Romans 1:23 point in the same direction. Idolatry involves the confusion of creation and Creator: "The difference between the immortal, eternal, and ascendant God and our own mortal, relative, and dependent existence is obliterated."[40] Barth observes that any number of created things may act as a substitute for the splendor of the immortal God, not only the images of birds, beasts, and creeping things (see Rom 1:23) but also "personality, the child, the woman . . . family, people, nation, church, homeland, and so on."[41] Barth's interpretation has proven to be influential in German Protestant theology. As Klaus Berger reports, much preaching since the Second World War in Germany has followed Barth in finding this form of idolatry repeated in every act of sin.[42] Sin consists of placing such a high value on something that it effectively replaces God in some sense.

Luke T. Johnson's definition of idolatry, which he applies to various aspects of modern life, is very similar: "Idolatry means treating what is not ultimate as though it were ultimate, making absolute what is only relative. . . . The idolatrous impulse can express itself variously, although the basic options are drearily predictable. We can fix our freedom on just about anything, can serve anything as the be-all and end-all of our existence, the source of our hope and our worth."[43]

In another book that attempts to expose the idols of modernity, Vinoth Ramanchandra propounds the same understanding of idolatry. For

---

37. Ibid., 224, 222, respectively. Cf. 226: "Collective pride is thus man's last, and in some respects most pathetic, effort to deny the determinate and contingent character of his existence."

38. Ibid., 225.

39. Ibid., 137-38.

40. Barth, *Römerbrief*, 25.

41. Ibid., 26.

42. Berger, *Theologischegeschichte des Urchristentums*, 509.

43. Johnson, *Faith's Freedom*, 61 and 63.

Ramanchandra idolatry occurs when we "elevate some aspect of the created order to the central place that the Creator alone occupies."[44] In a wide-ranging critique (of Western culture in particular), Ramanchandra attacks the gods of science, nation, ethnicity, sexuality, and so on. The sin of idolatry becomes a danger, he argues, "when we forget that these are human creations."[45]

Both the strength and weakness of this view of idolatry lie in its being so general. On the one hand, it can be readily applied to almost anything.[46] On the other hand, perhaps for this very reason, it lacks explanatory power, never getting much beyond saying that idolatry involves elevating something into the place of God. To label all sin idolatry, as attractive as this may sound, does not do justice to the variety and depth of the Bible's treatment of sin. Lawbreaking, lawlessness, impurity, and the absence of love are just a few of the many other ways in which Scripture conceives of different forms of sin. Romans 1 does not take idolatry to be the pattern of all subsequent sins, but rather portrays indulgence in further sin, being given up to various vices, as being the appropriate punishment for giving up God in idolatry. In attempting to understand idolatry the theologians mentioned above take a top-down approach, focusing on God as the absolute one. Another way of proceeding is to go from the bottom up, looking at what it is that idolaters do with their idols, what the charge of idolatry consists of, and to what the sin of idolatry is compared. Rather than taking our cue from the notion of contingency alone, such an approach may draw from a wide range of biblical material, including both laws and narrative pertaining to idolatry.

The Marital Model

The Bible uses a number of anthropomorphic metaphors to elucidate how God relates to humankind. God is at different points king, father, bridegroom, woman in labor, judge, and so on. The relevant metaphor for the dominant and most familiar conception of idolatry in the Old Testament

44. Ramanchandra, *Gods That Fail*, 107.
45. Ibid., 109.
46. Cf. Calvin, *Institutes*, 1.11.8: "From this we may gather that man's nature, so to speak, is a perpetual factory of idols."

is that of marital relations. The depiction of idolatry as sinful sexual relations is introduced in the Pentateuch (Exod 34:15-16) and is used extensively in the Prophets, especially Hosea, Jeremiah, and Ezekiel.[47]

The marital model also finds its way into some Jewish interpretation of biblical texts relating to idolatry. In the Talmud *b. Shabbat* 88b and *Gittin* 36b compare the sin of the golden calf to "a shameless bride who plays the harlot within her bridal canopy." And *b. Abodah Zarah* 44a asserts that Moses made the Israelites drink the water which contained the powdered remains of the calf (Exod 32:20) in order to test them as one would test a woman suspected of adultery.

Common to all uses of the image is the idea that Israel is married to God but is unfaithful to her husband. The betrayed husband experiences both a fierce desire for revenge and a strong urge to win back his beloved wife. If Hosea describes idolatry as prostitution, even more daring is Ezekiel, for whom it is outright nymphomania.

The marital model of idolatry renders obvious support for the love and devotion interpretation of "greed is idolatry." However, the marital model is not the sole conception of idolatry in the Old Testament.

The Political Model

Another major conception of idolatry appears in the Prophets, namely, the political model, in which God is seen as king and his people as his subjects. If when God is conceived of as the husband he demands exclusive love and devotion, as king he demands trust and confidence in his ability to provide for and protect those under his care. Whereas the marital model fits well with the love-and-devotion interpretation of "greed is idolatry," the political model supports and clarifies the trust-and-confidence interpretation.

The metaphor of marital relations, with the scenario of the couple and the rival lover, is doubtless more readily applicable to idolatry, as Halbertal and Margalit explain: "on the face of it the marital metaphor creates a tie of loyalty that is more exclusive than that created by the political metaphor. An erotic relationship, according to the sexual morality of monogamy, is not transferable. Political authority, in contrast, is transferable by

47. Greenberg, *Ezekiel 1–20*, 297-99, supplies a good summary.

its very nature."[48] This may in part account for the neglect of the political model in most accounts of idolatry in the Bible. Nonetheless, the image of king and subjects is clearly used as a way of describing the sin of idolatry. As Halbertal and Margalit observe, "Within the traditional discourse of idolatry there is an interesting extension of what worship is. The prophets condemned Israel's protective treaties with the superpowers of the ancient world as a form of idolatry."[49]

The path for the political model of idolatry is paved in several ways. First, titles of political sovereignty, such as "king," "savior," "Elohim," and "Lord of hosts," are used to describe God, and the Israelites are correspondingly described as his subjects.[50] Second, some of the covenants between God and Israel are modeled on those between a suzerain and his vassals.[51] Third, Israel's demand for a monarchy is met with reluctance at first (cf. Judg 8:23), and then interpreted as a waiver of God's exclusive political role (cf. 1 Sam 8:7).

In both the marital and political models the choice of metaphor was reinforced or perhaps even occasioned by a potent literal association. Temple prostitution and the deification of human leaders made both the marital and the political models of idolatry all the more appropriate.

Idolatry as a betrayal of God's political domain can be seen in the Old

48. Halbertal and Margalit, *Idolatry*, 215.

49. Ibid., 245. Cf. 20: "the prohibition against worshipping other gods is more general and broader than the narrow sense of ritual, and it involves other areas, such as reliance upon a regime."

50. Cf. ibid., 216: "The heads of the great powers in the geopolitical arena of the Bible are described as people who have dared to cross the boundary between the human and divine." See Isa 14:12-16 on the king of Babylon; Ezek 28:1-2, 6-7 on the prince of Tyre; Ezek 29:3 on Pharaoh, king of Egypt. Halbertal and Margalit, *Idolatry*, 217, state: "The tendency of powerful political leaders to arrogate divine attributes to themselves clashes with the principle of exclusivity of God's political leadership." For a report of such a challenge to God's leadership see the words of Rabshakeh, the Assyrian King's emissary, in Isa 36:18-20 and God's answer in 37:23-24, 29, which interprets the situation as a direct threat to his sovereignty. Self-deification is taken to be irreconcilable to the exclusivity of God's rule. Furthermore, the conceptions of monarchy in Egypt, where the king was one of the gods, and Mesopotamia, where he was either their representative or their incarnation, were based upon the unique status of the king in the cosmic order (see Frankfort, *Kingship and the Gods*, 259-312). By contrast, the Israelite king's power is limited in Deuteronomy, in order that "he will not act haughtily toward his fellows" (17:20), pride being the first step toward self-deification. The link between pride and idolatry can also be observed in Isa 2:7-8.

51. Cf. Weinfeld, *Deuteronomy and the Deuteronomic School*, 59-157.

Testament in (a Jewish interpretation of) the tower of Babel story, in God's response to the institution of the monarchy, and most clearly in the arena of international politics when the prophets denounce Israel's treaties with Assyria and Egypt, and in the New Testament with teaching about the beast and Babylon in Revelation. The case of Zealot opposition to Roman rule supplies an intriguing first-century Jewish example. In such cases, as Halbertal and Margalit explain:

> Idolatry is a challenge to God's exclusive position as king, and the sin represents a crisis in a political system. The political model provided us with a different understanding of the sin of idolatry. Instead of whoredom and nymphomania, instead of the forgetful woman who loses her identity, it uses the image of a rebellious slave who becomes a pretender to the throne when he is driven insane by jealousy and a craving for power.[52]

Midrash Genesis Rabbah 38:6 (on Gen 11:1) explains the rebellion of the tower of Babel in terms of idolatry:

> R. Eleazar said, "Which is worse, the person who says to the king, 'Either you or I in the palace,' or the person who says, 'Neither you nor I in the palace'? The one who says 'Either you or I' is worse. Thus the generation of the flood said, 'Who is God that we should worship Him?' but the generation that built the Tower said, 'Will he choose the upper world for Himself and give us the lower world? Therefore let us make a tower for ourselves and put an idol at its top and put a sword in its hand, so that it will look as though it is making war on Him.'"

The midrash draws a distinction between the generation of the flood, who denied God, and those who built the tower, who attempted to usurp God's throne. The words "to make a name for ourselves" (Gen 11:4) are taken to mean "to make an idol." In terms similar to Isaiah 14:14, "I will mount the back of a cloud — I will catch the Most High," the tower builders declare war on God. In this case the strength of feeling inherent in the accusation of idolatry is not the jealousy of a betrayed partner, but the wrath of a sovereign ruler against open rebellion.

When the Israelites requested a king in 1 Samuel 8, Samuel was dis-

---

52. Halbertal and Margalit, *Idolatry*, 233-34.

pleased and prayed to the Lord. The Lord's comforting reply in 8:7-9 compares their rejection of God's kingship to idolatry: "And the LORD told him: 'Listen to all that the people are saying to you; it is not you they have rejected, but they have rejected me as their king. As they have done from the day I brought them up out of Egypt until this day, forsaking me and serving other gods, so they are doing to you.'"

The prophets Isaiah, Jeremiah, and Ezekiel denounce Israel's treaties with Assyria and Egypt in terms that add up to nothing less than the charge of idolatry, even though the literal worship of other gods is nowhere in view. Isaiah 31:1-3 chides the nation for her treaty with Egypt against the threat of Assyria. The reliance upon Egypt is regarded as a form of deification. Since God is Israel's ruler, the nation is supposed to seek protection only from him. To seek it elsewhere is effectively to look to another "god":

> Woe to those who go down to Egypt for help, who rely on horses, who trust in the multitude of their chariots and in the great strength of their horsemen, but do not look to the Holy One of Israel, or seek help from the LORD. Yet he too is wise and can bring disaster; he does not take back his words. He will rise up against the house of the wicked, against those who help evildoers. But the Egyptians are men and not God; their horses are flesh and not spirit. When the LORD stretches out his hand, he who helps will stumble, he who is helped will fall; both will perish together.

Isaiah 30:7 describes Egyptian help against the Assyrians as הבל, as futility, the same word that Isaiah 57:13 and Jeremiah 2:5 employ to condemn the idolatry of the fathers.

In similar fashion Jeremiah 2:17-19 describes the treaties with the Egyptians and with the Assyrians as a forsaking of God in favor of someone else. The nation is guilty of idolatry because it sought protection from, trusted, and relied upon something other than God. The use of such verbs in explaining the sin of idolatry calls to mind Luther's confidence-and-trust interpretation of "greed is idolatry."

The third prophet to associate political treaties with idolatry is Ezekiel. Here, however, the political and marital models merge, with the treaties being described in the familiar terms of marital unfaithfulness: "You engaged in prostitution with the Egyptians, your lustful neighbors, and provoked me to anger with your increasing promiscuity. . . . You engaged in prostitution with the Assyrians too" (16:26, 28). In this case the request to foreign powers for protection is compared to adultery and the relation between God the king and the nation to a husband and wife.[53]

With a throne room, from which God rules the world, and twenty-four elders who sit on thrones and wear crowns, ruling the heavenly world on God's behalf, the book of Revelation is not short on political imagery. As Richard Bauckham contends, Revelation portrays God's rule over against that of the Roman Empire, which, "like most political powers in the ancient world, represented and propagated its power in religious terms. Its state religion, featuring the worship both of the deified emperors and of the traditional gods of Rome, expressed political loyalty through religious worship. In this way it absolutized its power, claiming for itself the ultimate, divine sovereignty over the world."[54] Revelation presents an alternative, theocentric vision of the world, referring frequently to worship in its graphic portrayal of the conflict of sovereignties. Glimpses of worship in heaven punctuate the reports of God's victory over false worship on earth. Christians are called to resist the deification of military and political power, represented by the beast, and of economic prosperity, represented by Babylon (see Rev 18:12-17), by worshiping the true God and living under his rule.[55]

As Halbertal and Margalit observe, "In moving to a discussion of the relation between idolatry and politics we take the idea of God's exclusivity out of the realm of ritual worship and into broader areas."[56] The political model is thus itself an extension of the strictest sense of idolatry and is as such of keen interest to the metaphorical sense of idolatry evident in

---

53. The French theologian and ethicist Jacques Ellul, *Money and Power,* 105, also stresses the relevance of Israel's treaties to the question of trusting in material prosperity rather than God, using the words "trust" and "confidence" (but without reference to "greed is idolatry"): "This is the enormous lesson of the prophets: if God is Israel's protector, Israel has no need to protect itself by treasonous alliances with Egypt or Babylon (Is 30 and 36, Jer 42, for example). It is exactly the same thing with savings accounts. For ultimately there is no way to share: either our confidence is in God or it is in our savings account. To claim that we can thus insure ourselves and still put our trust in God is to add hypocrisy to mistrust of God. . . . But in reality, what we call trust in God is only a word, and without daring to admit it, we really put our trust in money." Cf. 47: "wealth is temptation because it urges us to put our confidence in money rather than in God."

54. Bauckham, *Theology of Revelation,* 34.

55. Ibid., 160.

56. Halbertal and Margalit, *Idolatry,* 234.

Colossians 3:5 and Ephesians 5:5. It supports the confidence-and-trust interpretation of "greed is idolatry" by explaining the sense in which such behavior may constitute idolatry.

A Definition of Idolatry

Halbertal and Margalit are adamant that idolatry is too complex a notion to be distilled in a single definition.[57] Nonetheless, even if it is difficult to reduce Old Testament teaching on idolatry to a simple formula, one element common to both models, the marital and the political, is worth noting. In both cases the notion of *exclusivity* is central: in one, the exclusive claims of a husband to his wife's love and affection; in the other, the exclusive claims of a sovereign to protect and provide for his subjects and receive their trust in return.[58] Thus *idolatry is an attack on God's exclusive right to our love and trust.* This definition, which attempts to offer an abstraction of the concept, may have relevance to our attempt to understand metaphorical application of idolatry in Colossians and Ephesians. We shall return to it in chapter 10.

---

57. Cf. ibid., 241: "Our approach is therefore not to try to formulate one definition of idolatry that will capture its essence, but to show how diverse and problematic the concept itself is." It is worth noting that Halbertal and Margalit's interests are broader than the Jewish Scriptures, including the whole of Jewish tradition.

58. Halbertal and Margalit, *Idolatry,* 229, notice this feature, even if they stop short of regarding it as definitive: "the description of someone as an idolater entails that the worshipper ascribes to the powers he worships attributes that are essential and exclusive to God."

CHAPTER 10

Understanding Greed as Idolatry: Reaching the Summit

———⟋⟋⟋———

Having made adequate preparations, we are ready to embark on the expedition to which this book has been leading, namely the secure interpretation of greed as idolatry. The attempt to understand the words "greed is idolatry" as a metaphor involves four steps: before *feeling* and *mapping* the metaphor, it is helpful to notice how the way for it has been *prepared*. In conclusion, in order to provide some check on our interpretation, other *comparisons* of greed with idolatry, especially the mammon saying in Matthew and Luke, will be considered alongside the words "greed is idolatry" in Colossians and Ephesians.

Preparing the Metaphor

In the world of those who first wrote and read the words "greed is idolatry," greed and idolatry had up to seven things in common. These points of comparison do not in themselves lend much assistance in interpreting the metaphor in question. Some of them may help explain its origin. Like Frank's eyes, teeth, and beard, to recall our discussion of method in chapter 3, their main function is to suggest the metaphor to the one using it and to ease its reception with those who receive it. The common associations between greed and idolatry are so strong as to make their comparison more appealing, convincing, and effective. They might be called incidental features that facilitate the metaphor. The seven points are listed from the very specific to the more general.

First, both greed and idolatry focused attention on items made of gold and silver. In biblical and Jewish tradition these two metals are frequently associated with both the greedy, who can be called literally "lovers of silver," and the idols of pagan worship, beginning with the golden calf. Indeed, Philo arrives at his judgment that greed is idolatry in *Special Laws* 1.22-23 through this very observation, when he comments on Exodus 20:23 ("You shall not make gods of silver to be worshiped as well as me, nor shall you make yourselves gods of gold").

Second, both the greedy and the idolater visited pagan temples, the latter for obvious reasons, and the former since in antiquity the temples operated not only as places of worship but as the equivalent of banks, a place for safe deposit of valuables.

Third, both greed and idolatry, according to parenesis found in the New Testament, were considered to be of such gravity that one ought to flee (φεύγω) from them: greed in 1 Timothy 6:11 and idolatry in 1 Corinthians 10:14.[1]

Fourth, both greed and idolatry are thought to cause other forms of evil: Wisdom 14:27: "The worship of idols . . . is the beginning and cause and end of every evil" (cf. 14:12);[2] 1 Timothy 6:10: "The love of money is the root of all evils."

Fifth, in Jewish thought both greed and idolatry involved evil desire, greed in connection with covetous grasping and idolatry from the incident of the golden calf onward. The Hebrew verb for "covet" used in the tenth commandment, חמד ("desire, wish, crave, long for"), is used not only of another person's property (Exod 20:17; Deut 5:21) but also of silver and gold (Deut 7:25), treasure (Prov 21:20), and even idols (Isa 44:9).

Sixth, both greed and idolatry are treated in biblical and Jewish moral teaching as inherently futile and a folly. One of the main premises of the

---

1. It is noteworthy that the only other vice in the NT that calls for such action is the third typical pagan vice, sexual immorality, in 1 Cor 6:18.

2. The connection between idolatry and all kinds of other sins is evident in 3 Macc 6:11; Wis 13–15; *Let. Aris.* 134ff.; *Jub.* 9.4-7; Ep Jer 4–73; *2 En.* 10.6. In Rom 1 Paul blames idolatry for the sinful condition of the gentile world. To deny the existence of the true and living God inevitably entails moral corruption. In 1 and 2 Kings there is a clear pattern that the worship of idols leads to the mistreatment of other human beings (cf. 1 Kgs 21; 2 Kgs 16:1-4; 21:1-16).

biblical injunction against idolatry is that it is useless.[3] Although we must be careful not to overgeneralize concerning the religious conceptions of the nations surrounding Israel in the ancient Near East,[4] and we must not read the biblical polemic as if it were an impartial description of pagan religion, it is safe to say that many pagans believed that certain benefits like fertility, rain, and health resulted from worshiping idols. It is against this background that many Old Testament texts proclaim the ineffectualness and vanity of idolatry (e.g., Isa 41:23-24; 44:6-21; Jer 10:1-5). Likewise, wealth is ultimately unreliable, and trust in riches useless.[5] According to Proverbs 11:28; 18:11-12; 23:1-3, 5-8; and Ecclesiastes 5:10-12, wealth is fleeting and is not a firm basis of security. The reminder of the possibility of imminent death is also linked to the futility of storing up riches (cf. Ps 49:10-14, 16-17; Prov 10:2; 27:24; 28:22). Indeed, wealth will mean nothing on the day of wrath (Prov 11:4; Isa 10:3; Ezek 7:19; Zeph 1:18). The moth, rust, and thieves in Matthew 6:19-21[6] and the precariousness of wealth in 1 Timothy 6:17 demonstrate that this motif has not diminished for the early church.

Seventh, both greed and idolatry are distinguishing marks of the gentiles. Since this feature is fundamental to the rhetoric of both Colossians 3 and Ephesians 5, it calls for more extended comment. The distinguishing marks of the gentiles are often listed as idolatry and sexual immorality.[7] However, greed stakes a good claim to the same status. The self-perception of Jews in the first century was that they were a people under foreign domination, which was the outcome of wars waged for mercenary reasons.

3. Cf. Faur, "Biblical Idea of Idolatry," who adds a second premise: idolatry violates the covenant.

4. See inter alia Gaster, "Mythic Thought in the Ancient Near East"; and on Egyptian religion, Wilson, "Egypt," in Frankfort et al., *Before Philosophy,* 37-133.

5. Hellenistic sources also note the problem of the insecurity of wealth. On Aristotle, Menander, and Dio Chrysostom see Kidd, *Wealth and Beneficence,* chap. 3. Cf. 126: "protestations of the precariousness of wealth are very much part of contemporary ethical discourse."

6. Cf. Schmidt, *Hostility to Wealth,* 125: "the triple scourge of animal, mineral, and human destructive agents is a comprehensive statement of the futility of possessions for the sake of security."

7. E.g., Borgen, *Early Christianity and Hellenistic Judaism,* 240, notes that the vice lists of Gal 5:19-21 and 1 Cor 6:9-11, which in context contrast pagan and Christian lifestyles, contain only two identical sins, namely, idolatry and sexual immorality. They also occur in Col 3:5; Eph 5:5; Acts 15:20, 29; 21:25; Rev 22:15. Borgen (245) concludes: "These two vices are central in Jewish characterising of the pagan way of life."

Thus it is hardly surprising that they regarded Greeks and Romans as fundamentally greedy.[8]

Apart from the frequent appearance of greed in the New Testament vice catalogues,[9] many of which describe the lifestyle of believers' pagan past, the presentation of the gentiles in Luke-Acts supplies striking evidence that for the early church the gentiles were unmistakably and unquestionably greedy.[10] In Luke 12:22-34 the gentiles are a foil to the lifestyle and attitudes of the disciples. Whereas the gentiles anxiously strive after what they are to eat, drink, and wear (12:22), knowing nothing of the Father's providential care, the disciples are instead to seek God's kingdom and trust in his provision. C. Stenschke notes the relevance of Acts 14:11-13, 17, where the providential care the gentiles experienced was not perceived as testimony to the true God but was ascribed to idols." The description of Noah's contemporaries and the inhabitants of Sodom in Luke 17:26-29 is not unrelated. In eating, drinking, buying, selling, planting, and building they are characterized as those who are preoccupied with material things, "anxious about their lives," unaware that "life is more than food and the body more than clothing" (Luke 12:22, 23).

In Acts it is significant that the two occasions of exclusively non-Jewish opposition to the early Christian movement are both motivated by the threat posed to financial interests. In Philippi when Paul exorcises the slave girl (Acts 16:16-18), the missionaries are brought to trial and imprisoned for "disturbing" the city (16:20). However, the real reason for the grievance was the loss of income caused by the deliverance: the slave girl "brought her owners much gain by soothsaying" (16:16). The owners seized Paul and Silas "when they saw that their hope of gain was gone" (16:19). The cause of the riot in Ephesus is remarkably similar (19:23-41). In response to the success of Paul's message, which was perceived as competing with the worship of idols, "Demetrius, a silversmith who made silver shrines of Artemis" (19:24), gathered fellow workers and presented Paul as a threat to business.

8. We may add an eighth point based on later rabbinic tradition: both sins were thought to deserve severe punishment: If R. Yohanan ben Torta blamed the demise of the first temple on idolatry, illicit sexual relations, and bloodshed, he puts the blame for the second on greed and groundless hatred (t. Men. 13:22; y. Yoma 1:38c; b. Yoma 9a-b).

9. It is noteworthy that the three related vices ἅρπαξ, κλέπτης, and πλεονέκτης appear in 1 Cor 6:9-11, one of Borgen's key texts (see n. 7 above).

10. The following discussion builds on the work of Stenschke, Portrait of Gentiles Prior to Their Coming to Faith.

Demetrius, who is described as "bringing no little business to the crafts-men" (19:24), appeals directly to the financial self-interest of his audience: "Men, you know that from this business we have our wealth" (19:25; cf. v. 27). While he goes on to appeal to the potential loss of honor to Artemis (19:27), there is no escaping the impression that in the narrator's view the resistance was primarily due to the potential loss of income. Polycarp makes explicit the presupposition of this material, that greed was a typical sin of the gentiles: "If a man does not avoid love of money, he will be judged as one of the gentiles" (*Phil.* 11.2).[11]

Two of the clearest texts for determining the distinguishing marks for the gentiles are Colossians 3:5 and Ephesians 5:5. Both texts, as we shall see in the following section, are set in the context of polemic against the hea-then, describing the lifestyle of the heathen with which God's people have made a clean break. In both texts three sins are highlighted: sexual immo-rality (through a number of synonyms), greed, and idolatry. *Testament of Dan* 5.5-7 is a clear Jewish witness, where abandoning the Lord leads to "committing the revolting acts of the gentiles," which are described in terms of sexual immorality and greed.

Evidence may also be cited from the second century. When Aristides (*Apology* 15.1-10) attempted to characterize the Christians around AD 150 it was to the positive counterparts to idolatry, sexual immorality, and greed that he pointed. Christians are those who "worship no other God than him . . . God the Creator and Maker of all things. . . . They do not worship strange gods." Furthermore, "their wives . . . are pure as virgins, and their daughters modest and their men refrain from all unlawful intercourse and all uncleanness." Finally, "if they see a stranger, they bring him under their roof . . . if they hear that any of their number is imprisoned or oppressed . . . all of them provide for his needs. . . . And if there is among them a man that is poor and needy . . . they fast two or three days that they may supply the needy with their necessary food."

To recap, in the ancient world of Jews and Christians, greed and idola-try had so many things in common that they were ripe for comparison. Both were associated with items of silver and gold, pagan temples, and evil desire. Both were considered by Jews and Christians to be so dangerous that they must be fled. Both were thought to lead to other forms of evil and

---

11. Cf. Philo, *Virtues* 180-82, who states that the conversion of pagans from idolatry en-tails a new lifestyle, which is among other things "superior to the desire for money."

were disparaged as a pointless folly. Most importantly, both were considered to be distinguishing marks of those who do not know God, namely, the gentiles.

Feeling the Metaphor

To understand a metaphor like "greed is idolatry" is at first to be unsettled by it and then to be changed by it. In other words, it is to notice its affective impact and rhetorical function. The metaphorical shock that the words carry has to do with our former light assessment of the subject in comparison to the predicate. In order to account adequately for the intended and likely effect of the words "greed is idolatry," we must recall the unique status of the charge of idolatry in both ancient Judaism and early Christianity as the identifying characteristic of a pagan lifestyle.

The assumption behind many of the references to vices, and for that matter, virtues, in Paul's letters is that certain behavior is tied up with a particular identity. Paul does not draw the distinction between Christians and the heathen along the lines of ethnicity, culture, or languages; rather, the essential difference is accounted for on religious and particularly ethical grounds. Identity for Paul is, as Ulrich Heckel observes, "solely religious and tied up with ethical demands."[12]

When Paul mentions such vices, it is usually in connection with the new identity of believers, many of whom used to belong to "the heathen," in tandem, more or less explicitly, with a "once-now" motif (cf. Rom 6:19b; 1 Cor 6:9-11; Titus 3:3; and especially Eph 3:3ff.; Col 3:5-8). In every case in this schema the "once" is descriptive of the sins of the heathen past and the "now" proclaims a decisive break with this past. As Peter Tachau asserts, "the heathen past is for gentile Christians for all time a thing of the past."[13] Various expressions are used to describe the heathen past (see especially 1 Cor 12:2; 1 Thess 1:9; Eph 4:22; cf. 1 Pet 1:14). It is significant that Ephesians 2 represents the strongest expression of the scheme.[14] Of particular relevance to the words "greed is idolatry" is that much of this Pauline heathen

---

12. Heckel, "Bild der Heiden," 281. See especially Rom 10:12; Gal 3:28; 1 Cor 10:32; 1:22-24; 12:13; Col 3:11.

13. Tachau, *"Einst" und "Jetzt,"* 99.

14. Tauchau, ibid., 96, calls it "a highpoint."

polemic has connections with the first commandment (see 1 Thess 1:9; 1 Cor 12:2; 8:4-6; 1 Thess 4:5; cf. Jer 10:25; Ps 79:6; and with reference to Christians see 1 Cor 10:7, 14; Gal 4:8ff.).

Heckel is correct to stress the parenetic function of this material: "The main purpose of this polemic is the admonition of the churches."[15] Paul describes the vices of the heathen in order to exhort the believers not to behave that way. As we saw in chapter 9, idolatry is the heathen sin par excellence that marks them off as a group. As Heckel contends, idolatry is "the distinguishing characteristic of the heathen."[16] Whereas it is true to say that Paul took over the traditional motifs of Jewish polemic against the heathen, we do not find him employing it against the heathen as such, except perhaps in Romans 1, but more commonly in the realm of his moral exhortation.[17] It is found less often in the theological arguments of his letters than in the parenetic sections, where he reminds the believers of the significance of their conversion and its attendant new lifestyle.

Thus to feel the shock of the comparison of greed with idolatry is not only to reckon with the weight of the charge, evoking as it does horror and a dreadful fear of punishment (see "Opposition to Idolatry," the first section in chapter 9), but also with its penetration, reaching to the very heart of religious affiliation and identity. We can appreciate the function of the words "greed is idolatry" only when we recognize that idolatry was a Jewish and Christian way of identifying and referring to the heathen and that Paul used it in parenesis in descriptions of behavior inappropriate for Christians, who have left behind their pagan past.[18] That the charge of idolatry classes one among the heathen and puts one in danger of judgment is given early testimony in the Apostolic Fathers, in Polycarp's *Letter to the Philippians* 11.2, which alludes to our text: "If a man does not avoid love of money, he will be polluted by idolatry, and will be judged as one of the gentiles, who are ignorant of the Lord's judgment."

It may further clarify the effect and effectiveness of labeling greed as

---

15. Heckel, "Bild der Heiden," 278.

16. Ibid., 283. For Paul idolatry was perhaps even more important than sexual immorality as a typical gentile vice, since πορνεία is for him not a particularly heathen sin; cf. 1 Cor 5:1; 1 Thess 4:3, 5. Cf. Dabelstein, *Beurteilung der "Heiden,"* 55.

17. Cf. Heckel, "Bild der Heiden," 282: "Paul takes over the traditional topoi of Jewish anti-gentile polemic. But he uses it not so much against the gentiles but rather as a part of his positive ethics in the churches."

18. Cf. Pokorný, *Epheser,* 210.

idolatry if we analyze the words in terms of rival groups and core values. With the words "greed is idolatry," a particular group, the early church, is indicating its disapproval of greed by comparing it to something that is in the opinion of the group a defining characteristic of a rival group, the heathen. In this scheme to say that "greed is idolatry" is equivalent to saying that greed is a heathen behavior, but it has a stronger emotive appeal, since the early church took idolatry to be particularly abhorrent. To be greedy, then, is in the opinion of the group, to be guilty of flagrant disloyalty to group values, in effect, to betray the group's identity. To be a member of the group, one says implicitly that one is not greedy; in other words, one is no longer one of the heathen. Therefore, to charge that "greed is idolatry" carries a disturbing emotive appeal and deems greed totally inappropriate behavior for members of the group.

Comparison with analogous rhetorical strategies involving competing groups in the realm of politics is possible and may enable us to see, and more importantly feel, the effect of the judgment "greed is idolatry" more keenly. Political parties often form their identities not only by positively affirming certain values, but also by shunning those values that they take to be characteristic of the main opposing party. A left-of-center party, for instance, might say that it not only stands for equal opportunity and social welfare, but also that it stands against social injustice, which it takes to be the defining trait of many of the policies of the right-of-center party. The analogy could of course be turned around, with a conservative party regarding the opposing party as above all economically irresponsible. In a debate within the left-of-center party concerning some policy proposal, it might be said that the proposal is socially unjust.[19] Such rhetoric would communicate the inappropriateness of the policy for the group and carry a measure of emotive impact, depending on the strength of feeling against the notion of social injustice, and, more to the point, against the main opposing party.

To take the analogy a step further, it is noteworthy that in understanding the charge that a certain policy is socially unjust, it is not sufficient just to say that they communicate powerful disapproval of the policy. The question remains, in what sense is the proposed policy socially unjust? In the same way, explaining the rhetorical function of "greed is idolatry" is

19. Examples could be multiplied with reference to different groups of nationalities, in sport, etc.

only the first step in interpretation, and the task remains to make clear the points of comparison between greed and idolatry (see the next section, "Mapping the Metaphor").

This construal of the function of "greed is idolatry" fits well with the overall strategy of Colossians and Ephesians with respect to their use of polemic against the heathen in general and, in particular, with the thrust of Ephesians 5:3ff. and Colossians 3:5-8. Three Pauline terms that stand out as characterizing pre-Christian existence occur in Ephesians: ἄγνοια ("willful ignorance"; Eph 4:18; 1 Thess 4:5; Gal 4:8-9; cf. 1 Pet 1:14; Acts 17:30); ἀπαλλοτριοῦμαι ("estrangement, alienation"; Eph 2:12; 4:18; Col 1:21), a concept that is frequently associated with idolatry in the LXX (e.g., Hos 9:10; Jer 13:27; 19:4; Ezek 14:5; cf. also Ps 57:4; 3 Macc 1:3); and ἀκροβυστία ("uncircumcision"; Eph 2:11; Col 2:13; 3:11).[20] In context, each of these negative terms is accompanied by descriptions of sinful behavior and by calls not to behave in such a way. That the sins listed in Colossians 3:5 and Ephesians 5:3-5 are treated as belonging to the rival group of the heathen and as thereby totally inappropriate for Christians is clear not only from the mention of idolatry, but also from references to "the earth," "God's dreadful judgment," "the life you once lived," "the ways you yourselves followed," "the old humanity," and the "new humanity" in Colossians 3:5-11, and to "[behavior] as befits the people of God" and "things that are out of place" in Ephesians 5:3-5.

EXCURSUS 1:
Condemning Greed in Ancient Judaism and Early Christianity

To brand greed as idolatry is a most striking and effective means of emphatic condemnation. However, it was only one way in which the seriousness of the sin of greed was underscored. Even in Colossians (see nos. 1, 5, 9 below) and Ephesians (nos. 2, 5, 9) other means are employed. Greed was widely considered in early Jewish and Christian moral teaching to be among the most wicked vices. In this excursus some of the numerous ways in which greed was condemned in ancient Judaism and early Christianity are noted.

---

20. Cf. Tachau, *"Einst" und "Jetzt,"* 99-100.

1. Drastic action against greed is recommended with emotive verbs such as: νεκρόω ("put to death," Col 3:5); ἀποτίθημι ("put away," Col 3:8); φεύγω ("flee," 1 Tim 6:11); ὁράω ("be watchful of," Luke 12:15); φυλάσσω ("guard against," Luke 12:15).

2. Unflattering descriptions of greed are given, including: "the root of all evil" (1 Tim 6:10; Ps.-Phoc. 42; cf. Philo, *Virt.* 100: "covetousness . . . that insidious foe and source of all evils"); one of "the three nets of Belial" (CD 4:17-18); one of the twelve evil things that come out of the human heart and defile (Mark 7:22); evidence of a base mind (Eph 4:19; Rom 1:28-29).

3. Stories are told to illustrate the folly of greed, such as the parable of the rich fool in Luke 12:16-21.

4. Greed is compared to a grave disease (cf. Philo, *Spec. Laws* 4.5, "greed, a baseful passion and difficult to cure").

5. Greed is tainted by the "bad company" it keeps as it turns up in steady relationship to πορνεία (see the five synonyms in Col 3:5; Eph 5:5; and excursus 2 below); ἀδικία (Rom 1:29; *Let. Aris.* 277; Philo, *Rewards* 15, *Contempl. Life* 70; *Sacr.* 32; Josephus, *Ant.* 6.86); κακία (LXX Hab 2:9; Philo, *Spec. Laws* 1.278; 2:52; *Contempl. Life* 2); ἅρπαξ (1 Cor 5:10-11; 6:10; *T. Dan* 5.7; Philo, *Agriculture* 83); and less often with ὑπούμενοι ("presumption"; *T. Jud.* 21.8); ὕβρις (*T. Gad* 5.1); ἀταξία (Philo, *Decal.* 155); ἀκολασία ("licentiousness"; Philo, *Spec. Laws* 1.173); ἀντεπιθέσεις ("acts of hostility"; *Spec. Laws* 2.3).

6. Greed is set in contrast to certain virtues, tainted by the good company it shuns, such as justice (Josephus, *Ant.* 3.67; Philo, *Good Person* 159), God's statutes (LXX Ps 118:36).

7. Greed leads to other sins, such as violence and murder (Jer 22:17; cf. Ezek 22:27) and hubris (Ps.-Phoc. 62; see further the section on "Greed, Violence, and Corruption" in chapter 8).

8. Wicked individuals, like corrupt leaders (LXX Ezek 22:27; Wis 10:11; Philo, *Decalogue* 155; *Spec. Laws* 2.43; Josephus, *Ant.* 6.86) and the Pharisees (Luke 16:14), are condemned for their greed; and godly leaders, like Paul (1 Thess 2:5; 2 Cor 7:2) and Christian elders (1 Tim 3:3), are commended for not being greedy or at least expected to refrain from it.

9. The inappropriateness of greed to a group claiming to be saints is pronounced in Eph 5:3-5 and implied in Col 3:7, 9, with the once-now motif (greed belongs to the past life of the old man), and in Col 3:5 with the association of greed with that which is "earthly in you."

10. The greedy are to be excluded from the church (1 Cor 5:9-11).[21]
11. Warnings concerning the eschatological punishment of the greedy appear in Col 3:6 (it is the object of God's wrath), Eph 5:5 and 1 Cor 6:10 (it excludes from a share in God's kingdom), 1 Tim 6:9 (οἱ βουλόμενοι πλουτεῖν; ruin and destruction) and 2 Pet 2:3, 14 (the greedy are condemned, destroyed, accursed).

Mapping the Metaphor

If a metaphor is an expression that in speaking of one thing in terms of another draws on two sets of associations, one approach to the interpretation of the metaphor "greed is idolatry" is to consider how Paul and his readers would have conceived of the typical characterization of the two entities greed and idolatry. What do the greedy do with their wealth (that they ought not to do)? What do idolaters do with their idols? The overlap between the answers to these two questions will supply possible points of comparison that the metaphor could be exploiting. A third question is also worth posing. It concerns the implicit contrast of idolatry with true worship: What do believers do with God (that they ought to do)? Of interest also, in the light of our definition of idolatry, will be whether these ways of relating to God are intended to be exclusive. If believers are to respond to God in some particular way, are they to do it only with God? Our search will take biblical and Jewish texts into account, for reasons set out in chapter 3 and in accordance with our findings in part 2. The inquiry is not restricted to the mere occurrence of particular words (love, trust, etc.), but recognizes that concepts can be expressed in broader contexts in narrative and in other ways. The three metaphorical interpretations discovered in the history of interpretation (chapter 2) can be tested by these measures.

Love and Devotion

The evidence is clear that love and devotion were a fundamental description of at least two of the three relationships in question: the greedy love

---

21. Cf. Ps 15:5, where one of the conditions for inclusion is that a person does not lend money at interest and does not take a bribe; he or she is able to resist the temptation of greed.

their money, and believers are to love God. A virtual synonym for πλεονεξία in a broad range of material is "lover of money," φιλάργυρος (e.g., Luke 16:14; 1 Tim 3:3; 6:10; 2 Tim 3:2; 4 Macc 2:8; cf. *T. Jud.* 18.6; Eccl 5:10, "lover of wealth"), the thought of which is sometimes expressed in the form of an admonition (e.g., Heb 13:5: "Keep free from the love of money").

Furthermore, in the Jewish Scriptures the rich are not "to set their heart," the spiritual organ of love and devotion, on their riches (Ps 62:10; cf. 2 Pet 2:14). That such love should be reserved for God is spelled out in *Testament of Benjamin* 6.1-3: "the good man . . . does not accumulate wealth out of love for pleasure . . . the Lord is his lot." That love for God characterizes the people of God, and that this love is supposed to be exclusive is clear in numerous texts, most notably in Israel's famous Shema (Deut 6:5) and in Jesus' summary of the commandments (Matt 22:37-38) that alludes to it.

Idolaters are described less often as loving their idols, perhaps because such a positive description would be given only from the idolaters' viewpoint; the perspective of the biblical authors on idolatry is decidedly that of the opposing outsider. The few exceptions are Wisdom 14:30, which condemns "devotion to idols," and Ezekiel 14:3, 7; 20:16, which depict those who "set their hearts on idols."

In sum, evidence that love characterizes the behavior of the greedy and believers, and to a lesser extent idolaters, tallies with the dominant conception of idolatry in terms of marital relations that focuses on spurned and misdirected love. This adds further support to the marital model of idolatry for the love-and-devotion interpretation of "greed is idolatry."

Trust and Confidence

Trust and confidence are core, defining characteristics of the greedy with respect to their wealth, of idolaters in relation to their idols, and of believers with God.[22] Numerous texts not only observe that the rich trust in

22. Eichrodt, *Theology of the Old Testament*, 1:38, explains the essence of the loyalty demanded by the covenant precisely in terms of trust and confidence in God. In a section entitled "The Meaning of the Covenant Concept," Eichrodt explains what the exodus and the giving of the law meant for Israel: "With this God men know exactly where they stand; *an atmosphere of trust and security* is created, in which they find both the strength for a willing surrender to the will of God and joyful courage to grapple with the problems of life."

their riches, but warn against such reliance as being incompatible with and an unacceptable alternative to trust in God.

Jeremiah accuses Israel of trusting in its "strongholds and treasures" (48:7; cf. 22:21; 49:4; Ezek 28:4-5; Hos 12:7-8). Psalm 52:7 states that the one who "does not make God his refuge . . . trusts in his great wealth" (cf. 49:13, 15). In Proverbs "the wealth of the rich is their fortress" (10:15) and "their strong city" (18:11); but "those who trust in their riches will wither" (11:28). On the other hand, God is the only one the poor and those of humble means can trust (Pss 34:6; 40:17; cf. 68:10; 86:1; Isa 66:2). Proverbs 18:10-11 suggestively juxtaposes trust in God and trust in money: "The name of the LORD is a strong tower, where the righteous may run for refuge. A rich man's wealth is his strong city, a towering wall, so he supposes" (cf. 28:25). Sirach warns its readers not to "rely on their wealth" (5:1) or to "depend on wealth" (5:8; cf. 44:6). In Proverbs 28:25 "a greedy person" is contrasted with "the one who trusts in the LORD."[23] And in *Psalms of Solomon* 17.33-34 the coming "Lord Messiah" "will not rely on horse and rider and bow, nor will he collect gold and silver . . . the Lord himself is his king, the hope of the one who has a strong hope in God." The same teaching is put more positively when in noncanonical Jewish moral teaching trust in and fear of God are to be valued more highly than wealth (cf. Sir 5:13; 40:18-26; Bar 3:16-17; *Pss. Sol.* 1.4-6; *T. Job* 15.7-9; Ps.-Phoc. 53-54; cf. Sir 10:23-24).

The songs of trust in the Psalter (4, 16, 23, 27, 40, 46, 62, 115, 125, 129) express eloquently the dependence of the believer and the believing community upon God. Not only is the verb to trust, בטח, used frequently in these prayers, but also a host of synonymous expressions that expound its meaning (see especially Ps 16). Such trust is said to belong exclusively to the Lord; the Lord *alone* (MT LXX) gives safety (4:8); he *only* (אך) is the believer's salvation (62:1 [MT 2]) and rock (62:2 [MT 3]).[24]

Significantly, two of the alternatives to trusting God in these psalms are idols and riches. In Psalm 115:2-8 lifeless "idols of silver and gold" are contrasted with "our God [who] is in heaven." Verses 8-9 make plain the choice between trusting either idols or God:

23. Cf. Prov 28:26a: "He who trusts in himself. . . ."

24. Hebrew אך occurs six times in Ps 62 and may have either an affirmative meaning ("truly/surely/yes") or a restrictive meaning ("only/alone"). The LXX has πλήν, which is likewise ambiguous ("only/nevertheless/however/in any case"). Both meanings stress God as the proper object of trust.

Their makers grow to be like them,
and so do all who trust in them.
But Israel trusts in the LORD;
he is their helper and their shield.

Likewise Psalm 40:4 affirms: "Blessed is the man who makes the LORD his trust, and does not turn aside to falsehood."[25] Furthermore, in Psalm 62 God's people are exhorted to "trust always in God" and to "pour out your hearts before him" (62:8). Verse 10 warns against trusting in wealth in the same terms: "Do not trust in extortion, and take no pride in stolen goods: when wealth increases, do not set your heart upon it."

Such teaching is carried on in the New Testament, where the parable of the rich fool in Luke 12 warns "against all active striving for the increase of material possessions as a means of security";[26] and 1 Timothy 6:17 counsels the rich not to trust in their riches but in God. In the New Testament the notion of trusting God, not money, is also apparent in the instructions to the disciples in the mission charges (e.g., Mark 6:8-9); in the story of the widow's offering (Mark 12:41-44 par.); the calling of Peter and Matthew to leave all and follow Jesus (Mark 1:18-20; Luke 5:28); the example of Zacchaeus (Luke 19:1-10); the call to store up treasures in heaven, not on earth (Matt 6:19-21); and supremely in Matthew 6:25-34, the Lukan version of which is introduced by the parable of the rich fool (12:13-34). Hebrews 13:5-6 encourages its readers not to love money and promises the Lord's help, implying that faith in God is the alternative to finding security in money.

Trust and confidence is also a frequent description of what people do with their idols. In the Song of Moses in Deuteronomy 32:37-38 the Lord asks about the idolatrous Israelites: "Now where are their gods, the rock they took refuge in . . . let them rise up to help you! Let them give you shelter." So too in Isaiah 44:17 the idol worshipers say to their idols, "save me, you are my god." In Psalm 81:8-10 the motivation for not having a foreign god is the Lord's promise to supply life's needs: "Open wide your mouth and I will fill it" (81:10b; cf. v. 16). According to Habakkuk 2:18 the one who fashions an idol "trusts in what he has made." In Wisdom of Solomon 14:1-5 pagan sailors are said to cry "to a piece of wood more fragile than the

25. The expression כֹזָב שָׂטֵי could refer to "false gods" (NIV) or to "these who spread lies."

26. Delling, "πλεονέκτης," 271.

ship which carries them" in order to find "a pathway through the sea and a safe course among the waves . . . [safe] from every danger."[27]

At various points in the Jewish Scriptures objects not originally intended to be idols become objects of trust and hence of worship.[28] In 2 Kings 18:4 Hezekiah, having "removed the high places, smashed the sacred stones and cut down the Asherah poles . . . broke into pieces the bronze snake Moses had made [cf. Num 21:4-9], for up to that time the Israelites had been burning incense to it." The following verse implies the significance that the nation had attached to such items: "Hezekiah trusted in the LORD, the God of Israel" (18:5). The implied logical connection between vv. 4 and 5 might be brought out with the word "instead": the king had replaced certain objects of trust with another more worthy one. A similar case of misplaced trust is seen in 1 Samuel 4–6, where the Israelites take the ark into battle against the Philistines, a strategy that led not only to defeat but also to the capture of the ark.

The synonymous parallelism of Psalm 49:6, where the wicked "trust in their riches and boast of their great wealth," suggests that trust and boasting are closely related. As we saw in the political model of idolatry, that to which one goes for security and protection is that about which one boasts. Significantly the greedy are consistently portrayed as boasting in and about their wealth (cf. Jer 9:23; Ezek 28:5; Wis 5:8). In Job 22:29 Eliphaz regards Job as the classic example of a man who is rich and proud and needs to be humbled. Indeed, the link between wealth and pride is common in Jewish texts.[29] In 1 Timothy 6:17 the call to the rich not to trust in riches amplifies the imperative not to be haughty, and in Luke 16:14-15 wealth is what is "exalted by human beings." That idolaters boast about their idols is stated less often, but does appear in Psalm 97:7. In the context of such boasting in wealth and material things, Paul insists in 1 Corinthians 1:31, quoting Jeremiah 9:23, that all boasting is to be reserved exclusively for God.

Thus the trust-and-confidence interpretation of "greed is idolatry" receives strong support not only conceptually from the political model of

27. That 14:3 deals with shipping in general and does not refer to Israel's passage through the Red Sea has been shown by Beentjes, "You have given a road."

28. Curtis, "Idolatry," 379. Cf. also the incident with Gideon's ephod (Judg 8:26-27), where the element of trust is not evident.

29. See Philo, *Posterity* 115; *Names* 214; *Dreams* 2.57-62; *Decalogue* 4; *Virtues* 174; *1 En.* 94.8; 97.8-9; and 46.7, where the wealthy are the proud; 1QpHab 8:3; 1QH 10:25; Sir 13:20.

idolatry, but from many texts that characterize the greedy as those who seek security in their possessions instead of in God and that conceive of the relationship between idolater and idol in terms of trust.

Service and Obedience

Texts involving the terms usually translated "to serve" and "to worship" supply unambiguous evidence that both idolaters and believers were conceived of as serving and obeying their respective deities. A primary action expected both of believers toward God and idolaters toward their gods in the Old Testament is designated by עבד and δουλεύειν. Even in ceremonial contexts these words signify more than just isolated acts of cultic worship. When it is said that the people "serve" Baal (Judg 10:6, 10, etc.) or other gods (e.g., 10:13) or the Lord (e.g., 10:16), the term implies not only the exclusive nature of the relationship but the total commitment and, in effect, obedience of the worshiper. That to "serve" a deity involved doing their bidding is not only implied by the nouns עבד and δοῦλος, but is made clear in passages like Matthew 6:24/Luke 16:13, where the "service" is rendered to a master.[30]

The numerous Greek terms commonly translated by the English word "worship" can be divided into three groups: (1) λατρεύω, λειτουργέω, and (possibly) σεβάζομαι — the worship of a deity by performing cultic acts; (2) εὐσεβέω, σέβομαι, and (probably) σεβάζομαι — worship as the exercise of personal piety; and (3) προσκυνέω and κάμπτω τὸ γόνη — worship as submitting to divine authority.[31] The third group are of particular interest in our attempt to answer the question whether "worship" in the New Testament world carried the connotations of service and obedience.

Although προσκυνέω occurs more frequently in the New Testament than any of the other words, it appears only once in Paul's letters (1 Cor 14:25). The sense of the word in Matthew 4:10, Luke 4:7-8, Acts 7:43, and Revelation 9:20 clearly includes the idea of submitting to a supreme authority, whether God, Jesus, angels, Satan, demons, or a pagan deity. In response to Satan's temptation Jesus states, "You shall worship (προσκυνέω)

---

30. The notion of divine service was commonplace in not only the Jewish world, but also with other Semitic peoples and with the Egyptians; cf. Rengstorf, "δοῦλος," 262.

31. See Jobes, "Distinguishing the Meaning."

the Lord your God and serve (λατρεύω) him only" (Matt 4:10; Luke 4:8). As Karen H. Jobes observes: "Here Jesus prescribes both submission to God's authority and the performance of religious duties devoted to him."[32]

Paul, on the other hand, is the only New Testament author to use the synonymous expression κάμπτω τὸ γόνυ, "bow the knee" (Eph 3:14; Rom 11:4; 14:11; Phil 2:10). In each case the words connote service and obedience. That both Romans' references appear in quotations of the Septuagint (1 Kgs 19:18 and Isa 45:23, respectively) point to the probable source. That the words occur in Ephesians shows that according to the book itself worship necessarily implied submission to an authority.

Thus it is clear that both idol worship and worship of the true God involve service and obedience. Little evidence, however, may be adduced that accuses the greedy of such a relationship to their wealth. *Testament of Judah* 8.6 indicates that the love of money is "contrary to God's commands" and "enslaves" a person. Furthermore, as we saw in chapter 8, much material indicates that the greedy disobey God in ignoring social justice and oppressing the poor. The notion of sin as a ruling power was certainly not out of place in the ancient world, in both pagan moral philosophy and Jewish moral teaching,[33] the main New Testament texts being John 8:30-36 and Romans 6. To accuse the greedy of serving and obeying their wealth would amount to a bold personification of wealth. For this reason the lack of evidence for the rich obeying their riches should not be taken as decisive.

To sum up our findings: in mapping the metaphor greed as idolatry profiles of the greedy and idolaters may be said to overlap unambiguously in terms of love and devotion and confidence and trust, and probably, if less obviously, with service and obedience.

Comparing the Metaphor

Another way of seeking validation for the three metaphorical interpretations of "greed is idolatry" is to inquire after the interpretation of analogous expressions. In part 2 we discovered four clear places in which greed was in some sense compared to idolatry: in Job, Philo, Matthew, and Luke.

---

32. Ibid., 188.
33. See Röhser, *Metaphorik und Personifikation*, 104-11.

In each case the context helps in the task of interpretation, more so than can be said for the expression in Colossians and Ephesians.[34] Is the comparison between greed and idolatry in these texts in terms of trust, love, or obedience?

In Job 31:24-28 Job indicates that to put confidence and trust in wealth is to be "unfaithful to God" (31:28), a charge that also applies to idolatry (31:26-27). Philo, on the other hand, consistently condemns greed as idolatrous in terms of inordinate and inappropriate love and devotion (see chapter 5 above). When we turn to the mammon saying in Matthew 6:24 and Luke 16:13, we may glean support for all three metaphorical senses.

Matthew 6:24 gives clear support to the idea that mammon (money, property, possessions, wealth) calls for both service and obedience and love and devotion, with the term δουλεύειν supporting the former sense and ἀγαπάω and ἀντέχομαι the latter.[35] Indeed, wealth is presented as God's rival for the human heart.[36] However, that the verse also implies a negative judgment on trusting in wealth is suggested by the verses that v. 24 effectively introduces, 6:25-34, which point to the birds and lilies in order to inspire trust in God's providential care, and by the likely etymology of μαμωνᾶς, which probably comes from a *maqtal* form of the root אמן with the meaning, "that in which one puts trust," with "money and riches" as the derivative meaning.[37] Thus in Matthew 6:19-34 we find sup-

---

34. For example, Davies and Allison, *Matthew,* 1:625, give the section 6:19-34 the heading "God and Mammon." The two masters are set alongside the two eyes (6:22-23) and the two treasures (6:19-21), all three of which introduce the priority of seeking the kingdom instead of worrying about material things (6:25-34).

35. On the notion of service and obedience cf. ibid., 1:642: "Mammon, once it has its hooks in human flesh, will drag it where it wills"; and Hagner, *Matthew,* 1:160: "Only the rarest of individuals can possess much of this world's wealth without becoming enslaved to it." That "devotion" here probably also implies trust is suggested by the appearance of ἀντέχεσθαι with δουλεύειν and ἀγαπᾶν in Jer 8:2 and with ζητεῖν in Zeph 1:6, where it means "to look to for support and help" (Schmidt, *Hostility to Wealth,* 127; cf. Isa 57:13; 1 Thess 5:14; Titus 1:9).

36. Cf. Percy, *Botschaft Jesu,* 91: "either one serves God or mammon, either one sets one's heart on God or on mammon."

37. Fitzmyer, *Luke,* 2:1109; for other etymologies see Hauck, "μαμωνᾶς," 390. Even if the etymology of μαμωνᾶς has little bearing on the meaning of the word in Matthew, where it means wealth, it supplies indirect evidence for the notion that people put too much trust in their possessions.

port for all three senses of idolatry. In this sense 6:24 is the point at which the passage finds its unifying focus.

In Luke the mammon saying, as part of 16:10-13, applies the lessons of the parable of the unjust steward (16:1-9). It is identical to Matthew 6:24 except for the addition of οἰκέτης, which makes even more explicit that everyone has a master. Thus as in Matthew 6:24 love and service are implied. Furthermore, some commentators suggest that the etymological connection of μαμωνᾶς with trust is alluded to and used for a play on words with πιστός and πιστεύω in 16:11. And in 16:14-15 the Pharisees, who are effectually charged with the idolatry of serving mammon rather than God, are accused of being "lovers of money" and of exalting that which is an abomination, βδέλυγμα, a word used of idolatry in the LXX (cf., e.g., Deut 7:25-26; 1 Kgs 14:24; Ezra 9:11; Isa 44:19; see also Mark 13:14; Matt 24:15; Rom 2:22).

Thus the teaching of Matthew 16:19-34 and Luke 16:1-15 can be seen as expanding on the warning not to serve mammon by loving, trusting, and obeying wealth instead of God, and demonstrating that all three demands may be implied in a comparison of greed with idolatry.

EXCURSUS 2:
Idolatrous Greed as Implicit Religion

In terms of contemporary evaluation and application, the biblical judgment that greed is idolatry raises a host of theological, economic, sociological, cultural, and practical issues. While the focus of this book has been firmly on the relationship between greed and idolatry in the ancient world, a brief look at its possible relevance to the modern world is only fitting.

Since the 1980s sociologists have begun to investigate phenomena that have often, but by no means exclusively, been described as implicit religion.[38] These include sport, politics, nationalism, complementary therapies, health, fitness and dietary regimes, various philosophies of life, and organizations such as Alcoholics Anonymous, Scientology, and Transcendental Meditation. This diverse grouping, it is thought, have in common that they either express the idea of something that is rather like but not

---

38. See especially the works of Bailey, "Implicit Religion of Contemporary Society"; *Implicit Religion: An Introduction; Implicit Religion in Contemporary Society;* and the international journal, *Implicit Religion,* which he edits.

quite like religion, or while they may not appear to be religion on the surface, they reveal themselves to be so on closer inspection.

Accepting the biblical worldview expounded in this study, greed, and the related modern system of thought and behavior, materialism, would seem to be a worthy candidate for consideration and investigation under the rubric of implicit religion. Before suggesting ways in which greed might be construed as a religion in the modern world, we must address the question of definition and classification. The ideas, beliefs, and practices listed above differ in important respects. This suggests that "implicit religion" may be too inclusive a definition to be heuristically helpful.

Whereas all of the phenomena in question resemble religion to some extent, albeit differently, not all of them have a religious self-understanding and few if any could be said to be "objectively religious." Malcolm Hamilton has surveyed the various labels in current use in this broad field of sociological inquiry and suggests the following typology that takes into account such differences.[39] For those cases that are not objectively religion, he offers three subcategories: (1) "secularised religion" describes those groups that bear a clear resemblance to religion and that also perceive themselves to be religious, but, defining religion strictly, they do not qualify as objectively religious (e.g., some mainstream churches that do not believe in God as a supreme being with supernatural power); (2) "pseudo-religion" refers to groups that are not objectively religious but present themselves as being religious unambiguously (e.g., Alcoholics Anonymous); (3) "quasi-religion" describes ostensibly nonreligious phenomena that resemble or share certain characteristics of religion (e.g., sport). All three might be called implicit religion, but the distinctions seem to be valid. If secularized religion resembles religion and understands itself as such, pseudo-religion has a religious self-understanding but does not resemble religion, and quasi-religion merely resembles religion in certain ways.[40]

On this reckoning the biblical charge that greed is idolatry would best be understood as an assertion that greed is a quasi-religion. There is no suggestion that the greedy have a religious self-understanding, but rather simply that greed substantially resembles religion. This opens up the possibility of undertaking an exercise in practical theology and suggesting

---

39. Hamilton, "Implicit Religion."

40. Other terms that have been proposed for the varying shades of implicit religion include invisible religion, surrogate religion, para-religion, and novel religion.

where the similarities between greed and religion today might lie. The following comments are merely provisional soundings designed to underscore the potential for more serious and rigorous reflection with the aid of sociological tools and expertise.

Secular commentators in fact regularly point to the "religious" role that money and possessions play in many people's lives in the West today. Two articles in *The Times* demonstrate this point. Alexander Frean writes: "Bereft of employment security and increasingly detached from traditional faith in religion, people appear to have elevated material objects . . . virtually to objects of faith"; and Dorothy Rowe asserts: "Even if we achieve what the world is pleased to acknowledge as success, we discover that the seizing of it fails to satisfy the hunger of our spiritual expectation."[41] In Australia stories in the *Sydney Morning Herald* about materialism allude to the religious role of money in their headlines: "In greed we trust" (instead of "In God we trust"); and "A city obsessed — Through its worship of land and buildings, Sydney has found the stories that tell us who we are and what matters in life." The *Sydney Morning Herald* review of the best-selling book, *Rich Dad, Poor Dad: What the Rich Teach Their Kids about Money That the Poor and Middle Class Do Not,* by Robert Kiyosaki, commented wryly: "*Rich Dad* isn't just a wealth creation manual, it's a religious tract. . . . Kiyosaki has created a cosmology of fiscal winners and sinners. Its economic evangelism culminates in a misquoting of St Paul's admonition to Timothy: 'The lack of money is the root of all evil.' Blessed are the rich; they won't inherit the kingdom because they've got it right now, and the poor can go to hell."[42] Another example is an obituary for high-profile stockbroker Rene Rivkin, which speaks of his "once-loyal entourage of supporters who worshipped their high priest at the altar of wealth."[43]

In popular culture, songs by the band Extreme and the artist Shania Twain draw on traditional religious categories to satirize greed. The lyrics from Extreme's song "Money (In God We Trust)," off their 1990 album *Pornograffiti,* which opens with the sounds of "bed time" and recounts a child's prayers, contain numerous religious allusions: "Hallelujah — Now I lay me down to sleep, Hallelujah — almighty dollar, I praise the Lord. Afford my roll to keep. Hallelujah — almighty dollar." The chorus chants:

---

41. See, respectively, September 5, 1997, p. 11; September 1, 1997, p. 34.
42. November 17-18, 2001, "Spectrum," p. 2.
43. Ian Verrender, "Pity the Poor Man," *The Sydney Morning Herald,* May 3, 2005, p. 8.

"Money, my personal savior. Money, material lust. Money, life's only treasure. Money, in God we trust." On her 2002 *Up!* album, which sold over ten million copies, Shania Twain's "Ka-Ching" laments the religious fervor of the consumerism of the Western world: "We've created us a credit card mess. We spend the money that we don't possess. Our religion is to go and blow it all."

The task of comparing greed and religion is complicated by the fact that the latter is notoriously difficult to define. It is possible to define religion in psychological terms, stressing the notion of the holy or the sacred, and people's response to it. Alternatively, the functions of religion can be taken as critical, such as the quest to make sense of the ultimate problems of life and human existence and the attempt to integrate people into social units or communities of faith. A more popular approach notices elements common to all religions, including belief systems, rituals, symbols, and ceremonies. However, no matter how religion is defined, whether using the disciplines of psychology, sociology, phenomenology, or theology, a good case can be made for seeing considerable resemblances between greed and religion in the modern world.[44]

In Western society in general the economy could be said to have achieved what could be described as a status comparable to that of the sacred. Sociologist John Boli, in homiletical mode, in an essay entitled "The Economic Absorption of the Sacred," warns: "We must come to terms with the depth of the problem [of materialism]: We are dealing with a highly institutionalized economic religion . . . and many of the cultural underpinnings of that religion are, I believe, sacred to us all."[45]

To fill out the similarities with some imaginative license, it is thought that the economy, like God, is capable of supplying people's needs without limit. Also like God, the economy is fundamentally mysterious, unknowable, and intransigent. It has both great power and, despite the best managerial efforts of its associated "clergy," great danger. It is an inexhaustible well of good(s) and is credited with prolonging life, giving health, and enriching our lives. Money, in which we put our trust, and advertising, which we adore, are among its rituals. The economy also has its sacred symbols, which evoke undying loyalty, including company logos, product names, and credit cards.

44. Cf. Wuthnow, ed., *Rethinking Materialism.*
45. In ibid., 95.

170

Individuals in Western economies could also be conceived as conducting their lives primarily in terms of economic religiosity. The economy is the ultimate source of value and, as a religion, confers value on those who participate in it. As a religion, it supplies solutions to the basic puzzles of life and help in negotiating them. The meaning of a person's life is found in full participation in the economy, both as a producer and consumer. The purpose of life consists in the full development of the individual's economic potential and the pursuit of material progress and gain. As Boli explains: "Religion may help us save our souls, but it cannot help us to obtain the vast array of goodnesses, meanings and purposes that are preferred in the economic realm."[46]

For many people, arguably, the vivid and intense experiences once found in traditional religion have been replaced with money rituals, whether at work, on holidays, or shopping. The traditional center of the community, the city cathedral, finds its substitute in the huge, costly edifices with awe-inspiring architecture, which often include aesthetically pleasing internal spaces made of stone and glass — the shopping malls. More profoundly, as our study of the ancient comparison of greed with idolatry suggests, many people may implicitly love, trust, and serve their money and possessions in ways that traditional religion reserved for God.

The purpose of this short excursus has been to suggest fruitful lines of practical theological investigation that would be enhanced by an explicit partnership with the various disciplines of the social sciences, in particular, psychology and sociology.

46. Ibid., 113.

CHAPTER 11

Conclusions:
Final Debrief and a Look Ahead

The goal of this book has been to investigate the origin and meaning of the words "greed is idolatry," making a modest contribution along the way, I hope, to a biblical theology of both greed and idolatry and providing a case study in the interpretation of a biblical metaphor. In this final chapter I briefly summarize the main findings and explore a few of the implications for Christian ethics and theology.

Greed Is Idolatry

In order to understand the words "greed is idolatry," we must grasp idolatry as a concept, recognize the typical behaviors of the greedy and of idolaters, and investigate other comparisons of greed with idolatry. To equate greed with idolatry is a powerful means of condemning greed, since idolatry was the most serious of sins, being the distinguishing mark of those who do not know God (the gentiles), which elicited the most disdainful polemic, prompted the most extreme measures of avoidance, and evoked an expectation of frightening judgment from a God who demands exclusive worship and tolerates no rivals. It is in effect to charge that the greedy do not belong in the church.

Investigating the link between greed and idolatry also uncovered good

172

evidence that the frequently asserted view that ancient Judaism and early Christianity were similarly characterized, especially in polemics against the heathen, by hostility toward idolatry and sexual immorality is deficient.[1] Greed deserves to join this pair of vices to form an unholy triad that, according to Jews and Christians, are the distinguishing marks of those who do not know God.

What do the greedy, idolaters, and believers have in common? In each case they relate to their objects of worship in terms of love, trust, and obedience. Thus, at the risk of blunting the affective impact of the metaphor, "greed is idolatry" may be paraphrased as teaching that *to have a strong desire to acquire and keep for yourself more and more money and material things is an attack on God's exclusive rights to human love and devotion, trust and confidence, and service and obedience.*

But can three innocent words mean so much? Whether they signified this to their original author and hearers is of course impossible to say with certainty. However, that they could have legitimately been taken to involve one, two, or all three demands is clear from similar comparisons of greed with idolatry in Job and Philo, which involve misplaced trust and inordinate love, respectively, and especially in the mammon saying in Matthew and Luke that in context supports all three senses. The modern consensus found in biblical commentaries, which limits the meaning of the words to love and devotion, needs to be supplemented by Luther's focus on trust and Chrysostom's on obedience.

Is only greed idolatry? Other vices could conceivably be compared to idolatry, the two most commonly suggested being sexual immorality and pride. In biblical and Jewish tradition, however, sexual immorality is more readily conceived of as desecrating God's temple rather than worshiping elsewhere. Philo calls pride idolatry, although deification usually involves others rather than oneself in biblical thought.[2] More work on the concept of pride could well be fruitful in clarifying its status in relation to other sins.

That the equation of greed with idolatry is anticipated in biblical and Jewish tradition by much teaching on the dangers of wealth undermining faithfulness to God and that greed and idolatry overlap in numerous sig-

---

1. For example, Dunn, "Who Did Paul Think He Was?" 174, speaks of Paul's "characteristically Jewish hostility to idolatry and sexual licence."

2. The major exception is the antichrist theme of Daniel, 2 Thessalonians, and Revelation.

nificant ways indicate that, rather than being an ill-considered exaggeration, it sits comfortably in Christian theology and ethics.

Indeed, among the vices, greed arguably stakes a claim to being the best candidate for the label idolatry, since it is portrayed throughout Scripture and Jewish moral teaching as a potent and insidious rival to God that competes for the human heart. Not only do the many texts treated in parts 2 and 3 help us to understand Colossians 3:5 and Ephesians 5:5, but the reverse is also true. One can better grasp the meaning and significance of those texts that deal with the dangers of greed, such as Job 31:24-28 and Proverbs 30:7-9, when one fully appreciates the senses in which greed is idolatry.[3]

All in all, there is a good case to be made for a positive assessment of the Pauline comparison of greed with idolatry as a genuine and valuable insight in Christian theology and ethics. Chrysostom and Gregory of Nazianzus were right to label greed the second idolatry. Idolatry is a typical sin of the gentiles, a vain folly and an evil desire that leads to other sins and ought to be treated with the greatest vigilance since it evokes stern divine judgment. According to a range of texts in the Bible, so is greed. Idolatry involves trusting, loving, and serving gold and silver objects rather than the true and living God. So does greed.

The Fight against Greed

In the fight against greed there is no more effective weapon in Christian ethics than the recognition that greed is idolatry. If there was ever a time in the history of Christendom when greed needed condemning again, it is now. If greed was a major vice in the New Testament, it was treated extensively and repeatedly warned against in all earnestness by the church fathers and in the Middle Ages. In the Reformation greed had no better reputation, as we saw in the case of Martin Luther, who regularly prayed for help against the vice, a practice carried on by the Lutheran hymn writer Paul Gerhardt.[4] All of this contrasts starkly with greed's status today as ei-

---

3. It is intriguing that not only is greed idolatry, but according to Phil 4:18 the opposite of greed, generous giving, is the opposite of idolatry, namely, true worship.

4. Shortly before his death Gerhardt wrote a six-point *Testament,* the last point of which stresses the prayer against greed: "Flee greed as energetically as one flees hell" (cited in Erb, *Paul Gerhardt und seine Lieder*).

ther a public good or a triviality.[5] Greed has been whitewashed and is a forgotten sin.

Obviously any attempt to deal with the problem of greed in the modern world has to take account of the major differences between the economic systems today and those of New Testament times. To love, serve, and trust money meant something radically different then than it does now. Such a task, however, is beyond the scope of the present study.[6]

Nonetheless, it is possible to notice some general principles that apply in most conditions. To oppose greed it is instructive to observe how idolatry is typically opposed. Polemic involves both running down the opposition and protesting the corresponding superiority of the thing being commended. This can be seen in idol polemic that ridicules the idols, labeling their worship an ineffective folly, and that extols the Lord appropriately.

Such a strategy can be seen with greed when the futility of amassing wealth is underscored and, more subtly, when being rich toward God is presented as the attractive alternative. The latter is an abundant and neglected strand of teaching, the relevance of which to the fight against greed is often missed. In discussing Job 22:22-30 in chapter 4 above, I mentioned some of the main Old Testament examples of such material. In noncanonical Jewish moral teaching trust in and fear of God are sometimes contrasted with wealth and said to be valued more highly (cf. Sir 5:13; 40:18-26; Bar 3:16-17; *Pss. Sol.* 1.4-6; *T. Job* 15.7-9; cf. Sir 10:23-24). For example, in Pseudo-Phocylides 53-54 the motivation for not "priding oneself in riches" is the existence of the "only God . . . [who is] rich in blessings."

The promise of true riches both now and in the age to come is also offered often in the New Testament, frequently in the context of and as a comfort for financial loss. In 1 Corinthians 6:9-11 Paul encourages Christians to suffer being defrauded (6:7-8) with the promise of inheriting God's kingdom.[7] In 2 Corinthians 8:9 Paul reminds the Corinthians of their becoming rich through Christ's poverty in part to undergird his plea for their involvement in the collection for the poor in Jerusalem. In

5. Cf. Volf, "In the Cage of Vanities," 172, who has observed: "cultural acceptance, even encouragement, of insatiability is unique to modernity. . . . The inactive virus of insatiability broke out with capitalism in a general epidemic." It is probably fair to say that even though greed remains a vice in most people's minds, it has been devalued.

6. See my *How to Get Really Rich* (2nd ed.: *Beyond Greed*).

7. See my "Origin and Meaning."

Philippians 4:19 the Christians are promised blessing "according to God's glorious riches in Christ Jesus" in return for their financial contribution to Paul's support. By asserting that godliness with contentment brings great spiritual rather than material gain (πορισμός), 1 Timothy 6:5-6 turns the tables on the false teachers who are looking to get rich (πορισμός) through religion. The rich in 1 Timothy 6:18-19 are to be "rich in noble actions" by giving generously, thereby acquiring "a treasure that will form a good foundation for the future." Likewise in Revelation 3:17-18, Mark 10:29-30, and Hebrews 10:34, spiritual prosperity is contrasted with and is to be preferred to financial prosperity.

The same notion of true riches is underscored by Clement of Alexandria. He emphasizes the now-familiar themes of the generous sharing of possessions and the futility of riches:

Ὁ μὲν ἄρα ἀληθῶς καὶ καλῶς πλούσιός ἐστιν ὁ τῶν ἀρετῶν πλούσιος καὶ πάσῃ τύχῃ χρῆσθαι ὁσίως καὶ πιστῶς δυνάμενος, ὁ δὲ νόθος πλούσιος ὁ κατὰ σάρκα πλουτῶν καὶ τὴν ζωὴν εἰς τὴν ἔξω κτῆσιν μετενηνοχὼς τὴν παρερχομένην καὶ φθειρομένην καὶ ἄλλοτε ἄλλου γινομένην καὶ ἐν τῷ τέλει μηδενὸς μηδαμῇ.

The man who is truly and nobly rich, then, is he who is rich in virtues and able to use every fortune in a holy and faithful manner; but the spurious rich man is he who is rich according to the flesh, and has changed his life into outward possessions which are passing away and perishing, belonging now to one, now to another, and in the end to no one at all.[8]

The people of God who are told to "come out" of doomed Babylon with all her riches in Revelation 18:4 are given a vision of the new Jerusalem in the following chapters that more than compensates. If Babylon's wealth is to fall, the new Jerusalem's is eternal and incorruptible, "having the glory of God, its radiance like a most rare jewel, like a jasper, clear as crystal." Significantly, the description of the city in 21:18-21 recalls Ezekiel's dirge over Tyre in Ezekiel 28:13, a passage to which Revelation 18 alludes in announcing the fall of Babylon. The βύσσινον (fine linen) that clothed "the great city" in 18:16 is eclipsed by the βύσσινον that adorns the Lamb's bride in 19:8. In Isaiah a repeated refrain celebrating the glory of the restored Je-

8. Clement of Alexandria, *Rich Man's Salvation* 19 (trans. Butterworth).

rusalem is the "wealth of the nations" (60:5; 60:11; 61:6; cf. 45:1).[9] The new Jerusalem's wealth far outweighs that which Revelation's readers are called to shun.[10]

If idolatrous greed is an evil desire, then according to the biblical and Jewish tradition such desire needs to be not only resisted but replaced by holy desire. The importance of replacing evil desires with holy ones was seen by Augustine, "let not these occupy my soul; rather let God occupy it."[11] Thus it is no accident that in Colossians 3 believers are not only to put earthly greed, which is idolatry, to death (3:5), but also and instead to seek (ζητέω) and set their minds on things above and not on things that are on the earth (3:1-2). Likewise in the context of the mammon saying in Matthew 6 the teaching against greed is introduced with the injunction to lay up treasures not on earth but in heaven (6:19), and closes with the call to seek (ζητέω) first God's kingdom and righteousness (6:33) instead of the material things that the gentiles seek (ἐπιζητέω; 6:32). In 1 Timothy 6:10-11 it is not enough just to run away from greed; the person of God is also to run after something: the way to flee (φεύγω) the love of money is to pursue (διώκω) godly virtues.

Along with noticing that greed can replace God, we ought also to ask what sort of God can replace greed. Which conception of God is called on when the prophets assert the Lord's superiority and incomparability over against the idols? Isaiah stresses that the Lord alone is the creator and redeemer. The polemic against the idols in Isaiah 44, for example, opens with the words, "This is what the Lord says — Israel's King and Redeemer" (44:6a), and closes with the exhortation: "Remember these things, O Jacob, for you are my servant, O Israel. I have made you, you are my servant; O Is-

---

9. In Isa 60 the gates of the city remain open because of the constant stream of wealth from the nations into the city, including gold, silver, and frankincense. Cf. Tob 13:16-17, "The gates of Jerusalem will be built with sapphire and emerald, and all your walls with precious stones. The towers of Jerusalem will be built with gold, and their battlements with pure gold. The streets of Jerusalem will be paved with ruby and with stones of Ophir." Rev 21:21 is a remarkably close parallel. Robert M. Royalty's survey of wealth imagery in ancient Jewish literature, *Streets of Heaven*, chapter 2, concludes that Revelation's portrayal of an opulent new Jerusalem stands in a tradition not only with Isaiah and Tobit but also with 5QNJ, which describes the main street passing through the middle of the city as "paved with white stone . . . marble and jasper."

10. As Royalty, *Streets of Heaven*, 4, puts it: "Babylon's merchants and sea captains trade in the same luxury goods that adorn the heavenly armies and the New Jerusalem."

11. Augustine, *Confessions* 10.51.

rael, I will not forget you. I have swept away your offenses like a cloud, your sins like the morning mist. Return to me, for I have redeemed you" (44:21-22).[12] Werner H. Schmidt observes that the goal in such passages in Isaiah and Hosea is to elicit trust and confidence in the Lord.[13] The implicit message is that the people are to trust God their creator and love God their redeemer rather than idols. In Deuteronomy 6 and 8 a third dimension is introduced, where God the lawgiver is to be obeyed rather than the foreign gods.

If the way one conceives of idolatry says something about who God is, then the love, trust and obedience senses of idolatrous greed presuppose different conceptions of God. In combating greed it is thus helpful to ponder God as the Creator and Provider to be trusted instead of wealth (the very strategy employed in Matt 6:25-33), the Savior and Redeemer to be loved, and the Ruler and Lawgiver to be obeyed. Such positive teaching should not be ignored in moral discourse and preaching that seeks to deal effectively with the vice and is precisely the strategy employed by the prophets in their polemic against the idols. The recognition that greed is idolatry shows that the root cause of greed is not psychological, economic, cultural, or societal, but rather theological. People are greedy because they ignore the Creator, forget the Redeemer, and spurn the Ruler of the world.

Finally, the alternatives to the grasping and hoarding aspects of greed, contentment and giving, respectively, need to be modeled and promoted.

Idolatry and the Knowledge of God

Nothing is more fundamental to Old and New Testament religion than the rejection of idolatry. Hence it is disappointing that modern Christian theology and preaching have not explored the contemporary significance of the concept more thoroughly and put it to use more often.[14] While most

---

12. Cf. Isa 43:10-11; 44:6, 24; 45:5-18; 46:9; cf. Hos 13:4; see Schmidt, *Zehn Gebote*, 44-47.

13. Schmidt, *Zehn Gebote*, 47.

14. By way of contrast, several modern Jewish philosophers and theologians have given serious attention to different forms of idolatry, including the worship of the state, persons, and isms of various kinds. Cf. Jacobs, *Jewish Religion*, 264; and Halbertal and Margalit, *Idolatry*, 242-50, who in their discussion of modern discourse on idolatry treat, among others, the works of Bacon, Marx, Wittgenstein, and Hume. On idolatry in modern theology see the section on "The Concept of Idolatry" in chapter 9.

modern Christians are not tempted literally to worship idols, at least in the West, the biblical and early Jewish material covered in the present study lays a foundation for the recovery of the concept based on the example of Jesus and Paul. Understood narrowly, idolatry has little significance to the modern world. Taken broadly, however, that powerful and disturbing accusation is relevant whenever and wherever the exclusive rights of God are transgressed.

If doing theology is to speak about God, then properly undertaken all theological inquiry should lead and contribute to our knowledge of God. To base a biblical doctrine of God only on the names and attributes of God, or even on the acts of God in salvation history, as is often the case, is unacceptably narrow. The fundamental question of theology, what do we mean by "God," can be answered from a variety of angles by exploring God's various relations to the world and to ourselves. Ironically, the study of idolatry affords us some insight into the nature of the true and living God. Thus the narrow focus of the present study, the origin and meaning of a Pauline metaphor, may at this point be broadened out to answer the most fundamental question of all: the identity of God.

If greed is idolatry, then what constitutes a god?[15] Luther's answer, reflecting on the first commandment in his Larger Catechism, was: "whatever your heart clings to and relies upon, that is your God; trust and faith of the heart alone make both God and idol." My findings confirm his view, but wish also to supplement his emphasis on trust in two respects: *a god is that which one trusts, loves and obeys above all else.* This definition suggests both the possibility and urgency of making clear the relevance of idolatry to the modern world.

---

15. Put differently, we could also ask, if greed is idolatry, what constitutes worship? Our findings support a broad definition that includes the elements of love, trust, and obedience.

Bibliography

꧁ꕥ꧂

Primary Sources

Ante-Nicene Christian Library: Translations of the Writings of the Fathers down to A.D. 325. Ed. A. Roberts and J. Donaldson. 24 vols. Edinburgh: T. & T. Clark, 1867-1872.

The Apostolic Fathers. Text and Translation. Trans. Kirsopp Lake. LCL. 2 vols. Cambridge: Harvard University Press, 1912-1913.

Apostolic Fathers. Trans. J. B. Lightfoot and J. R. Harmer. Ed. and rev. Michael W. Holmes. 2nd ed. Grand Rapids: Baker, 1989.

Baillet, M., et al. *Discoveries in the Judaean Desert.* Vols. 1-. Oxford: Clarendon, 1955-.

Basil the Great. *Letters and Select Works.* Trans. with notes by Blomfield Jackson. NPNF 2/8. 1894. Repr. Grand Rapids: Eerdmans, 1983.

Berger, Klaus, ed. *Die Weisheitsschrift aus der Kairoer Geniza: Erstedition, Kommentar und Übersetzung.* Texte und Arbeiten zum neutestamentlichen Zeitalter 1. Tübingen: Francke, 1989.

Biblia Hebraica Stuttgartensia. Ed. K. Elliger and W. Rudolph. Stuttgart: Deutsche Bibelgesellschaft, 1977.

Biblia Patristica. Index des citations et allusions bibliques dans la littérature patristique. 3 vols. Paris: Centre d'analyse et de documentation patristiques, 1975-1981.

Blackman, Philip, ed. *Mishnayoth.* 7 vols. New York: Judaica Press, 1964.

Bibliography

Cathcart, Kevin J., and Robert P. Gordon. *The Targum of the Minor Prophets.* ArBib 14. Edinburgh: T. & T. Clark, 1989.

Charlesworth, James H., ed. *The Old Testament Pseudepigrapha.* 2 vols. Garden City, NY: Doubleday, 1983-1985.

Chrysostom, John. *Homilies on Galatians, Ephesians, Philippians, Colossians, Thessalonians, Timothy, Titus, and Philemon.* Ed. Philip Schaff. NPNF 1/13. Repr. Grand Rapids: Eerdmans, 1979.

Clement of Alexandria. *The Exhortation to the Greeks, The Rich Man's Salvation and To the Newly Baptised.* Trans. G. W. Butterworth. LCL. Cambridge: Harvard University Press, 1919.

Danby, Herbert, trans. *The Mishnah.* Oxford: Oxford University Press, 1933.

de Jonge, M. *The Testaments of the Twelve Patriarchs: A Critical Edition of the Greek Text.* PVTG 1/2. Leiden: Brill, 1978.

Epstein, Isadore, ed. *Hebrew-English Edition of the Babylonian Talmud.* 20 vols. London: Soncino, 1972-1984.

Finkelstein, Louis, ed. *Sifre on Deuteronomy.* New York: Jewish Theological Seminary of America, 1969.

Freedman, H., and M. Simon. *Midrash Rabbah.* 10 vols. London: Soncino, 1939.

García Martínez, Florentino. *The Dead Sea Scrolls Translated: The Qumran Texts in English.* Trans. Wilfred G. E. Watson. 2nd ed. Grand Rapids: Eerdmans, 1996.

Gregory of Nyssa. *Homilies on Ecclesiastes: An English Version with Supporting Studies. Proceedings of the Seventh International Colloquium on Gregory of Nyssa; St. Andrews, 5-10 September 1990.* Ed. Stuart George Hall. Berlin: de Gruyter, 1993.

Heilmann, Alfons, ed. *Texte der Kirchenväter: Eine Auswahl nach Themen geordnet.* Vol. 1. Munich: Kösel, 1963.

Holl, K., ed. *Die griechischen christlichen Schriftsteller.* Leipzig: J. C. Hinrichs, 1922.

Horst, P. W. van der. *The Sentences of Pseudo-Phocylides with Introduction and Commentary.* SVTP 4. Leiden: Brill, 1978.

Josephus. Trans. H. St. J. Thackeray et al. LCL. Cambridge: Harvard University Press, 1926-1965.

Knibb, Michael A. *The Book of Enoch: A New Edition in the Light of the Aramaic Dead Sea Fragments.* 2 vols. Oxford: Clarendon, 1978.

Lauterbach, Jacob Z., ed. *Mekilta de-Rabbi Ishmael.* 3 vols. Philadelphia: Jewish Publication Society of America, 1933-1935.

Metzger, Bruce M., ed. *The Apocrypha of the Old Testament: Revised Standard Version.* Oxford Annotated Apocrypha. New York: Oxford University Press, 1977.

Migne, J.-P., ed. *Patrologia cursus completus: Series graeca.* 162 vols. Paris: Garnier, 1857-1891.

Migne, J.-P., ed. *Patrologia cursus completus: Series latina.* 221 vols. Paris: Garnier, 1844-1864.

Nestle, Eberhard, et al., eds. *Novum Testamentum Graece.* 27th ed. Stuttgart: Deutsche Bibelstiftung, 1995.

Origen. *Die griechisch erhaltene Jeremiahomilien.* Ed. Erwin Schadel. Bibliothek der griechischen Literatur 10. Stuttgart: Anton Hiersemann, 1980.

Origenes Werke, vol. 3: *Jeremiahomilien, Klageliederkommentar, Erklärung der Samuel- und Königsbücher.* Die griechischen christlichen Schriftsteller der ersten drei Jahrhunderte. Leipzig: Hinrichs'sche Buchhandlung, 1901.

Philo. Trans. F. H. Colson et al. LCL. Cambridge: Harvard University Press, 1929-1953.

Rahlfs, Alfred, ed. *Septuaginta: Id est Vetus Testamentum graece iuxta LXX interpretes.* 2 vols. in 1. Stuttgart: Deutsche Bibelgesellschaft, 1935.

Rüger, Hans Peter, ed. *Die Weisheitschrift aus der Keiroer Geniza: Übersetzung und philologischer Kommentar.* WUNT 53. Tübingen: Mohr-Siebeck, 1991.

Sifre: A Tannaitic Commentary on the Book of Deuteronomy. Trans. R. Hammer. New Haven: Yale University Press, 1986.

Sparks, H. F. D., ed. *The Apocryphal Old Testament.* Oxford: Clarendon, 1984.

Sperber, Alexander, ed. *The Bible in Aramaic: Based on Old Manuscripts and Printed Texts.* 4 vols. Leiden: Brill, 1959-1968.

Tacitus. *The Histories.* Trans. Clifford H. Moore. 2 vols. LCL. Cambridge: Harvard University Press, 1937-1943.

Talmud Yerushalmi. 1866. Repr. Jerusalem: Shiloh, 1967.

Targum Neofiti 1: Exodus. Trans., with introduction and apparatus by Martin McNamara and notes by Robert Hayward. *Targum Pseudo-Jonathan: Exodus.* Trans., with notes by Michael Maher. ArBib 2. Collegeville, MN: Liturgical Press, 1994.

The Targum Onqelos to Deuteronomy. ArBib 9. Trans., with Apparatus, and Notes by Bernard Grossfeld. Wilmington, DE: Michael Glazier, 1988.

The Targums of Onkelos and Jonathan ben Uzziel on the Pentateuch with the Fragments of the Jerusalem Targum; From the Chaldee. Trans. J. W. Etheridge. New York: Ktav, 1968.

Tertullian. *De idololatria.* Critical Text, Translation and Commentary by J. H. Waszink and J. C. M. van Winden. Vigiliae christianae Sup 1. Leiden: Brill, 1987.

Ulrich von Pottenstein. *Dekalog-Auslegung: Text und Quellen.* Vol. 1. Ed. Gabriele Baptist-Hlawatsch. Tübingen: Niemeyer, 1995.

Ziegler, Joseph, et al. *Septuaginta: Vetus Testamentum Graecum Auctoritate Academiae Scientiarum Gottingensis editum.* Göttingen: Vandenhoeck & Ruprecht, 1931-.

Bibliography

Secondary Sources: Works Cited

Aaron, David H. *Biblical Ambiguities: Metaphor, Semantics and Divine Imagery.* Brill Reference Library of Ancient Judaism 4. Leiden: Brill, 2001.

Achenbach, Reinhard. *Israel zwischen Verheissung und Gebot: Literarkritische Untersuchungen zu Deuteronomium 5–11.* EH 23. Frankfurt am Main: Peter Lang, 1991.

Assmann, Hugo, and Franz J. Hinkelammert. *Götze Markt.* Trans. Horst Goldstein. Düsseldorf: Patmos, 1989.

Bailey, E. I. *Implicit Religion: An Introduction.* Middlesex: Middlesex University Press, 1998.

Bailey, E. I. *Implicit Religion in Contemporary Society.* Leuven: Peeters, 2001.

Bailey, E. I. "The Implicit Religion of Contemporary Society: An Orientation and Plea for Its Study." *Religion* 13 (1983): 69-83.

Barclay, John M. G. *Jews in the Mediterranean Diaspora: From Alexander to Trajan (323 BCE–117 CE).* Edinburgh: T & T Clark, 1996.

Barclay, John M. G. "Ordinary but Different: Colossians and Hidden Moral Identity." *Australian Biblical Review* 49 (2001): 34-52.

Barnes, Albert. *Notes, Explanatory and Practical, on the Epistles of Paul to the Ephesians, Philippians, and Colossians.* New York: Harper Brothers, 1845.

Barr, James. *The Semantics of Biblical Language.* New York: Oxford University Press, 1961.

Barrett, C. K. *A Commentary on the Epistle to the Romans.* London: A. and C. Black, 1957.

Barth, Karl. *Der Römerbrief.* 5th ed. Zurich: Evangelischer Verlag, 1954.

Barth, Markus. *Ephesians: Translation and Commentary on Chapters 4–6.* AB 34A. Garden City, NY: Doubleday, 1974.

Barth, Markus, and Helmut Blanke. *Colossians: A New Translation and Commentary.* Trans. Astrid B. Beck. AB 34B. Garden City, NY: Doubleday, 1994.

Bauckham, Richard. *The Climax of Prophecy: Studies on the Book of Revelation.* Edinburgh: T & T Clark, 1993.

Bauckham, Richard. *The Theology of the Book of Revelation.* New Testament Theology. Cambridge: Cambridge University Press, 1993.

Baumgarten-Crusius, L. F. O. *Commentar über den Brief Pauli an die Epheser und Kolosser.* Jena: Friedrich Mauke, 1847.

Beasley-Murray, G. R. *The Book of Revelation.* NCBC. Grand Rapids: Eerdmans, 1981.

Becker, Jürgen. *Paulus: Der Apostel der Völker.* Tübingen: Mohr, 1992.

Becker, Jürgen, Hans Conzelmann, and Gerhard Friedrich. *Die Briefe an die Galater, Epheser, Philipper, Kolosser, Thessalonicher und Philemon.* 15th ed. NTD 8. Göttingen: Vandenhoeck & Ruprecht, 1981.

183

Beentjes, Pancratius C. "'You have given a road in the sea': What Is Wisdom 14,3 Talking About?" *Ephemerides theologicae lovanienses* 68 (1992): 137-41.

Berger, Klaus. *Die Gesetzauslegung Jesu: Ihr historischer Hintergrund im Judentum und im Alten Testament.* Part 1: *Markus und Parallelen.* WMANT 40. Neukirchen-Vluyn: Neukirchener Verlag, 1972.

Berger, Klaus. *Theologischegeschichte des Urchristentums: Theologie des Neuen Testaments.* Tübingen: Francke, 1994.

Bickerman, Elias J. *The Jews in the Greek Age.* Cambridge: Harvard University Press, 1988.

Bieder, Werner. *Der Kolosserbrief.* Zurich: Zwingli, 1943.

Black, M. "More about Metaphor." In *Metaphor and Thought.* Ed. A. Ortony. Cambridge: Cambridge University Press, 1993. Pp. 19-41.

Bockmuehl, Markus. *The Epistle to the Philippians,* 14th edition. London: A. and C. Black, 1997.

Bockmuehl, M. N. A. *Epistle to the Philippians.* Black's New Testament Commentary. Peabody, MA: Hendrickson, 1998.

Bockmühl, Klaus. *Christliche Lebensführung: Eine Ethik der Zehn Gebote.* Giessen: Brunnen, 1993.

Bockmühl, Klaus. *Gesetz und Geist: Eine kritische Würdigung des Erbes protestantischer Ethik.* Vol. 1: *Die Ethik der reformatorischen Bekenntnisschriften.* Giessen: Brunnen, 1987.

Bonhoeffer, Dietrich. *Nachfolge.* Ed. Martin Kuske and Ilse Tödt. Werke 4. Munich: Chr. Kaiser, 1989.

Booth, A. "The Art of Reclining and Its Attendant Perils." In *Dining in a Classical Context.* Ed. W. J. Slater. Ann Arbor: University of Michigan Press, 1991.

Borgen, Peder. "Catalogues of Vices, the Apostolic Decree, and the Jerusalem Meeting." In *The Social World of Formative Christianity and Judaism: Essays in Tribute to Howard Clark Kee.* Ed. Jacob Neusner, Peder Borgen, Ernest S. Frerichs, and Richard Horsley. Philadelphia: Fortress, 1988. Pp. 126-41.

Borgen, Peder. *Early Christianity and Hellenistic Judaism.* Edinburgh: T. & T. Clark, 1996.

Bori, Pier Cesare. *The Golden Calf and the Origins of the Anti-Jewish Controversy.* South Florida Studies in the History of Judaism 16. Atlanta: Scholars Press, 1990.

Bradley, Ian. *The Book of Hymns.* Woodstock, NY: Overlook, 1989.

Braune, Karl. "Epistle of Paul to the Ephesians." Trans., with additions by M. B. Riddle. In *Commentary on the Holy Scripture.* Vol. 11: *Galatians–Hebrews.* Ed. John Peter Lange. Trans. and ed. Philip Schaff. Edinburgh: T. & T. Clark, 1871.

Brock, Sebastian. "The Two Ways and the Palestinian Targum." In *A Tribute to Geza Vermes: Essays on Jewish and Christian Literary History.* Ed. Philip R. Davies and Richard T. White. JSOTSup 100. Sheffield: Sheffield Academic Press, 1990. Pp. 139-52.

Bibliography

Brooks, Roger. *The Spirit of the Ten Commandments: Shattering the Myth of Rabbinic Legalism*. New York: Harper & Row, 1990.

Brown, Lesley, ed. *The New Shorter Oxford English Dictionary*. 3rd ed. 2 vols. Oxford: Clarendon, 1993.

Brown, Raymond. *The Epistles of John*. AB 30. Garden City, NY: Doubleday, 1983.

Bruce, F. F. *1 + 2 Thessalonians*. WBC 45. Waco: Word, 1982.

Bruce, F. F. *The Epistles to the Colossians, to Philemon, and to the Ephesians*. NICNT. Grand Rapids: Eerdmans, 1984.

Bruce, F. F. "Review of *Die Tugend- und Lasterkataloge im Neuen Testament* by Siegfried Wibbing." *JTS* 11 (1960): 389-91.

Caird, G. B. *Paul's Letters from Prison*. Clarendon Bible. Oxford: Oxford University Press, 1976.

Calvin, John. *Commentaries on the Epistles of Paul to the Galatians and Ephesians*. Repr. Grand Rapids: Eerdmans, 1948.

Calvin, John. *The Institutes of the Christian Religion*. Trans. Ford Lewis Battles. Ed. John T. McNeill. 2 vols. Library of Christian Classics 20-21. Philadelphia: Westminster, 1960.

Calvin, John. *The Sermons of John Calvin upon the Fifth Book of Moses Called Deuteronomy*. London: Henry Middleton, 1583.

Calvin, John. *Sermons on the Epistle to the Ephesians*. Edinburgh: Banner of Truth, 1973.

Carpenter, H. J. "Popular Christianity and the Theologians in the Early Centuries." *JTS* 14/2 (1963): 294-310.

Carson, Herbert M. *The Epistles of Paul to the Colossians and Philemon: An Introduction and Commentary*. TNTC. Grand Rapids: Eerdmans, 1960.

Ceresko, Anthony R. *Job 29–31 in the Light of Northwest Semitic: A Translation and Philological Commentary*. BibOr 36. Rome: Biblical Institute Press, 1980.

Chesnutt, Randall D. *From Death to Life: Conversion in Joseph and Asenath*. JSPSup 16. Sheffield: Sheffield Academic Press, 1995.

Childs, Brevard. *Exodus: A Commentary*. OTL. Philadelphia: Westminster, 1974.

Choi, Deok-Soon. "Economic Aspects of the Fall of Babylon/Rome in Rev. 18:1-19:8." Unpublished M.Th. diss., University of Aberdeen, 1998.

Ciampa, Roy E. *The Presence and Function of Scripture in Galatians 1 and 2*. WUNT 102. Tübingen: Mohr Siebeck, 1998.

Clark, Gordon H. *Ephesians*. Jefferson, MD: Trinity Foundation, 1985.

Clarkson, David. *The Practical Works*. 3 vols. Edinburgh: Banner of Truth, 1988.

Clifford, Richard. "Idol." *Harper's Bible Dictionary*. Ed. Paul J. Achtemeier. San Francisco: Harper & Row, 1985. Pp. 416-18.

Collins, John J. "Review of Hans Peter Rüger, *Die Weisheitsschrift aus der Kairoer Geniza*." *JBL* 111 (1992): 705-7.

Comfort, P. W. "Idolatry." *DPL*, 424-26.

Conzelmann, Hans. "Der Brief an die Epheser." In Jürgen Becker, Hans Conzelmann, and Gerhard Friedrich, *Die Briefe an die Galater, Epheser, Philipper, Kolosser, Thessalonicher und Philemon*. 15th ed. NTD 8. Göttingen: Vandenhoeck & Ruprecht, 1981.

Conzelmann, Hans. "Korinth und die Mädchen der Aphrodite: Zur Religionsgeschichte der Stadt Korinth." In *Theologie als Schriftauslegung*. BEvT 65. Munich: Kaiser, 1974. Pp. 152-66.

Countryman, L. William. *Dirt, Greed, and Sex: Sexual Ethics in the New Testament and Their Implications for Today*. Philadelphia: Fortress, 1988.

Cranfield, C. E. B. "Riches and the Kingdom of God: St. Mark 10.17-31." *SJT* 4/3 (1951): 302-12.

Cranfield, C. E. B. *Romans*. 2 vols. ICC. Edinburgh: T. & T. Clark, 1975-1979.

Crouch, James E. *The Origin and Intention of the Colossian Haustafel*. FRLANT 109. Göttingen: Vandenhoeck & Ruprecht, 1972.

Curtis, Edward M. "Idol, Idolatry." *ABD*, 3:376-81.

Dabelstein, R. *Die Beurteilung der "Heiden" bei Paulus*. BBET 14. Frankfurt am Main: Lang, 1981.

Dahood, Mitchell. *Psalms I: 1–50*. AB 16. Garden City, NY: Doubleday, 1965.

Daillé, Jean. *An Exposition of the Epistle of Saint Paul to the Colossians*. Trans. F. S. Repr. Minneapolis: Klock & Klock, 1983.

Daillé, Jean. *Sermons upon the Whole Epistle of St. Paul to the Colossians*. Trans. F. S. London: Parkhurst, 1672.

Dautzenberg, Gerhard. "Biblische Perspektiven zum Problemfeld Eigentum und Reichtum." In *Handbuch der Christlichen Ethik*. Vol. 2. Ed. Anselm Hertz et al. Freiburg: Herder, 1993. Pp. 353-62.

Dautzenberg, Gerhard. "Φεύγετε τὴν πορνείαν (1 Kor 6,18): Eine Fallstudie zur paulinischen Sexualethik in ihrem Verhältnis zur Sexualethik des Frühjudentums." In *Neues Testament und Ethik: Für Rudolf Schnackenburg*. Ed. Helmut Merklein. Freiburg: Herder, 1989. Pp. 271-98.

Davies, Philip R. *The Damascus Covenant: An Interpretation of the "Damascus Document."* JSOTSup 25. Sheffield: JSOT Press, 1983.

Davies, W. D., and Dale C. Allison. *A Critical and Exegetical Commentary on the Gospel according to Saint Matthew*. 3 vols. ICC. Edinburgh: T. & T. Clark, 1988-1997.

de Wette, W. M. L. *Kurze Erklärung der Briefe an die Colosser, an Philemon, an die Epheser und Philipper*. Leipzig: Weidmann'sche Buchhandlung, 1847.

Delling, G. "πλεονέκτης." *TDNT*, 6:266-74.

Dexinger, F. "Der Dekalog im Judentum." *Bibel und Liturgie* 59 (1986): 86-95.

Dibelius, Martin. *An die Kolosser, Epheser, an Philemon*. HNT 12. Tübingen: Mohr (Siebeck), 1953.

Dickens, Charles. *A Christmas Carol*. Oxford: Oxford University Press, 1988.

Dunn, James D. G. *The Epistles to the Colossians and to Philemon.* NIGTC. Grand Rapids: Eerdmans, 1996.

Dunn, James D. G. "Judaism in the Land of Israel in the First Century." In *Judaism in Late Antiquity.* Part 2: *Historical Syntheses.* Ed. Jacob Neusner. Leiden: Brill, 1995. Pp. 229-61.

Dunn, James D. G. *Romans.* 2 vols. WBC 38A-B. Dallas: Word, 1988.

Dunn, James D. G. "Who Did Paul Think He Was? A Study of Jewish-Christian Identity." *NTS* 45 (1999): 174-93.

Easton, Burton Scott. "New Testament Ethical Lists." *JBL* 51 (1932): 1-12.

Eaton, J. H. *Job.* OTG. Sheffield: JSOT Press, 1985.

Edwards, C. *The Politics of Immorality in Ancient Rome.* Cambridge: Cambridge University Press, 1993.

Eichrodt, Walther. *Theology of the Old Testament.* Trans. J. A. Baker. 2 vols. OTL. Philadelphia: Westminster, 1961-1967.

Eidevall, Göran. *Grapes in the Desert: Metaphors, Models, and Themes in Hosea 4–14.* ConBOT 43. Stockholm: Almqvist & Wiksell, 1996.

Ellicott, Charles J. *A Critical and Grammatical Commentary on the Epistles of Saint Paul.* Vol. 1: *Galatians, Ephesians, 1 Thessalonians and 2 Thessalonians.* 1855. Repr. Buffalo: William S. Hein, 1986.

Ellul, Jacques. *Money and Power.* Trans. LaVonne Neff. Downers Grove, IL: InterVarsity Press, 1979.

Epstein, L. M. *Sex Laws and Customs in Judaism.* New York: Ktav, 1948.

Erb, Jörg. *Paul Gerhardt und seine Lieder.* Lahr: St.-Johannis-Druckerei, 1974.

Ernst, Josef. *Die Briefe an die Philipper, an Philemon, an die Kolosser, an die Epheser.* Regensburger Neues Testament. Regensburg: Pustet, 1974.

Faur, José. "The Biblical Idea of Idolatry." *JQR* 69 (1978): 1-15.

Fauth, W. "Sakrale Prostitution im Vorderen Orient und im Mittelmeerraum." *JAC* 31 (1988): 24-39.

Fee, Gordon D. *Paul's Letter to the Philippians.* NICNT. Grand Rapids: Eerdmans, 1995.

Feldman, Louis H. *Jew and Gentile in the Ancient World: Attitudes and Interactions from Alexander to Justinian.* Princeton: Princeton University Press, 1993.

Fitzmyer, J. A. *The Gospel according to Luke.* 2 vols. AB 28-28A. Garden City, NY: Doubleday, 1981-1985.

Floss, J. P. *Jahwe dienen, Göttern dienen. Terminologische, literarische und semantische Untersuchung einer theologischen Aussage zum Gottesverhältnis im Alten Testament.* BBB 45. Köln: Hanstein, 1975.

Flusser, David. "The Parable of the Unjust Steward: Jesus' Criticism of the Essenes." In *Jesus and the Dead Sea Scrolls.* Ed. James H. Charlesworth. New York: Doubleday, 1992. Pp. 176-97.

Fohrer, Georg. *Studien zum Buche Hiob (1956-1979)*. 2nd ed. Beihefte zur Zeitschrift für die alttestamentliche Wissenschaft 159. Berlin: de Gruyter, 1983.

Foulkes, Francis. *The Epistle to the Ephesians*. TNTC. Grand Rapids: Eerdmans, 1963.

France, R. T. "God and Mammon." *TynBul* 51 (1979): 3-21.

Frank, K. S. "Habsucht." *RAC*, 13:226-47.

Frankfort, Henri. *Kingship and the Gods*. Chicago: University of Chicago Press, 1948.

Frankfort, Henri, H. A. Frankfort, John A. Wilson, and Thorkild Jacobsen. *Before Philosophy: The Intellectual Adventure of Ancient Man*. 1946. Repr. Baltimore: Penguin, 1973.

Gaster, Theodore. "Mythic Thought in the Ancient Near East." *Journal of the History of Ideas* 16 (1955): 422-66.

Gerhardsson, Birger. *The Shema in the New Testament: Deut 6:4-5 in Significant Passages*. Lund: Novapress, 1996.

Gerhart, Mary, and Allan Melvin Russell. *Metaphoric Process: The Creation of Scientific and Religious Understanding*. Fort Worth: Texas Christian University Press, 1984.

Gestrich, Christof. *The Return of Splendor in the World: The Christian Doctrine of Sin and Forgiveness*. Trans. Daniel W. Bloesch. Grand Rapids: Eerdmans, 1997.

Gnilka, Joachim. *Der Epheserbrief*. HTKNT 10/1. Freiburg: Herder, 1971.

Gnilka, Joachim. *Der Kolosserbrief*. HTKNT 10/2. Freiburg: Herder, 1980.

Godet, Frederic. *Commentary on St. Paul's Epistle to the Romans*. Trans. A. Cusia. 2 vols. Edinburgh: T. & T. Clark, 1881-1883.

Goldenberg, Robert. "The Septuagint Ban on Cursing the Gods." *JSJ* 28/4 (1997): 381-89.

Gonzalez, Justo L. *Faith and Wealth: A History of Early Christian Ideas on the Origin, Significance, and Use of Money*. San Francisco: Harper & Row, 1990.

Goodfriend, E. A. "Prostitution." *ABD*, 5:509ff.

Gordis, Robert. *The Book of Job: Commentary, New Translation and Special Studies*. New York: Jewish Theological Seminary of America, 1978.

Gray, J. "Idolatry." *IDB*, 2:675-78.

Greenberg, Moshe. *Ezekiel: A New Translation with Introduction and Commentary*. 2 vols. AB 22-22A. Garden City, NY: Doubleday, 1983-1997.

Griffith, Terry Michael. "'Little children, keep yourselves from idols' (1 John 5:21): The Form and Function of the Ending of the First Epistle of John." Unpublished Ph.D. thesis, King's College, University of London, 1996.

Gundry, R. H. *Matthew: A Commentary on His Literary and Theological Art*. Grand Rapids: Eerdmans, 1982.

Habel, Norman C. *The Book of Job*. CBC. Cambridge: Cambridge University Press, 1975.

Hafemann, Scott J. "Paul and His Interpreters." *DPL*, 666-79.

Hafemann, Scott J. *Paul, Moses, and the History of Israel: The Letter/Spirit Contrast and the Argument from Scripture in 2 Corinthians 3.* WUNT 81. Tübingen: Mohr (Siebeck), 1995.

Hagner, Donald A. *Matthew.* 2 vols. WBC 33A-B. Dallas: Word, 1993-1995.

Hahn, M. Ph. Matthäus. *Erbauungsreden über den Brief Pauli an die Kolosser.* Stuttgart: J. G. Sprandel, 1845.

Halbertal, Moshe, and Avishai Margalit. *Idolatry.* Trans. Naomi Goldblum. Cambridge: Harvard University Press, 1992.

Hamilton, Malcolm. "Implicit Religion and Related Concepts: Seeking Precision." *Implicit Religion* 4/1 (2001): 5-13.

Hanson, Anthony Tyrrell. *Studies in Paul's Technique and Theology.* Grand Rapids: Eerdmans, 1974.

Harless, Gottlieb Christoph Adolph von. *Commentar über den Brief Pauli an die Epheser.* Erlangen: Carl Heyder, 1834.

Harrington, D. J. "Paul the Jew." *Catholic World* 235 (1992): 68-73.

Harris, Murray J. *Colossians and Philemon.* Grand Rapids: Eerdmans, 1991.

Hartley, John E. *The Book of Job.* NICOT. Grand Rapids: Eerdmans, 1988.

Hartman, Lars. "Code and Context: A Few Reflections on the Parenesis of Colossians 3:6–4:1." In *Tradition and Interpretation in the New Testament: Essays in Honor of E. Earle Ellis for His 60th Birthday.* Ed. Gerald F. Hawthorne with Otto Betz. Grand Rapids: Eerdmans, 1987. Pp. 236-47.

Hauck, F. "μαμωνᾶς." *TDNT*, 4:388-90.

Hauck, F., and W. Kasch. "πλοῦτος, κτλ." *TDNT*, 6:318-32.

Hausmann, Jutta. *Studien zum Menschenbild der älteren Weisheit (Spr 10ff).* FAT 7. Tübingen: Mohr, 1995.

Hawthorne, Gerald F. *Philippians.* WBC 43. Dallas: Word, 1983.

Hays, Richard B. *The Moral Vision of the New Testament: A Contemporary Introduction to New Testament Ethics.* Edinburgh: T. & T. Clark, 1997.

Heckel, Ulrich. "Das Bild der Heiden und die Identität der Christen bei Paulus." In *Die Heiden: Juden, Christen und das Problem des Fremden.* Ed. Reinhard Feldmeier and Ulrich Heckel. Tübingen: Mohr (Siebeck), 1994. Pp. 269-96.

Hellerman, Joseph H. "Wealth and Sacrifice in Early Christianity: Revisiting Mark's Presentation of Jesus' Encounter with the Rich Young Ruler." *Trinity Journal* 21 (2000): 143-64.

Hengel, Martin. *Property and Riches in the Early Church.* Trans. John Bowden. Philadelphia: Fortress, 1974.

Hengel, Martin. *The Pre-Christian Paul.* Trans. John Bowden. Philadelphia: Trinity Press International, 1991.

Hengel, Martin. "Die Septuaginta als 'christlicher Schriftsammlung,' ihre Vorgeschichte und das Problem ihres Kanons." In *Die Septuaginta zwischen Judentum und Christentum.* Ed. Martin Hengel and Anna Maria Schwemer. Tübingen: Mohr (Siebeck), 1994. Pp. 182-284.

Héring, Jean. *1 Corinthians.* Trans. A. W. Heathcote and P. J. Allcock. London: Epworth, 1962.

Herter, Hans. "Die Soziologie der Antiken Prostitution im Licht des heidnischen und christlichen Schriftums." *JAC* 3 (1960): 72-73.

Hollander, H. W., and M. de Jonge. *The Testaments of the Twelve Pariarchs: A Commentary.* SVTP 8. Leiden: Brill, 1985.

Holtz, Traugott. *Der erste Brief an die Thessalonicher.* EKK 13. Zurich: Benziger, 1986.

Hooker, Morna. "Paul — Apostle to the Gentiles." *Epworth Review* 18/2 (1991): 79-89.

Hopkins, Ezekiel. *Works.* Vol. 1. London: L. B. Seeley, 1809.

Hoppe, Rudolf. *Epheserbrief, Kolosserbrief.* Stuttgarter kleiner Kommentar 10. Stuttgart: Katholisches Bibelwerk, 1987.

Horst, Pieter W. van der. "Mammon, μαμωνᾶς." In *Dictionary of Deities and Demons in the Bible.* Ed. Karel van der Toorn, Bob Becking, and Pieter W. van der Horst. 2nd ed. Grand Rapids: Eerdmans, 1999. Pp. 542-43.

Horst, Pieter W. van der. "'Thou Shalt Not Revile the Gods': The LXX Translation of Ex. 22:28 (27), Its Background and Influence." *Studia Philonica Annual* 5 (1993): 1-8.

Huther, Joh. Ed. *Kommentar über den Brief Pauli an die Colosser.* Hamburg: Johann August Meissner, 1841.

Ireland, D. J. *Stewardship and the Kingdom of God: An Historical, Exegetical, and Contextual Study of the Parable of the Unjust Steward in Luke 16:1-13.* NovTSup 50. Leiden: Brill, 1992.

Jacobs, Louis. *The Jewish Religion: A Companion.* Oxford: Oxford University Press, 1995.

Jobes, Karen H. "Distinguishing the Meaning of Greek Verbs in the Semantic Domain for Worship." *Filologia Neotestamentaria* 4 (1991): 183-92.

Johnson, Luke T. *Faith's Freedom: A Classic Spirituality for Contemporary Christians.* Minneapolis: Fortress, 1990.

Jüngel, Eberhard. "Gewinn im Himmel und auf Erden: Theologische Bemerkungen zum Streben nach Gewinn." *Zeitschrift für Theologie und Kirche* 94/4 (1997): 532-52.

Kamlah, Ehrhard. *Die Form der katalogischen Paränese im Neuen Testament.* WUNT 7. Tübingen: Mohr (Siebeck), 1964.

Käsemann, Ernst. *Commentary on Romans.* Grand Rapids: Eerdmans, 1980.

Kaufmann, Stephen. "The Structure of Deuteronomic Law." *Maarav* 1/2 (1978): 105-58.

Kidd, Reggie M. *Wealth and Beneficence in the Pastoral Epistles: A "Bourgeois" Form of Early Christianity?* SBLDS 122. Atlanta: Scholars Press, 1990.

Kittay, Eva Fedder. *Metaphor: Its Cognitive Force and Linguistic Structure*. Oxford: Clarendon, 1987.

Klöpper, Albert. *Der Brief an die Kolosser*. Berlin: G. Reimer, 1882.

Knight, Douglas A. "Idols, Idolatry." In *The Oxford Companion to the Bible*. Ed. Bruce M. Metzger and Michael D. Coogan. New York: Oxford University Press, 1993. Pp. 297-98.

Koch, Traugott. *Zehn Gebote für die Freiheit: Eine kleine Ethik*. Tübingen: Mohr, 1995.

Koenig, John. *New Testament Hospitality*. OBT. Philadelphia: Fortress, 1985.

Kraftchick, Steven J. "A Necessary Detour: Paul's Metaphorical Understanding of the Philippian Hymn." *Horizons in Biblical Theology* 15/1 (1993): 1-37.

Kuhn, K. G. "The Epistle to the Ephesians in the Light of the Qumran Texts." In *Paul and Qumran*. Ed. J. Murphy O'Connor. London: Geoffrey Chapman, 1968. Pp. 115-31.

Kümmel, Werner. "Die älteste Form des Aposteldekrets." In *Heilsgeschehen und Geschichte*. Vol. 1: *Gesamelte Aufsätze, 1933-64*. Marburg: Elwert, 1965. Pp. 278-88.

Laato, Timo. *Paulus und das Judentum: Anthropologische Erwägungen*. Abo: Akademis Förlag, 1991.

Lake, Kirsopp, and Henry J. Cadbury, eds. *Additional Notes and Commentary*. Vol. 5 of *The Beginnings of Christianity*, part 1: *The Acts of the Apostles*. Ed. F. J. Foakes Jackson and Kirsopp Lake. 5 vols. Repr. Grand Rapids: Baker, 1966.

Lakoff, G., and M. Johnson. *Metaphors We Live By*. Chicago: Chicago University Press, 1980.

Lansing, Richard, ed. *The Dante Encyclopedia*. New York: Garland, 2000.

Lenski, R. C. H. *Interpretation of St. Paul's Epistles to the Colossians, to the Thessalonians, to Timothy, to Titus and to Philemon*. Columbus, OH: Wartburg Press, 1937.

Léon-Dufour, Xavier. *Dictionary of the New Testament*. Trans. Terence Prendergast. New York: Harper & Row, 1980.

Lichtenberger, Hermann. "'Im Lande Israel zu wohnen wiegt alle Gebote der Tora auf': Die Heiligkeit des Landes und die Heiligung des Lebens." In *Die Heiden: Juden, Christen und das Problem des Fremden*. Ed. Reinhard Feldmeier and Ulrich Heckel. Tübingen: Mohr (Siebeck), 1994. Pp. 92-107.

Lieu, Judith M. *Image and Reality: The Jews in the World of the Christians in the Second Century*. Edinburgh: T. & T. Clark, 1996.

Lightfoot, J. B. *Saint Paul's Epistles to the Colossians and to Philemon: A Revised Text with Introductions, Notes, and Dissertations*. London: Macmillan, 1904.

Lillie, W. "The Pauline House-Tables." *ExpTim* 86 (1974/75): 179-83.

Lincoln, Andrew T. *Ephesians*. WBC 42. Dallas: Word, 1990.

Lindemann, Andreas. *Der Epheserbrief*. Zürcher Bibelkommentare. Zurich: Theologischer Verlag, 1985.

Lloyd-Jones, D. M. *Darkness and Light: An Exposition of Ephesians 4:17–5:17.* Edinburgh: Banner of Truth, 1982.

Lock, John. *A Paraphrase and Notes on the Epistles of St. Paul to the Galatians, Romans, Corinthians, and Ephesians.* London: John Churchill, 1709.

Lohfink, Norbert. *Das Hauptgebot.* Analecta biblica 20. Rome: Biblical Institute Press, 1963.

Lohmeyer, Ernst. *Die Brief an die Philipper, Kolosser und an Philemon.* KEK 9. Göttingen: Vandenhoeck & Ruprecht, 1964.

Lohse, Eduard. *Colossians and Philemon.* Trnas. William R. Poehlmann and Robert J. Karris. Philadelphia: Fortress, 1971.

Louw, Johannes P., and Eugene A. Nida. *Greek-English Lexicon of the New Testament Based on Semantic Domains.* 2 vols. New York: United Bible Societies, 1988.

Lovejoy, A. O. *Essays in the History of Ideas.* New York: G. P. Putnam's Sons, 1948.

Lugt, Pieter van der. *Rhetorical Criticism and the Poetry of the Book of Job.* Oudtestamentische Studiën 32. Leiden: Brill, 1995.

Luther, Martin. *D. Martin Luthers Werke: Kritische Gesamtausgabe.* 93 vols. Weimar: Bohlau, 1883-1990.

Lyman, Stanford M. *The Seven Deadly Sins: Society and Evil.* Rev. ed. New York: General Hall, 1989.

Macky, Peter. *The Centrality of Metaphors to Biblical Thought.* Lewiston, NY: Edwin Mellen, 1990.

Maclaren, Alexander. *The Epistles of St. Paul to the Colossians and Philemon.* London: Hodder & Stoughton, 1909.

Maclean, H. B. "Omri, King." *IDB,* 3:600-601.

Malherbe, A. J. *Moral Exhortation: A Greco-Roman Sourcebook.* Philadelphia: Westminster, 1986.

Malherbe, A. J. *Social Aspects of Early Christianity.* Philadelphia: Fortress, 1983.

Malina, Bruce J. *The New Testament World: Insights from Cultural Anthropology.* Atlanta: John Knox, 1981.

Manton, Thomas. *The Complete Works.* London: James Nisbet, 1874.

Marshall, I. Howard. *1 and 2 Thessalonians.* NCBC. Grand Rapids: Eerdmans, 1983.

Marshall, I. H. *Acts.* TNTC. Grand Rapids: Eerdmans, 1980.

Martin, Ralph P. *Colossians: The Church's Lord and the Christian's Liberty: An Expository Commentary with a Present-Day Application.* Grand Rapids: Zondervan, 1973.

Marx, Karl. *Writings of the Young Marx on Philosophy and Society.* Trans. L. D. Easton and K. H. Cuddat. New York: Doubleday, 1967.

Matthies, Conr. Stephan. *Erklärung des Briefes Pauli an die Epheser.* Greifswald: C. A. Koch, 1834.

Mays, James Luther. *Psalms.* Interpretation. Louisville: John Knox, 1994.

McKane, William. *Proverbs: A New Approach.* OTL. Philadelphia: Westminster, 1970.

Merendino, R. P. "Die Zeugnisse, die Satzungen und die Rechte: Überlieferungsgeschichtliche Erwägungen zu Deut 6." In *Bausteine biblischer Theologie: Festgabe für G. Johannes Botterweck.* Ed. H.-J. Fabry. BBB 50. Bonn: Hanstein, 1977. Pp. 161-208.

Merk, Otto. *Handeln aus Glauben: Die Motivierungen der paulinischen Ethik.* Marburg: N. G. Elwert, 1986.

Moberly, R. W. *At the Mountain of God: Story and Theology in Exodus 32–34.* JSOTSup 22. Sheffield: JSOT Press, 1983.

Monk, W. H., and C. Steggall. *Hymns Ancient and Modern.* London: William Clowes and Sons, 1906.

Moo, Douglas J. *The Epistle to the Romans.* NICNT. Grand Rapids: Eerdmans, 1996.

Moritz, Thorsten. *A Profound Mystery: The Use of the Old Testament in Ephesians.* Leiden: Brill, 1996.

Morris, Leon. *The First Epistle to the Corinthians: An Introduction and Commentary.* TNTC. Grand Rapids: Eerdmans, 1969.

Moule, C. F. D. *An Idiom Book of New Testament Greek.* 2nd ed. Cambridge: Cambridge University Press, 1960.

Moxnes, Halvor. *The Economy of the Kingdom: Social Conflict and Economic Relations in Luke's Gospel.* OBT. Philadelphia: Fortress, 1988.

Müller, Christoph Gregor. *Gottes Pflanzung — Gottes Bau — Gottes Tempel: Die metaphorische Dimension paulinischer Gemeindetheologie in 1 Kor 3, 5-17.* Fuldaer Studien 5. Frankfurt am Main: Josef Knecht, 1995.

Murphy, Frederick J. "Retelling the Bible: Idolatry in Pseudo-Philo." *JBL* 107/2 (1988): 275-87.

Murphy-O'Connor, Jerome. *St. Paul's Corinth: Texts and Archaeology.* Wilmington, DE: Glazier, 1983.

Mussner, Franz. *Der Brief an die Epheser.* ÖTNT 10. Gütersloh: Gütersloher Verlagshaus — Gerd Mohn, 1982.

Nanos, Mark D. *The Mystery of Romans: The Jewish Context of Paul's Letter.* Minneapolis: Fortress, 1996.

Nebe, G. Wilhelm. *Text und Sprache der hebräischen Weisheitschrift aus der Kairoer Geniza.* Heidelberger orientalische Studien 25. Frankfurt am Main: Peter Lang, 1993.

Newhauser, Richard. *The Early History of Greed: The Sin of Avarice in Early Medieval Thought and Literature.* Cambridge Studies in Medieval Literature 41. Cambridge: Cambridge University Press, 2000.

Niebuhr, Karl-Wilhelm. *Gesetz und Paränese: Katechismusartige Weisungsreihen in der frühjüdischen Literatur.* WUNT 28. Tübingen: Mohr (Siebeck), 1987.

Niebuhr, Karl-Wilhelm. *Heidenapostel aus Israel: Die jüdische Identität des Paulus nach ihrer Darstellung in seinen Briefen.* WUNT 62. Tübingen: Mohr (Siebeck), 1992.

Niebuhr, Reinhold. *The Nature and Destiny of Man.* Vol. 1: *Human Nature.* New York: Scribner's, 1949.

Norris, Alfred. *The Ten Commandments in the Twentieth Century.* Lichfield: Tamarisk, 1988.

O'Brien, Peter T. *Colossians, Philemon.* WBC 44. Dallas: Word, 1982.

O'Brien, Peter T. *The Epistle to the Philippians: A Commentary on the Greek Text.* NIGTC. Grand Rapids: Eerdmans, 1991.

Olson, Dennis T. *Deuteronomy and the Death of Moses: A Theological Reading.* OBT. Minneapolis: Fortress, 1994.

Osborne, Grant R. *The Hermeneutical Spiral: A Comprehensive Introduction to Biblical Interpretation.* Downers Grove, IL: InterVarsity Press, 1991.

Owen, John. *Hebrews.* 7 vols. Repr. Edinburgh: Banner of Truth, 1979.

Percy, E. *Die Botschaft Jesu: Eine traditionskritische und exegetische Untersuchung.* Lund: Gleerup, 1953.

Plöger, Otto. *Sprüche Salomos.* BKAT 17. Neukirchen-Vluyn: Neukirchener Verlag, 1984.

Pokorný, Petr. *Der Brief des Paulus an die Epheser.* THKNT 10/2. Leipzig: Evangelische Verlagsanstalt, 1992.

Pokorný, Petr. *Der Brief des Paulus an die Kolosser.* THKNT 10/1. Leipzig: Evangelische Verlagsanstalt, 1987.

Polhill, John B. *Acts.* New American Commentary. Nashville: Broadman, 1992.

Provan, Iain W. *1 & 2 Kings.* OTG. Sheffield: Sheffield Academic Press, 1997.

Ragaz, Leonhard. *Die Gleichnisse Jesu: Seine soziale Botschaft.* Bern: H. Lang, 1944.

Ramanchandra, Vinoth. *Gods That Fail: Modern Idolatry and Christian Mission.* Downers Grove, IL: InterVarsity Press, 1996.

Reinmuth, Eckart. *Geist und Gesetz: Studien zu Voraussetzungen und Inhalt der paulinischen Paränese.* Theologische Arbeiten 44. Berlin: Evangelische Verlagsanstalt, 1985.

Rengstorf, K. H. "Die neutestamentlichen Mahnungen an die Frau, sich dem Manne unterzuordnen." In *Verbum Dei manet in Aeternum: Festschrift für O. Schmitz.* Ed. W. Foerster. Witten: Luther, 1953. Pp. 131-45.

Rengstorf, Karl Heinrich. "δοῦλος." *TDNT,* 2:261-80.

Richard, Pablo. "Unser Kampf richtet sich gegen die Götzen: Biblische Theologie." In Hugo Assmann et al., *Die Götzen der Unterdrückung und der befreiende Gott.* Trans. Antonio Reiser et al. Münster: Edition Liberacion, 1984.

Ricoeur, Paul. *Interpretation Theory: Discourse and the Surplus of Meaning.* Fort Worth: Texas Christian University Press, 1976.

Ricoeur, Paul. *The Rule of Metaphor: Multi-Disciplinary Studies in the Meaning of Language.* Toronto: University of Toronto Press, 1977.

Bibliography

Riesner, Rainer. *Die Frühzeit des Apostels Paulus: Studien zur Chronologie, Missionsstrategie und Theologie.* WUNT 71. Tübingen: Mohr (Siebeck), 1994.

Rieth, Ricardo. *"Habsucht" bei Martin Luther.* Arbeiten zur Kirchen- und Theologiegeschichte 1. Weimar: Böhlau, 1996.

Roberts, Richard. "The Beatitude of Giving and Receiving." *ExpTim* 48 (1936/37): 438-41.

Robertson, A. T. *A Grammar of the Greek New Testament in the Light of Historical Research.* 4th ed. Repr. Nashville: Broadman, 1934.

Robinson, J. Armitage. *St. Paul's Epistle to the Ephesians.* London: Macmillan, 1904.

Rogerson, J. W., and J. W. McKay. *Psalms 1–50.* CBC. Cambridge: Cambridge University Press, 1977.

Röhser, Günter. *Metaphorik und Personifikation der Sünde: Antike Sündenvorstellungen und paulinische Harmartia.* WUNT 2/25. Tübingen: Mohr (Siebeck), 1987.

Rosner, Brian S. "The Concept of Idolatry." *Themelios* 24/3 (1999): 28-32.

Rosner, Brian S. "Habsucht — Eine Vergessene Sünde." *Theologische Beiträge* 2 (2000): 75-81.

Rosner, Brian S. *How to Get Really Rich: A Sharp Look at the Religion of Greed.* Leicester: InterVarsity Press, 1999. (2nd ed.: *Beyond Greed.* Sydney: Matthias, 2004.)

Rosner, Brian S. "The Origin and Meaning of 1 Corinthians 6,9-11 in Context." *Biblische Zeitschrift* 40/2 (1996): 250-53.

Rosner, Brian S. *Paul, Scripture and Ethics: A Study of 1 Corinthians 5–7.* AGAJU 22. Leiden: Brill, 1994.

Rosner, Brian S. "Secret Idolatry." *Ex Auditu* 15 (2000): 73-86.

Rosner, Brian S. "Temple Prostitution in 1 Corinthians 6:12-20." *Novum Testamentum* 40/4 (1998): 336-51.

Rosner, Brian S. "'Written for Us': Paul's View of Scripture." In *A Pathway into the Holy Scripture.* Ed. Philip E. Satterthwaite and David F. Wright. Grand Rapids: Eerdmans, 1994. Pp. 81-105.

Rowland, Christopher. *Revelation.* London: Epworth, 1993.

Rowley, H. H. *The Book of Job.* NCBC. Grand Rapids: Eerdmans, 1980.

Royalty, Robert M. *The Streets of Heaven: The Ideology of Wealth in the Apocalypse of John.* Macon, GA: Mercer University Press, 1998.

Rückert, L. J. *Der Brief Pauli an die Epheser.* Leipzig: R. J. Köhler, 1834.

Rüger, Hans Peter. *Die Weisheitsschrift aus der Kairoer Geniza: Text, Übersetzung und philologischer Kommentar.* WUNT 53. Tübingen: Mohr (Siebeck), 1991.

Saffrey, H. D. "Aphrodite à Corinthe: Réflexions sur une idée reçue." *RB* 92 (1985): 359-74.

Sampley, J. Paul. "Scripture and Tradition in the Community as Seen in Eph 4,15ff." *ST* 26 (1972): 101-9.

Sandelin, Karl-Gustav. "The Danger of Idolatry According to Philo of Alexandria." *Temenos* 27 (1991): 109-50.

Sandnes, Karl Olav. *Belly and the Body in the Pauline Epistles.* SNTSMS 120. Cambridge: Cambridge University Press, 2002.

Sandnes, Karl Olav. *A New Family: Conversion and Ecclesiology in the Early Church with Cross-Cultural Comparisons.* Studien zur interkulturellen Geschichte des Christentums 91. Bern: Peter Lang, 1994.

Sandnes, Karl Olav. *Paul, One of the Prophets? A Contribution to the Apostle's Self-Understanding.* WUNT 2/43. Tübingen: Mohr (Siebeck), 1990.

Schimmel, Solomon. *The Seven Deadly Sins: Jewish, Christian, and Classical Reflections on Human Nature.* New York: Free Press, 1992.

Schlatter, Adolf. *Erläuterungen zum Neuen Testament.* Vol. 2: *Die Briefe des Paulus.* Stuttgart: Calwer, 1923.

Schlier, Heinrich. *Der Brief an die Epheser: Ein Kommentar.* Düsseldorf: Patmos, 1962.

Schmidt, Thomas E. *Hostility to Wealth in the Synoptic Gospels.* JSNTSup 15. Sheffield: JSOT Press, 1987.

Schmidt, Werner H. *Die Zehn Gebote im Rahmen alttestamentlicher Ethik.* Ertrag der Forschung 281. Darmstadt: Wissenschaftliche Buchgesellschaft, 1993.

Schmithals, Walter. *Paul and the Gnostics.* Trans. John E. Steely. Nashville: Abingdon, 1972.

Schnackenburg, Rudolf. *Der Brief an die Epheser.* EKK 10. Zurich: Denziger, 1982.

Schottroff, Luise. "Die Befreiung vom Götzendienst der Habgier." In *Wer ist unser Gott? Beiträge zu einer Befreiungstheologie im Kontext der "ersten" Welt.* Ed. Luise and Willy Schottroff. Munich: Chr. Kaiser, 1986. Pp. 137-52.

Schrage, Wolfgang. "Zur Ethik der neutestamentlichen Haustafeln." *NTS* 21 (1975): 1-22.

Schroeder, D. "Die Haustafeln des NT: Ihre Herkunft und ihr theologischer Sinn." Ph.D. thesis, Hamburg, 1959.

Schroeder, D. "Lists, Ethical." *IDBSup,* 546-47.

Schürer, Emil. *The History of the Jewish People in the Age of Jesus Christ* (175 B.C.– A.D. 135). Rev. and ed. Geza Vermes, Fergus Millar, and Matthew Black. Vol 2. Edinburgh: T. & T. Clark, 1979.

Schweizer, Eduard. *The Letter to the Colossians.* Trans. Andrew Chester. Minneapolis: Augsburg, 1982.

Schweizer, Eduard. "Traditional Ethical Patterns in the Pauline and Post-Pauline Letters and Their Development (Lists of Vices and House-tables)." In *Text and Interpretation: Studies in the New Testament Presented to Matthew Black.* Ed. Ernest Best and R. McL. Wilson. Cambridge: Cambridge University Press, 1979. Pp. 195-209.

Schweizer, Eduard. "Die Weltlichkeit des Neuen Testaments: Die Haustafeln." In

Bibliography

Beiträge zur alttestamentlichen Theologie: Festschrift für Walther Zimmerli zum 70. Geburtstag. Ed. H. Donner, R. Hanhart, and R. Smend. Göttingen: Vandenhoeck & Ruprecht, 1977. Pp. 397-413.

Scott, James M. *Paul and the Nations: The Old Testament and Jewish Background of Paul's Mission to the Nations with Special Reference to the Destination of Galatians.* WUNT 84. Tübingen: Mohr (Siebeck), 1995.

Scott, R. B. Y. *Proverbs, Ecclesiastes.* AB 18. Garden City, NY: Doubleday, 1965.

Seccombe, D. P. *Possessions and the Poor in Luke-Acts.* Freistadt: Linz, 1982.

Seifrid, Mark A. *Justification by Faith: The Origin and Development of a Central Pauline Theme.* Leiden: Brill, 1992.

Shepherd, J. W. *A Commentary on the New Testament Epistles.* Vol. 4: *Ephesians, Philippians, and Colossians.* Repr. Nashville: Gospel Advocate, 1976.

Siegert, F. "Gottesfürchtige und Sympathisanten." *JSJ* 4 (1973): 109-64.

Simeon, Charles. *The Entire Works.* Vol. 17: *Galatians–Ephesians.* London: Henry G. Bohn, 1847.

Skehan, P. W. "The Structure of the Song of Moses in Deuteronomy." *CBQ* 13 (1951): 159-70.

Smolar, Leivy, and Moshe Aberbach. "The Golden Calf Episode in Post-Biblical Literature." *HUCA* 39 (1970): 91-116.

Sölle, Dorothee. "Sünde und Entfremdung." In *Die Theologie des 20. Jahrhunderts: Ein Lesebuch.* Ed. Karl-Josef Kuschel. Munich: Piper, 1986. Pp. 333-44.

Soskice, Janet Martin. *Metaphor and Religious Language.* Oxford: Clarendon, 1985.

Soskice, Janet Martin. "Metaphor." In *A Dictionary of Biblical Interpretation.* Ed. R. J. Coggins and J. L. Houlden. Philadelphia: Trinity Press International, 1990. P. 447.

Spicq, Ceslas. "πλεονεξία, pleonexia." *Theological Lexicon of the New Testament.* Trans. J. D. Ernest. 3 vols. Peabody, MA: Hendrickson, 1994. 3:117-19.

Stamm, J. J., and M. E. Andrew. *The Ten Commandments in Recent Research.* SBT 2/2. London: SCM, 1967.

Stegner, W. R. "A Jewish Paul." *Asbury Theological Journal* 47/1 (1992): 89-95.

Stenschke, C. *Luke's Portrait of Gentiles Prior to Their Coming to Faith.* WUNT 2.108. Tübingen: Mohr (Siebeck), 1999.

Stuhlmacher, Peter. "Christliche Verantwortung bei Paulus und seinen Schülern." *EvT* 28 (1968): 165-86.

Stuhlmacher, Peter. *Biblische Theologie des Neuen Testaments.* Vol. 1: *Grundlegung: Vom Jesus zu Paulus.* Göttingen: Vandenhoeck & Ruprecht, 1992.

Sweet, John. *Revelation.* Pelican. London: SCM, 1979.

Tachau, Peter. *"Einst" und "Jetzt" im Neuen Testament: Beobachtungen zu einem urchristlichen Predigtschema in der neutestamentlichen Briefliteratur und zu seiner Vorgeschichte.* FRLANT 105. Göttingen: Vandenhoeck & Ruprecht, 1972.

Tauberschmidt, G. "The MT and the LXX Compared." Unpublished M.Phil. thesis, Aberdeen, 1997.

Thielman, Frank. *From Plight to Solution: A Jewish Framework for Understanding Paul's View of the Law in Galatians and Romans.* NovTSup 61. Leiden: Brill, 1989.

Thomas, Johannes. *Der jüdische Phokylides: Formgeschichtliche Zugänge zu Pseudo-Phokylides und Vergleich mit der neutestamentlichen Paränese.* Göttingen: Vandenhoeck & Ruprecht, 1992.

Thompson, G. H. P. *The Letters of Paul to the Ephesians, to the Colossians and to Philemon.* Cambridge: Cambridge University Press, 1967.

Tod, D. MacRae. "Avarice." *Encyclopaedia of Religion and Ethics.* Ed. James Hastings. 13 vols. New York: Scribner, 1924-1927. Vol. 2:261-62.

Tomson, Peter J. *Paul and the Jewish Law: Halakha in the Letters of the Apostle to the Gentiles.* CRINT 3/1. Minneapolis: Fortress, 1990.

Toorn, Karel van der. "Prostitution (Cultic)." *ABD,* 5:510-13.

Tow, S. H., ed. *Revival Hymns and Choruses.* Singapore: Bible Presbyterian Banner.

Tscho, Kyong Tscheol. "Die Ethischen Weisungen und ihre theologische Begründung im Epheserbrief." Unpublished Ph.D. thesis, Evangelisch-theologische Fakultät, Eberhard-Karls-Universität, Tübingen, 1991.

Turner, Nigel. *Syntax.* Vol. 3 of James Hope Moulton, *A Grammar of New Testament Greek.* Edinburgh: T. & T. Clark, 1963.

Tur-Sinai, N. H. *The Book of Job: A New Commentary.* Rev. ed. Jerusalem: Kiryath Sepher, 1957.

Ulrichsen, Jarl Henning. *Die Grundschrift der Testamente der Zwölf Patriarchen: Eine Untersuchung zu Umfang, Inhalt und Eigenart der ursprünglichen Schrift.* Acta Universitatis Upsaliensis Historia religionum 10. Uppsala: Almqvist & Wiksell, 1991.

Van Leeuwen, Raymond. "On the Structure and Sense of Deuteronomy 8." *Proceedings of the Eastern Great Lakes Midwest Biblical Societies* 4 (1984): 237-49.

Vaughan, Curtis. "Colossians." In *The Expositor's Bible Commentary.* Vol. 11. *Ephesians–Philemon.* Ed. Frank E. Gaebelein. Grand Rapids: Zondervan, 1978. Pp. 161-226.

Vögtle, A. *Die Tugend- und Lasterkataloge im Neuen Testament: Exegetisch, religions- und formgeschichtlich untersucht.* NTAbh 16. Münster: Aschendorff, 1936.

Volf, Miroslav. "In the Cage of Vanities: Christian Faith and the Dynamics of Economic Progress." In *Rethinking Materialism.* Ed. Robert Wuthnow. Grand Rapids: Eerdmans, 1995. Pp. 169-91.

von Flatt, D. Johann Friedrich. *Vorlesungen über die Briefe Pauli an die Galater und Epheser.* Tübingen: Ludwig Friedrich Fues, 1828.

Walton, John H. "Deuteronomy: An Exposition of the Spirit of the Law." *Grace Theological Journal* 8/2 (1987): 213-25.

Wanamaker, Charles A. *The Epistles to the Thessalonians: A Commentary on the Greek Text.* NIGTC. Grand Rapids: Eerdmans, 1990.

Warne, Graham J. *Hebrew Perspectives on the Human Person in the Hellenistic Era: Philo and Paul.* Mellen Biblical Press 35. Lewiston, NY: Edwin Mellen, 1995.

Weinfeld, Moshe. "The Decalogue: Its Significance, Uniqueness, and Place in Israel's Tradition." In *Religion and Law: Biblical-Judaic and Islamic Perspectives.* Ed. Edwin B. Firmage, Bernard G. Weiss, and John W. Welch. Winona Lake, IN: Eisenbrauns, 1990. Pp. 3-47.

Weinfeld, Moshe. *Deuteronomy 1–11: A New Translation with Introduction and Commentary.* AB 5. New York: Doubleday, 1991.

Weinfeld, Moshe. *Deuteronomy and the Deuteronomic School.* Oxford: Clarendon, 1972.

Weinfeld, Moshe. "Instructions for Temple Visitors in the Bible and in Ancient Egypt." In *Egyptological Studies.* Ed. Sarah Israelit-Groll. Scripta hierosolymitana 28. Jerusalem: Hebrew University, 1982. Pp. 224-50.

Weinfeld, Moshe. "What Makes the Ten Commandments Different?" *Bible Review* 7/2 (1991): 35-41.

Wengst, Klaus. *Pax Romana and the Peace of Jesus Christ.* London: SCM, 1987.

Whybray, R. N. *Proverbs.* NCBC. Grand Rapids: Eerdmans, 1994.

Whybray, R. N. *Wealth and Poverty in the Book of Proverbs.* JSOTSup 99. Sheffield: JSOT Press, 1990.

Wibbing, Siegfried. *Die Tugend-und Lasterkataloge im Neuen Testament und ihre Traditionsgeschichte unter besonderer Berücksichtigung der Qumran-Texte.* BZNW 25. Berlin: Töpelmann, 1959.

Wilcken, Ulrich. *Des Brief an der Römer.* Vol. 3. EKK 6. Köln: Neukirchener, 1980.

Williams, David J. *Paul's Metaphors: Their Context and Character.* Peabody, MA: Hendrickson, 1999.

Wilson, Daniel. *Expository Lectures on Paul's Epistles to the Colossians.* London: J. Hatchard and Son, 1845.

Wilson, S. G. *Luke and the Law.* SNTSMS 50. Cambridge: Cambridge University Press, 1983.

Winter, Bruce. *Seek the Welfare of the City.* Grand Rapids: Eerdmans, 1994.

Witherington, Ben, III. *Conflict and Community in Corinth.* Grand Rapids: Eerdmans, 1995.

Wolter, Michael. *Der Brief an die Kolosser. Der Brief an Philemon.* ÖTNT 12. Gütersloh: Gütersloher Verlagshaus — Gerd Mohn, 1993.

Wright, N. T. *The Epistles of Paul to the Colossians and to Philemon: An Introduction and Commentary.* TNTC. Grand Rapids: Eerdmans, 1987.

Wright, N. T. *Jesus and the Victory of God.* Minneapolis: Fortress, 1996.

Wright, N. T. "Monotheism, Christology and Ethics: 1 Corinthians 8." In *Climax of* the Covenant: Christ and the Law in Pauline Theology. Minneapolis: Fortress, 1992. Pp. 120-36.

Wright, N. T. The New Testament and the People of God. Minneapolis: Fortress, 1992.

Wright, N. T. What Saint Paul Really Said: Was Paul of Tarsus the Real Founder of Christianity? Grand Rapids: Eerdmans, 1997.

Wuthnow, Robert, ed. Rethinking Materialism: Perspectives on the Spiritual Dimension of Economic Behavior. Grand Rapids: Eerdmans, 1995.

Zerwick, Max. Biblical Greek: Illustrated by Examples. Repr. Rome: Pontifical Biblical Institute Press, 1994.

Zerwick, Max, and Mary Grosvenor. A Grammatical Analysis of the Greek New Testament. Repr. Rome: Pontifical Biblical Institute Press, 1988.

Zwingli, Huldrych. Schriften. Vol. 2. Zurich: Theologischer Verlag, 1995.

Index of Names

Index of Names

Ireland, D. J., 90

Jacobs, Louis, 132, 135
Jobes, Karen H., 164, 165
Johnson, Luke T., 140, 141
Johnson, M., 60, 61
Jüngel, Eberhard, 37

Kamlah, Ehrhard, 52
Käsemann, Ernst, 95
Kidd, Reggie M., 151
Kittay, Eva Fedder, 66
Koch, Traugott, 36
Koenig, John, 123
Kraftchick, Steven J., 63
Kümmel, Werner, 114

Laato, Timo, 50
Lakoff, G., 60, 61
Lansing, Richard, 128
Lenski, R. C. H., 12, 13, 110
Léon-Dufour, Xavier, 120
Lieu, Judith M., 139
Lightfoot, J. B., 10, 18, 29, 54, 109
Lillie, W., 58, 59
Lincoln, Andrew T., 57, 104, 107
Lindemann, Andreas, 12
Lloyd-Jones, D. M., 30, 31
Lohfink, Norbert, 70, 71
Lohmeyer, Ernst, 11, 54
Lohse, Eduard, 10, 54, 57
Louw, Johannes P., 107, 120 121, 122
Lugt, Pieter van der, 77, 78
Luther, Martin, 35, 36, 36, 46, 71, 174
Lyman, Stanford M., 20

Maclaren, Alexander, 37
Maclean, H. B., 131
Malherbe, A. J., 107
Malina, Bruce J., 117
Manton, Thomas, 4, 42

Margalit, Avishai, 3, 13, 14, 20, 140, 143, 144, 145, 147, 148, 178
Marshall, I. Howard, 107, 127
Martin, Ralph P., 104
Marx, Karl, 8, 19, 20, 21, 26, 178
Matthies, Conr, 12
Mays, James Luther, 74
McKane, William, 75, 76
McKay, J. W., 74
Merk, Otto, 57, 106
Moberly, R. W., 73
Monk, W. H., 31
Moo, Douglas J., 96
Moritz, Thorsten, 56, 57
Morris, Leon, 109
Moule, C. F. D., 110
Moxnes, Halvor, 117
Müller, Christoph Gregor, 26
Murphy, Frederick J., 137, 138
Murphy-O'Connor, Jerome, 112
Mussner, Franz, 12

Nanos, Mark D., 83
Nida, Eugene A., 107, 120 121, 122
Niebuhr, Karl-Wilhelm, 51, 71
Niebuhr, Reinhold, 140, 141

O'Brien, Peter T., 4, 30, 95
Olson, Dennis T., 72
Osborne, Grant R., 60
Owen, John, 42, 43, 128

Percy, E., 166
Pokorný, Petr, 12, 56, 155
Polhill, John B., 127
Provan, Iain W., 69

Ragaz, Leonhard, 20
Ramanchandra, Vinoth, 140, 141, 142
Reinmuth, Eckart, 51, 107, 108
Rengstorf, K. H., 57, 58, 164
Richard, Pablo, 21

Index of Subjects

Index of Scripture References

—✦—